JOSSEY-BASS CLASSICS
are works of enduring value that have
shaped thought and practice in their fields.
Practical and authoritative, these books
are timeless resources for professionals.
We are pleased to introduce these
important works to a wider readership
in a high-quality paperback format.

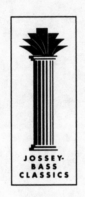

JOSSEY-
BASS
CLASSICS

ADULTS AS LEARNERS

K. Patricia Cross

ADULTS AS LEARNERS

Increasing Participation and Facilitating Learning

 Jossey-Bass Publishers • San Francisco

For sales outside the United States, please contact your local Simon & Schuster International Office.

Manufactured in the United States of America on Lyons Falls
TCF Pathfinder Tradebook. This paper is acid-free and 100 percent totally chlorine-free.

Library of Congress Cataloging-in-Publication Data

Cross, Kathryn Patricia, date.
    Adults as learners.

    Bibliography: p.
    Includes index.
    1. Adult education.   2. Continuing education.
I. Title
LC5219.C744   374   80-26985
ISBN 0-87589-491-7
ISBN 1-55542-445-7 (paperback)

FIRST EDITION
HB Printing   11
PB Printing   10 9 8 7 6 5 4 3   *Code 8105*
                                                        Code 9246

The Jossey-Bass
Higher and Adult Education Series

Contents

ix

Tables and Figures

Tables

Figures

Preface to the Classic Paperback

Ten years have passed since I wrote *Adults as Learners*. Two terms were in vogue in 1981 to describe adult learners—*lifelong learners* and *nontraditional students*. The term *nontraditional* has now virtually disappeared from the literature, whereas lifelong learning has become a reality for most adults.

My interest in adults as learners was first piqued by my assignment to work with the Commission on Non-Traditional Study, which was convened in the 1970s to formulate recommendations about how colleges should change to meet the needs of a new constituency. Colleges were interested in the recommendations of the commission primarily because adults were seen as a new "market" with excellent potential for filling the seats in college classrooms left vacant because of the scanty showing of "traditional" 18 year olds during the college-going years of the baby-bust generation. As far as colleges were concerned, students who were not 18-to-24-year-old full-time students were "nontraditional." As far as society and the workplace were concerned, adults were—and would continue to be—lifelong learners.

So what has changed in the decade since *Adults as Learners* appeared?

First, adults, while not the mainstream on many college campuses, are at least common enough to be simply one more element of the diversity that characterizes most college campuses today. The average age of the American undergraduate student is not 19 or 20, but 24. In community colleges, the segment of higher education that provides entry-level undergraduate education for the majority of the college-going population, the average age is approximately 28; students are overwhelmingly part-time, attending college intermittently, and most are workers as well as students. Evening classes are available almost everywhere, and most student services have evening hours.

Were one to visit evening classes, however, one would be quite likely to find a lecturer in a rectangular room with students taking notes on lined tablets. Thus, while services and attitudes have changed markedly, college classrooms and the delivery of education have not changed very much—or indeed even in the direction advocated by most adult educators. By and large, colleges have absorbed adult learners into their student bodies with scarcely a ripple. The principles of andragogy—whose legitimacy is still controversial in the 1990s—have not had much impact on the traditional classroom. Nor have nontraditional practices, so vigorously advocated in the 1970s, continued the tremendous spurt of growth that was stimulated by new models such as Open University, credit for experiential learning, and distance delivery. Whether innovation to serve the special needs of adults was adopted by traditional colleges and universities depended more on market forces than on an informed understanding of adult learning, it appears.

Second, it continues to be hard to document the trend in lifelong learning. How many adults are lifelong learners? Have their numbers increased significantly over the past decade? Somewhat facetiously, in *Adults as Learners* I cited research that placed estimates of adults engaged in learning at somewhere between 12 percent and 98 percent of the adults in the United States, depending on the definition of adult learning and on the sample polled. Estimates have not changed much over the past decade, either in precision or in percentages. Recent data from the triennial surveys of the National Center for Education Statistics (NCES) raise the floor from 12 percent to 14 percent of the adult population participating in some form of organized instruction, and ample documentation is still available for the widespread participation by adults in an enormous variety of learning opportunities. What has changed is the 1970s preoccupation with conducting surveys and counting participants. There appears to be less need today to convince people that lifelong learning is prevalent and here to stay.

Third, the demographic profile of the typical adult learner has not changed much. Women are still more likely than men to participate; whites more likely to than people of color. The middle and upper classes have higher rates of participation than lower classes, and educational attainment remains the strongest predictor of future participation in organized learning activities.

What has changed, and for the better, is our description of adult learners. In 1981, I deplored the fact that sociodemographic descriptors were used to the near-exclusion of other variables, despite research that found that such variables accounted for only 10 percent of the variance associated with participation in adult learning activities (p. 62). Fortunately, recent research has been directed toward more educationally relevant variables, such as motivation, stages of development, and the like. Research about adults as learners is more sophisticated than it was ten years ago. Much of what passed for research then consisted of surveys and the ubiquitous "needs assessments," purportedly conducted to see how educators could better serve the needs of adult learners.

Fourth, there is more theory in the field of adult education today, and it is more complex and more encompassing. In 1981, I expressed reluctant admiration for the pragmatism of adult education, while acknowledging that adult education as a field of study could not grow without a more systematic approach to the accumulation of knowledge. After analyzing the difficulties of theory building in adult education (pp. 110–111),

I concluded: "It is unlikely that there will ever be a single theory of adult education. Instead, there will be many theories useful in improving our understanding of adults as learners" (pp. 111–112). The trend among scholars of adult education, however, has been to call for wider, more inclusive theories. Merriam and Caffarella (1991, p. 119), for example, lament the fragmentation of theory in adult development, "since it represents a variety of perspectives that have yet to be integrated into a holistic picture of adulthood."

While I applaud the greater sophistication of today's research and theory in adult education, I would, in hindsight, recommend a more rigorous testing of tighter, smaller theories. Given my conviction that people will learn whatever they want to learn, I would select motivation for learning as potentially the most productive line of research, recognizing that the motivation to earn a college degree is something quite different from the motivation to undertake self-directed study.

Finally, there is greater interest today in adulthood itself than there was in 1981. Scientists and scholars of all stripes and in all fields—from psychology and sociology to demography and physiology—are adding daily to our understanding of the aging process, as well as inspiring us regarding the potential for self-actualization over the full span of a lifetime.

Berkeley, California   K. Patricia Cross
November 1991

Reference

Merriam, S. B., and Caffarella, R. S. *Learning in Adulthood: A Comprehensive Guide.* San Francisco: Jossey-Bass, 1991.

Preface

This book was motivated by my growing conviction that individuals living in today's world must be prepared to make learning a continuing lifelong activity. Lifelong learning is not a privilege or a right; it is simply a necessity for anyone, young or old, who must live with the escalating pace of change—in the family, on the job, in the community, and in the worldwide society.

As educators we have an obligation to aid lifelong learning by utilizing the best knowledge available. To that end, I proposed to the Carnegie Corporation of New York a synthesis of existing research and theory, so that we might see more clearly the implications of present knowledge for facilitating learning by adults. The Carnegie Corporation generously made the funds available, and I embarked on the task of conducting a comprehensive survey of the literature, looking especially for the implications of research and theory for improving practice. That task, while not unfamiliar to me as a synthesizer of educational research (Cross, 1971, 1976), posed two major problems. The first was how to focus on the diffuse concept of lifelong learning. The second was how to cope with the sheer volume of literature in adult education.

I wanted to preserve the concept of lifelong learning as involving learning on the part of people of all ages and from all walks of life using the multiple learning resources of society to learn whatever they wanted or needed to know. Understandably, it is hard to find a focus in a concept that seems to involve all people, learning all manner of subjects and skills, through all kinds of methods from multiple providers. I settled on the individual learner as the focus of the learning society and on two definitions of lifelong learning that I think provide better guidelines than any others for considering the future of education and learning. One definition was devised in the early 1970s, when education for adult part-time learners was emerging as a major interest of traditional colleges and universities. The Commission on Non-Traditional Study, although primarily concerned about adult learners in post-secondary education, composed one of the more eloquent, reformist definitions related to lifelong learning. In 1973, when the commission was making its recommendations, what many people in higher education now call "lifelong learning" was known as "nontraditional study," but the commission still had the problem of wrestling with the definition for an emerging phenomenon:

> Most of us agreed that nontraditional study is more an attitude than a system and thus can never be defined except tangentially. This attitude puts the student first and the institution second, concentrates more on the former's need than the latter's convenience, encourages diversity of individual opportunity rather than uniform prescription, and deemphasizes time, space, and even course requirements in favor of competence and, where applicable, performance. It has concern for the learner of any age and circumstance, for the degree aspirant as well as the person who finds sufficient reward in enriching life through constant, periodic, or occasional study [Commission on Non-Traditional Study, 1973, p. xv].

Tangential though the definition may be, it contains the seeds of the major theme of this book: Service to individual learners should be the goal of the learning society. Thus, "adults as learners" became my subject of study.

A second definition then helped to place the learner in the context of the learning society. In 1976 the following definition was adopted by UNESCO's supreme legislative body, the General Conference:

> The term "lifelong education and learning" denotes an overall scheme aimed both at restructuring the existing education system and at developing the entire educational potential outside the education system; in such a scheme men and women are the agents of their own education.

That definition contains three basic ideas about the nature of lifelong learning. One is that the entire formal educational system, from elementary school through graduate school, should be restructured to develop lifelong learners. Second, it is not just schools and colleges that are to serve as the targets for improved education. Rather, the world is full of people, organizations, and other learning resources that can be marshaled on behalf of lifelong learning. Third, this definition stresses the importance of helping people become self-directed learners, the active agents of their own education.

Thus, my solution to the problem of sharpening the book's focus was to seek knowledge helpful in developing learners capable of using the multiple resources of the learning society for their own growth. Limiting the book's scope to the study of adult learners did not, however, solve the problem of how to cope with the explosion of knowledge. There are thousands of books, articles, and reports on adult learning. The more I worked on the endless flow of literature, the more I became convinced of the need to go beyond the synthesis of research to search for an organizing framework in which to place this rapidly accumulating information.

At the present time, research efforts are piecemeal, faddishly duplicative in some areas (for example, life cycles and needs assessments) and virtually nonexistent in others (for example, the effect of early school experiences on adult attitudes toward learning). With this highly prolific but essentially primitive research base, there is the temptation to follow the same piecemeal, quick-fix pattern in implementation. Needs assessments, for example, have been especially popular, because they seem to lead directly to implementation. The rationale is: find out what people want and give it to them. The very concept of the learning society, however, calls for deeper understanding of the learner in the context of the learning environment.

For that reason this book does not lend itself easily to the statement of a research finding followed immediately by implications for practice. Rather, I have tried to build a holistic understanding of adults as learners through presenting research findings from varying methodological perspectives and then trying to develop a framework for understanding and interpreting the research. It is my hope that this approach, although more difficult to write and to read, will advance the cause of lifelong learning through promoting the deeper understandings that are essential both to the identification of missing blocks of knowledge and to the development of practical programs of action.

This book is not really a how-to-do-it book—although, of course, I have tried to interpret and suggest implementation whenever possible. The profession of adult education is more than amply supplied with a literature of advice from practitioners who can offer useful suggestions to their colleagues. It seemed to me that my greatest contribution might be to write a how-to-think-about-it book. I hope that these efforts to synthesize and organize research and theory will cause people to think about the coming learning society—and, of course, that such thought will lead to greater wisdom in planning for the future.

This book is organized to shed light on four questions: *Who* participates in adult learning? *Why* do they participate or, alternatively, why not? And *what* and *how* do they learn or want to learn? Chapter One sets the stage for the learning society by looking at trends—demographic, social, and technological—

that stimulate the increasing demand for learning opportunities. Chapter Two places the heady escalation of adult learning in perspective by presenting the views of those who see dangers in new pressures on adults to participate in organized learning activities. These critics fear that the freedom to engage in lifelong learning could easily turn into the compulsion of lifelong schooling. Chapter Three is a review of research findings about the characteristics of adult learners. Profiles of adults participating in the three common forms of adult learning (self-directed, organized instruction, and degree-credit) are developed to answer questions about *who* participates in adult learning. *Why* they participate—and why not—is addressed in Chapter Four, which is a synthesis of research about motivations and deterrents to adult learning. The chapter's review covers research conducted in a variety of formats and methodologies, ranging from surveys asking what people would like to learn (and what prevents them from learning it) to experimental studies documenting the impact on participation when certain barriers are removed or imposed. In Chapter Five, the search for organizational principles about adult learning motives begins. Various motivational theories are described, and synthesis is achieved through the identification of common elements in existing theories.

Chapter Six is one of two major summary chapters in the book. In it, I attempt to integrate what is known about motivation through research (Chapters Three and Four) and theory (Chapter Five) into an explanatory model of the motivation behind adult participation in learning activities. I hope that the Chain-of-Response (COR) Model will prove useful in identifying relevant variables in the motivation for adult learning, constructing explanatory hypotheses, and suggesting ways in which motivation can be enhanced and barriers lowered.

Chapters Seven and Eight are research reviews, synthesizing what is known about *what* and *how* adults learn. These questions are addressed in four research themes: learning processes as a function of aging, adult stages of development, phases of the life cycle, and preferences and practices of adult learners regarding subject matter, teaching methods, scheduling options, and the like.

Chapter Nine is the second summary chapter. Its purpose is to examine existing learning theories and to suggest a conceptual framework for analyzing the interactions between learners and their environments. The model provides for the consideration of physiological, social, and psychological dimensions.

Finally, I have added two appendices that emerged out of my efforts to find common threads in current definitions of lifelong learning. Appendix A illustrates the range of thought and opinion about lifelong learning; Appendix B lists agreements among scholars throughout the world on the basic concepts underlying the ideal of lifelong learning.

This book is addressed to all persons who have the need or desire to increase their basic understanding of adults as learners—educators in industry, community agencies, traditional and nontraditional schools and colleges, the military services, governmental agencies, and, in the spirit of the learning society, to "educators" who belong to no organization. I believe that the book will be especially useful in graduate programs helping to prepare future leaders of the learning society for the wide variety of educational positions in which they will work.

Any author owes debts of gratitude to numerous colleagues, past and present. I have consciously tried to draw as heavily as possible on the work of others in the conviction that progress will be made only through standing on the shoulders of those who went before us. I have strived to be both conscientious and accurate in acknowledging the source of all ideas and data, and I hope that this effort will make the book a useful bibliography as well as a presentation of my interpretation of the current state of knowledge.

I tender special thanks to the Carnegie Corporation for the kind of funding that permitted maximum effort on the content and concepts of the book without interruption by requests for progress reports and compliance to purely administrative procedures. I would also like to acknowledge the support of Educational Testing Service, which has offered throughout my fifteen years of employment maximum freedom and encouragement to pursue any knowledge to improve education. Finally, I thank Judy Kiffmeyer, my secretary, who worked as valued partner and friend through multiple drafts of this book and who assumed full responsibility for the extensive documentation.

Cambridge, Massachusetts   K. Patricia Cross
Berkeley, California
January 1981

The Author

K. Patricia Cross is the Elizabeth and Edward Conner Professor of Higher Education at the University of California, Berkeley. Cross has had a varied and distinguished career as university administrator (dean of students at Cornell University), researcher (distinguished research scientist at Educational Testing Service), and teacher (professor and chair of the Department of Administration, Planning, and Social Policy at the Harvard Graduate School of Education). Cross received her B.S. degree (1948) from Illinois State University in mathematics and her A.M. (1951) and Ph.D. (1958) degrees from the University of Illinois, in psychology and social psychology, respectively.

Author of eight books and more than 150 articles and chapters, Cross has been recognized for her scholarship by election to the National Academy of Education and receipt of the E. F. Lindquist Award from the American Educational Research Association. Past president of the American Association of Higher Education, she has been given numerous awards for leadership in education, among them the 1990 Leadership Award from the American Association of Community and Junior Colleges and the Outstanding Service Award from the Coalition of Adult Education Associations.

Cross serves on the editorial boards of six national or international journals of higher education and has won recognition for her own writing from the American Council on Education (the 1976 Borden Medal for *Accent on Learning*) and from the National Council of Instructional Administrators for her contributions to the improvement of instruction. She has lectured widely on American higher education in the United States and in France, Germany, the Soviet Union, Japan, Australia, and Holland. Her interests are primarily the changing college student populations and the improvement of teaching and learning in higher education.

ADULTS
AS LEARNERS

CHAPTER 1

Growth of the Learning Society

The learning society is growing because it must. It would be difficult to think of some way to live in a society changing as rapidly as ours without constantly learning new things. When life was simpler, one generation could pass along to the next generation what it needed to know to get along in the world; tomorrow was simply a repeat of yesterday. Now, however, the world changes faster than the generations, and individuals must live in several different worlds during their lifetimes. Margaret Mead once remarked that the world in which we are born is not the world in which we will live, nor is that the world in which we will die. Kenneth Boulding (1964) illustrated the pace of change by observing that the world in which he lives is as different from the world into which he was born as that world was from Julius Caesar's. Because of these rapid changes, Toffler (1970, p. 14) contends that "most people are

1

grotesquely unprepared to cope" with the pace of change and "mass disorientation" in the society may be the result.

In the face of such dramatic statements about the future, the observation that no education will last a lifetime seems conservative and even mundane. But change is now so great and so far reaching that no amount of education during youth can prepare adults to meet the demands that will be made on them. That reality should change the way schools and colleges prepare upcoming generations for their future as lifelong learners, and it should change the way societies think about education and learning. Already, many agencies whose primary function is not education have entered directly into the educational process. Just as schools no longer have a monopoly on education, businesses no longer tend strictly to business. Employers are increasingly involved in education, conducting on-the-job training for employees, workshops for professionals, and think-tanks for executives. Travel agencies are adding educational components to packaged tours at the same time that alumni offices and extension divisions are adding packaged tours to credit-bearing courses. Numerous new organizations are making their appearance as educators in the learning society. California's Continuing Education of the Bar is a self-supporting organization established by the State Bar to keep some 70,000 attorneys in California abreast of the latest developments in their profession through self-instructional materials. The Metropolitan Museum of Art offers semester-long parent-child workshops in which parents and young children learn the art of painting and the use of a variety of art materials. The spread of education to all people in the society and into the multiple organizations of society is the phenomenon that has become known as the learning society.

The present and anticipated growth of lifelong learning in the United States can be attributed to three influences. First are the demographic factors that result in larger numbers of adults in the population. Between 1975 and 1985, the number of adults between the ages of 25 and 45 will increase relative to other age groups—from 25 percent of the population to 31 percent (U.S. Bureau of the Census, 1977b). A second influence is social change—the rising educational level of the populace, the changing roles of women, early retirement, civil rights, increased leisure time, changing life styles, and so forth. Depending on individual circumstances, education for adults has become necessary for some, desirable for others, and more acceptable and attainable for almost everyone. The third pressure springs from technological change and the knowledge explosion. Almost any worker in the society has the problem of keeping up with new knowledge, but technological change is so fast and powerful that it wipes out entire industries and creates new ones in a single decade. Moreover, the people of a technological society have the problem of adapting to technological change as consumers as well as producers. The combined impact of demographic, social, and technological change is enormous, and it will almost certainly encourage the growth of the learning society. Let us look at these factors more carefully.

Demographic Change

The United States is becoming a nation of adults. By the year 2000, says the National Center for Education Statistics (Golladay, 1976, p. 12), "the United States population will be dominated by persons in their middle years." For most of the years of this century, the United States population has been numerically dominated by young people. With the exception of the World War II years, children under the age of 15 have always been the largest single age group in the nation. Table 1 shows that in 1980 numerical dominance shifted to those between the ages of 15 and 29. By the year 2000, the largest age group will be 30 to 44 year olds, with a rising curve for 45 to 64 year olds.

Most people are aware of the baby boom after World War II and the baby bust that followed, but few people realize how much the ebb and flow of births affect what we do and how we think as a society. In the 1960s, for example, most people assumed that the "youth culture," with its high visibility and influence on college campuses as well as in the marketplace, was the wave of the future. In hindsight, it seems apparent that the

Table 1. U.S. Population for Selected Age Groups, 1950-2000

| | Population Figures (in thousands) and Percentages | | | | | | | | | | | |
| | 1950 | | 1960 | | 1970 | | 1980 | | 1990 Projected | | 2000 Projected | |
Age	N	%	N	%	N	%	N	%	N	%	N	%
Under 15	40,530	27	55,595	31	57,900	28	51,202	23	58,089	24	58,564	22
15-29	34,400	23	34,782	19	48,919	24	60,430	27	54,913	22	55,348	21
30-44	33,009	22	35,920	20	34,519	17	42,926	19	57,450	23	59,304	23
45-64	30,662	20	36,015	20	41,811	21	43,688	20	45,693	19	58,679	22
65 and over	12,285	8	16,529	9	20,065	10	24,523	11	28,934	12	30,600	12
Totals	150,886	100	178,841	99	203,214	100	222,769	100	245,079	100	262,495	100

Source: Adapted from data presented in U.S. Bureau of the Census, 1977c, p. 23.

great amount of attention given to youth and the "new values" of the 1960s was achieved largely from the force of the unprecedented number of postadolescents in the population. In 1964, the year of the Free Speech Movement, 17 year olds became, almost suddenly, the single largest age group in the country. Drucker (1971) maintains that anyone who took the trouble to look at the population figures could have predicted some type of youth revolution in the 1960s.

Throughout its relatively brief history, the influence of the baby-boom generation on American life has been pervasive, affecting schools, recreation, the products marketed, and perhaps even the crime rate. As the baby-boom generation grew older, the pressures for educational expansion moved from elementary to secondary to postsecondary to adult education. Industry moved from emphasizing baby foods to pop records to recreational vehicles. The high crime rate of the 1960s and 1970s is thought to reflect, in part at least, the high proportion of 14 to 24 year olds in the population—the age when most crimes are committed.

Richard Easterlin, a University of Pennsylvania economist, has advanced the controversial social theory that demographics lies at the root of such social indicators as economic conditions, the divorce rate, fertility rates, even the women's movement. His work depends on cohort analysis (a cohort consists of all people born in the same calendar year). In large cohorts, there is a glut of people of that age group throughout their life span. When that group hits the labor market, there are not enough jobs, and there is a subjective feeling that times are tough. This in turn makes money tight and young people reluctant to marry and have children—a psychological factor which then in turn influences the birthrate of the next generation. In small cohorts, such as the baby-bust generation, young people find less competition for jobs; they are more willing to have children, and fertility rates rise. "A cohort carries its fortunes, good or bad, depending on its size, throughout its life cycle," says Easterlin (quoted in Collins, 1979, p. 37).

One of the "bad" ramifications for the baby-boom generation has been the increased competition generated among its members as a result of their large numbers. From the late 1940s into the 1960s, admission to college was intensely competitive, for example, because it took time for higher education to expand enough to accommodate the influx of students. In the 1970s and 1980s, the competition within the baby-boom cohort moves to the labor market, resulting in what has been termed the "promotion squeeze." Young people graduating from college and flooding into entry-level jobs are finding it difficult to move past the lower echelons of the occupational ladder (Best and Stern, 1976). Some career ladders have become severely congested, forcing people to look at a number of possible alternatives, all of which have ramifications for adult education. Some people, denied promotion in one career, may decide on midlife career changes, most of which will require further education. A recent study estimates that as many as forty million Americans are in a state of transition regarding their jobs or careers; 60 percent of them say that they plan to seek additional education (Arbeiter and others, 1978). Others may solve their problem of lack of career mobility through seeking satisfaction in other ways—through new hobbies or recreation or attention to family, all of which may encourage new learning. The greatest growth by subject area in adult education between 1969 and 1975 occurred in social life and recreation, closely followed by personal and family living (Boaz, 1978). Still other people may shift their search for personal fulfillment from career to learning for the joy of learning. Finally, those who are most dedicated to their careers will seek a competitive advantage through further education and specialization.

While many analyses have pointed to negative or depressive effects of being a member of a large cohort, it also seems that a large cohort, because of its political and economic strength, manages to gain the attention of the society throughout the life span of the cohort. The baby-boom generation, for all its problems, has not been ignored. Because of its sheer size, it has commanded the attention of education, industry, and government for some three decades now. There is no reason to think that the influence of America's largest generation will subside in the future. Should we expect an "adult revolution" within the next two decades comparable to the youth revolution in the 1960s? If so, how will it affect education? Whether a possible "adult revolution" will erupt into newsworthy events or quietly seep into all aspects of American life is not known, but we may expect that the impact of an aging population on education will be profound. Indeed, the handwriting is already on the wall, in bold relief in some areas. Let us look briefly at the impact of the high birthrate between 1946 and 1958 on adult education today.

Individuals born during the baby boom are now between 22 and 34 years of age—the adult age range of greatest participation in educational activities. Thus, increased participation in all forms of adult education is to be expected. Statistics document the expectation. Between 1967-68 and 1975-76, registration in noncredit adult education course in institutions of higher education increased 57 percent (Kemp, 1978, p. 3). The rise in part-time participation in all forms of organized learning[1] is equally impressive, increasing 31 percent in the six years between 1969 and 1975 (Boaz, 1978). Not all of that 31 percent increase, however, can be attributed to the birthrate alone—although, as we have seen, the impact of the birthrate is far more pervasive than mere numbers. For a 31 percent increase in part-time educational participation, there was only a 12.6 percent increase in the number of adults 17 years of age and older in the population. Thus, participation in educational activities increased two and a half times as fast as the growth of the eligible population. On the surface at least, the fact that educational participation is growing faster than the adult population suggests that more factors than "mere" demographics are at work.

Unfortunately, the National Center for Education Statistics, which has been monitoring adult education in the United States since 1969, has changed its definition of "part-time par-

---

[1]To the National Center for Education Statistics, "Organized learning involves a student-teacher relationship in which the learner is supervised or directed in learning experiences over a specified period of time for a recognized purpose. The teacher may be remote, such as on a recording or tape, or in a correspondence school headquarters. Short-term workshops and seminars are considered adult education" (Boaz, 1978, p. 109).

ticipant in adult education" just enough over the years to make it virtually impossible to present useful information about trends. Substantial changes in the 1978 data collection came at an especially critical time, because those data, had they been comparable to those collected in the three earlier surveys, would have shed some light on whether the increases in adult education herald the dawn of the learning society or whether the increases are not much more than the baby bulge pressing through the educational system. In a paper based on the NCES surveys of 1969, 1972, and 1975, O'Keefe (1977) suggested that the adult education boom peaked somewhere around the year 1972. He based his prediction on the fact that in the first interval of the triennial surveys, 1969-1972, participation in adult education increased 20.1 percent for a 6.6 percent increase in the adult population, whereas during the second interval, 1972-1975, participation slowed to an 8.4 percent increase for a 5.6 percent increase in the growth of the eligible population (Boaz, 1978). Data from the 1978 survey suggest that the recent gain in adult education has been very slight—from 12.3 percent of the eligible population in 1975 to 12.5 percent in 1978. The rise in numbers of participants from 18.1 million to 19.3 million indicates a 7 percent increase, which is still slightly ahead of the 5 percent increase in the eligible population.

While not much faith can be placed in the comparability of figures from survey to survey, two conclusions seem warranted. First, the extremely rapid increase in participation rates between 1969 and 1972 has not been repeated, and the *rate* of growth is slowing. Second, the activity in adult education probably cannot be attributed solely to the baby-boom generation, since the increase in participation rates has remained consistently ahead of the increase in eligible population. Nevertheless, the slowing of the rate of participation in adult education is enough to raise some questions. If the society gears up once again to serve the educational needs of the baby-boom generation as it passes through the educational pipeline, will providers of educational services for adults be faced with the same steady-state enrollments and retrenchments that face colleges serving 18 to 24 year olds today? Probably not. In the first place, adult education spans more than fifty years, which makes it much less subject to fluctuations in the birthrate than the four- to six-year time span embraced by traditional colleges. Second, the number of people participating in educational activities is a function of forces in society that extend beyond population statistics. Some are the result of social changes, such as the pressure for equal opportunity and the changing roles of women; some are a function of technological advances and occupational obsolescence; and some reflect complex side effects of the demographic fluctuations discussed above. Sorting out these various influences in order to analyze their possible impact introduces distortion because they inevitably occur in combination, interacting in complex rather than simple ways.

Social Change

It is difficult to think of any social change, presently occurring or predictable, that would not require increased attention to lifelong learning. Education has a generally supporting, and sometimes critical, role to play across a broad range of human endeavors—from improved job skills to enrichment of life for the individual, and from reducing unemployment to coping with worker alienation for the society. Thus, whether the individual wants to improve the quality of leisure or of work, education is usually perceived as helpful; and whether the society faces problems of assuring equal opportunity or environmental protection, education is frequently mentioned as a first step. However, specific social changes taking place now are encouraging the growth of the learning society.

From Linear to Blended Life Plan

So far in the history of industrialized nations, there has been a pronounced tendency to increase the separation between education, work, and leisure. The result has been termed the "linear life plan," a life pattern in which education is for the young, work for the middle aged, and leisure for the elderly. The linear life plan has been advancing in most countries of the world, even though most observers and analysts are convinced

that it promises serious social problems in the years ahead (Best
and Stern, 1976; Center for Educational Research and Innovation, 1977). In a careful analysis of the progression and influence of the linear life plan in the United States, Best and Stern
(1976, p. 24) warned: "There can be little doubt that many of
our most serious and persistent social problems stem from the
ways in which education, work, and leisure are distributed
throughout lifetimes." There are concerted efforts now, both in
the United States and abroad, to stem the social problems arising from the linear life plan.

The major social problem is unemployment. For the past
fifty years, society has been unable to provide jobs during
peacetime for everyone willing and able to work. The major vic-
tims of the chronic job shortage have been minority groups,
women, youth, and older people. While some progress has been
made in reducing unemployment among minority groups and
women, the position of youth and older people in the job market has been deteriorating for several decades—mainly because
those in midlife, who are at the peak of power on the job as
well as in political influence, have responded to the job shortage
by pushing "young persons back into school and older persons
into ever earlier retirement" (Best and Stern, 1976, p. 6). The
result over time has been the compression of work activities
into the middle years of life; nonwork time has increased substantially in the earlier and later years. In 1900, for example,
the average male in the United States spent thirteen years of his
youth in school, compared to a little over seventeen years today. On the other end of the life span, the typical worker in
1900 had only three years of retirement plus other nonwork
activities, compared to almost ten years today (Best and Stern,
1976, p. 8).

This general pattern of the concentration of work into
the middle years and nonwork into early and late years is a
problem plaguing all industrialized Western countries. Yet the
Center for Educational Research and Innovation (1977, p. 26)
admits that there is still pressure in some of the member countries of UNESCO to require an additional year of schooling for
young people in order to keep them off the labor market. In the

United States, however, there is growing dissatisfaction on the part of almost everyone with the linear distribution of education, work, and leisure. Youth and retirees want more work, independence, and responsibility while workers want more leisure (Best and Stern, 1976, p. 12).

The most prominent alternative to the linear life plan is the "cyclic life plan," ably presented by Best and Stern (1976). Its basic purpose is to redistribute work, education, and leisure across the life span. Descriptions of the cyclic life plan usually include charts with chunks of education and leisure time inserted into the working years and chunks of work time extended into early and late years. In Europe, the periods of education that are inserted into the work years are referred to as recurrent education. Recurrent education and the cyclic life plan stress alternating patterns of education, work, and leisure, implying that each would be a full-time activity while it lasted. Such plans call for some scheme for financing educational leaves for adult working people. However, in spite of a certain amount of discussion and experimentation with paid educational leaves (see Levine, 1974; von Moltke and Schneevoigt, 1977) and the proposals for vouchers and educational entitlements (Kurland, 1977), alternating periods of work and education probably are still a long way off. Nollen (1977, p. 75) observes that in the United States there has been little interest in full-scale recurrent education:

> Among the major labor contracts in 1974, there were few which included provisions for paid educational leaves of absence. Only 4 percent included unpaid educational leave. About 9 percent of private industrial firms authorized some workers to take sabbaticals of a month or longer in 1975, but almost none of these leaves were available to all workers in the firm. However, there is a

[2] "The essential characteristic of recurrent education is the distribution of education over the total life span of the individual in a recurring way—that is, in alternation with other activities, principally with work but also with leisure and retirement" (Organization for Economic Cooperation and Development, 1973, p. 16).

substantial amount of company-provided off-the-job education during working hours. About 3 million workers participate, or 4 percent of all industrial workers; three quarters of industrial firms provide such education. This education is not the type that involves alternation between work and education, in which the worker's job is left for any length of time, but it is one form of education for adult workers.

A variation on the theme of recurrent education does seem to be taking place in the United States without any comprehensive social planning. Young people are more likely than they were a decade ago to "stop out"; that is, to take a break between graduation from high school and entrance into college (Carnegie Commission on Higher Education, 1971). In 1973, 62 percent of the college freshmen entered college immediately following high school graduation; by 1976, the figure was down to 55 percent, with 22 percent waiting one to three years before entering college and 19 percent waiting five years or more (Henderson and Plummer, 1978, p. 25). The other way to break up the steady diet of education for young people is to blend work and leisure into the education years through part-time study combined with part- or full-time work. And that too appears to be happening. In fact, the trend toward a "blended life plan" appears much more likely, in the United States at least, than any widespread adoption of the cyclic life plan. By coining the phrase *blended life plan*, I mean to suggest that work, education, and leisure are concurrent, rather than alternating, at all points throughout life. Thus, instead of being a full-time worker, a typical 40 year old might spend fewer hours a day or week working, leaving more time for education and leisure; a 20 year old may cease being a full-time student to become a part-time student, part-time worker, and part-time vacationer; and a 60 year old might plan for a gradual withdrawal from work rather than full-time retirement. In other words, the blended life plan would consist of a blend of education, work, and leisure throughout most of the years of life.

Higher education in the United States may soon consist of a majority of learners who have adopted a blended life plan.

From 1966 to 1976, there was a 120 percent increase in part-time college students, compared to a 51 percent increase for full-time students. According to projections of the National Center for Education Statistics (1978), the trend toward part-time students will continue, with a 45 percent increase for part-time students and a 1 percent decrease for full-time students between 1976 and 1986. By 1986, 48 percent of all college students are expected to be part time, up substantially from 31 percent in 1966 and 39 percent in 1976 (Frankel, 1978, p. 4). Most of the new part-time students are coming from the ranks of full-time workers, but some are coming from the ranks of formerly full-time students. Many colleges are observing a steady decrease in the number of credit hours carried by younger students, as formerly full-time students opt for part-time study.

The workplace is experiencing a phenomenon similar to the part-time student revolution on college campuses. Labor experts report that the new demand for professional part-time jobs is growing much faster than the job market can handle (*Footnotes to the Future,* Feb. 1980). The new part-timers, unlike the old part-timers, are not working to supplement income. Rather, they are career people and primary wage earners—older workers seeking a transition before full retirement, women pursuing careers while raising children, people who want to work while returning to school, two-income couples who want flexible hours so that they can share home and child care duties, and disabled career people who cannot work all day. Because of costs and tax disincentives, industry has been slow to respond to the pressures for blended life plans. But the pressures on the institutions of society continue to build.

Older people too are reevaluating the linear life plan. They are not only resisting compulsory retirement but are participating in greater numbers in educational programs ranging from crafts and field trips at senior citizens' centers to credit classes at colleges and universities. Between 1969 and 1975, there was a 55 percent increase in the number of adults 55 and older who were participating in organized educational activities. The rate of educational participation by older people not only

increased faster than for other age groups; it also increased at a
rate five times as great as the increase of their numbers in the
population (Boaz, 1978, p. 4).

It appears, then, that many people across the span of ages
are opting for a blended life plan. Many upwardly mobile workers, however, are simply adding education to an already full
work schedule, rather than replacing some work hours with education hours. In effect, this eliminates the leisure component
from the blended life plan. Furthermore, it fails to solve one of
the most troublesome problems for society, which is the
chronic job shortage. The cyclic life plan addresses this issue by
moving workers out of their jobs temporarily; the blended life
plan could address the issue by job sharing, more part-time jobs,
and shorter workdays or workweeks, but so far these solutions
have not been forthcoming. Although there is evidence in atti-
tudinal surveys that workers want more free time, the work-
week has remained remarkably stable over the past three decades (Owen, 1976). Increased leisure time has come primarily in
the form of longer vacations and more holidays. That pattern
introduces more leisure into the life span of workers, but it is
difficult for educators to design programs that fit into
holidays—even if workers wanted to spend their leisure time in
educational pursuits, which research shows they do not (see
Chapter Eight).

In any event, the linear life plan that has predominated in
the industrialized nations of the world is destined to undergo
gradual transformation into blended and cyclic life plans. Education will play a major role, since both emerging life plans
offer new opportunities to adults as learners.

Rising Educational Attainment

As recently as 1940, only half of the adults in the United
States 25 years of age or older had completed elementary
school; by 1967 the median school years completed had risen to
12 (U.S. Bureau of the Census, 1975, p. 380). A more dramatic
way of illustrating the extremely rapid rise of educational
attainment in the United States is to look at the difference in
education between the generations now living. Eighty-four per-

cent of young people between the ages of 20 and 24 have completed four years of high school or more. For the cohort between the ages of 45 and 49, which can be considered the parent generation, only 66 percent have completed at least four years of high school. For the grandparent generation (age cohort 70 to 74 years of age), only 38 percent have completed four years of high school or more (U.S. Bureau of the Census, 1977a). Today a majority of the adults in the United States have completed high school (Golladay, 1977, p. 212), and 60 to 70 percent of today's high school graduates are likely to enroll in a postsecondary course sometime during their lives (Froomkin, 1978, p. 3).

The significance for lifelong learning in these statistics lies in the well-established research findings that the more education people have, the more education they want, and the more they participate in further learning activities (Cross, 1979a). Furthermore, there is the strong probability of an echo effect in rising educational attainment since the children of well-educated parents are also likely to become well educated. Thus, education is addictive not only for individuals but for entire societies.

The major increase in educational attainment in this century is the result of the dramatic increase in the number of people completing high school. With nearly 80 percent of the age group now completing high school, two questions arise with respect to whether we should expect a continuing rise of interest in education. First, does an 80 percent high school graduation rate represent a saturation point, beyond which progress will be slow? Second, will those with high school educations or more continue to seek further education? Answers to these questions are mixed.

There seems little doubt that raising the high school graduation rate from 80 percent to 100 percent will be much more difficult for the nation than raising it from 60 to 80 percent, which took only thirty years. Nevertheless, the value of a high school diploma is not questioned by anyone, and some minority groups are significantly below the national average in educational attainment. They might be expected to make rapid progress in the next decade or so. Hispanics, for example, are Ameri-

ca's most rapidly growing minority, and in 1977 only 61
percent of those between the ages of 20 and 24 had completed
four years of high school or more (U.S. Bureau of Census,
1977a). The number and proportion of blacks in the population
is also on the increase, and 25 percent of the 20- to 24-year-old
blacks lack a high school diploma. Another group, the handicapped, is being accepted into the mainstream of education
and more of them can be expected to complete high school in
the years ahead.

Whether high school graduates will continue to seek further education, either through college or through some other
form of continuing education, is more controversial. Some
argue, with good statistics to back up their position, that the
rate of return on the investment in a college degree has been
declining; thus, they expect the demand for degree-oriented
education to level off or even decrease (Dresch, 1975; Freeman,
1975; Froomkin, 1978). However, even though younger people
may be questioning the value of a college degree, their elders,
who missed the opportunity when they were younger, seem to
be increasingly interested in degrees and credit. Although only a
small percentage of adult learners now seek college degrees, the
rising educational attainment in the United States, combined
with the easier availability of credit for adult part-time learners,
makes it reasonable to suggest that more adults will seek degrees
in the future. Let us look separately, then, at predictions and
trends in credit and noncredit learning.

Credit Learning. There are any number of ways of analyzing the potential market for degree credit. The most optimistic
forecasts of possible futures come from equal opportunity arguments such as the one illustrated in Bowen's (1974, p. 150)
often-quoted paragraph:

> If women attended college at the same rate as men,
> if low-income people could attend at the same rate as
> high-income people, if attendance rates were as high
> throughout the country as they are in the leading states,
> enrollment would probably be increased by at least six or
> seven million. And if persons beyond the usual college

age began attending in rapidly growing numbers, as they show signs of doing, enrollments would grow even more. The doubling of college attendance is not beyond possibility.

Following this line of reasoning, we could make the ultra-optimistic assumption that all high school graduates who have not completed four years of college are potential college degree candidates. In 1977 almost sixty million adults—about half of the adult population in the United States—had completed high school but not four years of college (see Table 2). The equal

Table 2. Years of School Completed by Persons 25 Years Old and Older, March 1977

	N (in thousands)	Percent[a]
Eight years of elementary school	11,224	9.3
Four years of high school	43,602	36.1
One year of college	6,018	5.0
Two years of college	7,536	6.2
Three years of college	2,693	2.2
Four years of college	10,959	9.1
Five years of college	7,668	6.3

[a]Percents do not add to 100 because some years of educational attainment have been omitted from this table.
    Source: Adapted from U.S. Bureau of the Census, 1977a.

opportunity argument would then go like this: Since the college-going rate of high school graduates hovers at around 50 percent for young people today, if older generations were to catch up with the younger generation in educational attainment, approximately thirty million adults would be potential college students.

A more conservative—but still wildly optimistic—interpretation of the figures in Table 2 would suggest that the most likely candidates for college degrees are adults who started college but failed to finish. And research does show that adults with some college are more likely than any other group to aspire to college degrees (Carp, Peterson, and Roelfs, 1974;

Medsker and others, 1975; Sosdian and Sharp, 1978). Moreover, as Table 2 shows, relatively few people complete one or three years of college; instead, most people complete either two years (presumably associate degrees from community colleges) or four years (presumably bachelor's degrees). Thus, we could assume that some six million adults who have completed one year of college would like, for personal satisfaction and financial reasons, to get at least a two-year college degree; and ten million more may have unfulfilled aspirations for a four-year degree. In other words, as many as sixteen million adults can be considered in the college degree pipeline, a figure one and a half times the total number of students currently enrolled. If half of them pursued their degrees as half-time students, their numbers would more than replace the diminishing 18-year-old population.

Despite idealistic predictions about the potential adult market for college degrees, most college planners scale their aspirations down considerably to conform more closely to actions and expressions of interest on the part of adult learners. The national study of adult learners sponsored by the Commission on Non-traditional Study (Carp, Peterson, and Roelfs, 1974) found that 77 percent of the adults between the ages of 18 and 60 expressed an interest in continued learning, but only 12 percent of those would-be learners (9 percent of the adult population) said that they would like credit toward a two- or four-year college degree, and only 5 percent of the adult learners (less than 2 percent of the adult population) were receiving degree credit. (Learners were defined as the 31 percent of the adult population between the ages of 18 and 60 who reported receiving instruction in any subject.) These figures might jolt the optimism of those who hope to replace 18-year-old college students with 25 to 60 year olds. Nevertheless, even a seemingly insignificant 2 percent of the adult nonschool population represents almost three million part-time college students.

A realistic, but still optimistic, prediction for adult college enrollments would be that by 1985, 5 percent of the adult population 22 years of age or older could be attracted to undergraduate courses for college credit. According to population estimates by the U.S. Bureau of the Census (1977b, p. 45), there will be 155 million adults 22 and older by 1985. If 5 percent of them took classes for college credit, they would represent a substantial learning force of 7.75 million people. Presumably, most of them would be studying part time, but even at a conservative average of one course per term, the adult learning force would constitute approximately one and a half million full-time-equivalent students.

These admittedly speculative figures, if they are even close to reality, suggest three things. First, pursuing a college degree at age 22 or older will still represent a significant departure from the norm, and the 5 percent of the population who undertake it will be a selected group—more highly motivated, more successful as students, more achievement oriented, and probably better off occupationally and financially than their peers who are not involved in such learning activities. Second, although the proportion of adults seeking traditional credentials may rise, the total volume, over the next decade at least, is probably not sufficient to cause alarm about a significant extension of the overcredentialed, overschooled society into the adult years. (See Ziegler, 1977, for a provocative expression of concern on this issue.) Third, adults learning for college credit—although small in number when compared to their numbers in the population or even to the numbers pursuing noncredit learning options—are likely to constitute a significant portion of the college student population. The National Center for Education Statistics predicts that part-time students (of all ages and pursuing all degrees) will rise to 48 percent of the collegiate student body by 1986—up from 39 percent a decade earlier (Frankel, 1978, p. 4).

Noncredit Learning. Most adult would-be learners are interested primarily in noncredit learning options or in some kind of certificate that would add to their value to employers. Colleges in particular have responded vigorously to the growing interest in noncredit education. Between 1967 and 1975, the number of colleges offering noncredit adult education courses more than doubled, rising from 1,102 colleges to 2,225. The increase in student registration was no less impressive—up 57 percent, with an incredible 464 percent increase for the community colleges over the eight-year period (Kemp, 1978, p. 3). Some of the increase in college and university noncredit activities is directly attributable to the relatively recent practice of requiring professionals to keep up with their field of study through continuing education. "Mandated" education for a wide variety of professions, ranging from physicians to realtors, makes up the largest part of some university extension divisions today, and it is estimated that half of all the licensed professions are now subject to mandated continuing education (Watkins, 1977). (For further discussion of the hotly controversial issue of mandated continuing education, see Chapter Two.)

Changing Career Patterns

In most studies of adult learning interests, over half of the respondents say that they are learning (or that they would like to learn) in order to get a new job, advance in their present job, or get a better job (Aslanian and Brickell, 1980; Boaz, 1978; Carp, Peterson, and Roelfs, 1974; Cross, 1979a; Johnstone and Rivera, 1965). Moreover, a majority of people interested in upward mobility in the labor market think that education is the best way to achieve their goal. Of the forty million Americans who were reported in one recent study to be in the process of changing jobs or thinking of doing so, 62 percent said that they planned to seek further education (Arbeiter and others, 1978). In a related study, Aslanian and Brickell (1980) found that job or career change is the most common of all life's transitions and the most likely to motivate people to seek new learning opportunities. When adult learners were asked, in a national telephone survey, what motivated their learning activities, 83 percent mentioned some change in their life, and for 56 percent of them the change was related to job or career.

Although most adults claim that they are satisfied with their jobs (U.S. Bureau of the Census, 1977c, p. 389), a number of other factors contribute to the apparent restlessness of adults in their careers today. Among factors most frequently mentioned as stimulants to job-related education are the following:

- Job obsolescence. Jobs become obsolete because of technological advances or social change or occasionally because of
  sudden demographic change, such as that presently experienced in the declining need for teachers of children and
  young people. Further education in the development of new
  skills may be completely voluntary on the part of the worker,
  or it may be requested, rewarded, or required by an employer
  or by a professional association or state licensing agency.
- Increased participation of women in the labor market. In
  1960 only one third of American women worked outside the
  home; by 1977 half of all women over the age of 16 were in
  the labor market (National Commission on the Observance of
  International Women's Year, 1978, p. 43). Not only has it become more socially acceptable for wives and mothers to work
  outside the home, but the rising proportion of unmarried
  women in the population has made it economically necessary
  for large numbers of single, separated, divorced, and widowed
  women to develop careers of their own.
- Increased longevity. In 1900 the average worker spent
  twenty-one years of his or her life in the labor market; by
  1970 the work span of life had increased to thirty-seven
  years. It would be hard to find a job today that has not
  changed significantly in thirty-seven years, and probably even
  harder to find a person who has kept the same job duties over
  a lifetime.
- Job competition. Increased job competition is generally be-
  lieved to stimulate employers to raise educational requirements and workers to gain the competitive edge through further education.
- Higher aspirations. Certain groups in society—such as ethnic
  minorities, women, the elderly, and the handicapped—are
  seeking job advancement because it is more realistic than ever
  before for them to aspire to challenging jobs that require further education. In another respect, families are increasingly
  likely to need two wage earners to fulfill their aspirations for
  the "good life" depicted in national media.
- Social acceptability of career change. Whereas a worker was

once considered "unstable" if there were too many job
changes on the record, changing jobs now has some social
value as indicative of a more "interesting" or "adventuresome" person.
• The portability of pension plans. With the advent of social
security plus other nationwide employee benefits, workers
need not remain with a single employer throughout their lifetimes.

Despite all the above reasons for expecting greater job
mobility in the years ahead, some argue that the boom market
in adult education is to be found in education for leisure and
recreation rather than in job-related education. Arbeiter (1979),
in a provocative paper, maintains that the extent of midlife
career change has been greatly exaggerated. He bases his argument largely on national statistics showing that job mobility decreases with age. Families are most mobile at age 25, when 56
percent of the age cohort move to a different house, usually because of a job change. After that peak age of mobility, there is a
rather steady decline until by age 45 only 18 percent of the age
cohort are changing residences. Moreover, after the age of 40,
most people feel settled with respect to their careers; only 8
percent consider themselves in career transition, and relatively
few adults are interested in information about new career opportunities as they approach midlife (Arbeiter and others,
1978).

Increased Leisure

Although job-related education continues to dominate
the scene in adult education, learning for recreation and leisure
is the most rapidly growing field of study for adults, increasing
75 percent between 1969 and 1975, closely followed by learning for personal growth and family living, with a 60 percent increase (Boaz, 1978, p. 24).

There are a number of reasons for the substantial growth
of learning for recreation and personal enjoyment. First, of
course, we must take account of the rather small base of participants for recreational learning when compared with occupa-

tional training. To grow from 12 percent to 16 percent (for recreation) requires far fewer participants than to grow from 45 percent to 49 percent (for occupational-related education). Beyond that, however, certain social trends have contributed to the growth of learning for leisure and recreation. Among them are the following:

- The greatest growth in adult education is occurring among the well-educated, more affluent classes, who can afford education for leisure.
- The elderly constitute a major market for recreational learning, and the number of people 65 and older has been rising steadily. In 1950 they constituted 8 percent of the population (a little over twelve million people). By 1976 there were twenty-three million people 65 and over, and they made up 11 percent of the population (U.S. Bureau of the Census, 1977b, p. 10).
- There is more leisure for the average worker in the United States. The hours of leisure for the average urban resident increased from thirty-five hours per week in 1965 to thirty-nine in 1975 (U.S. Bureau of the Census, 1977c, p. 509). A small amount of the weekly increase in leisure time came from decreased working hours, but most of the increase in leisure time during the week seems to have come from decreased time spent in family care. Another source of leisure time comes from the reduction of the work year. In 1960 only 27 percent of plant workers and 38 percent of office workers had three weeks of paid vacation after ten years of service; by 1974 the proportion had increased to 75 percent and 87 percent, respectively, and about one third of all workers now have a month or more of vacation after fifteen years of service (U.S. Bureau of the Census, 1977c, p. 388).
- Concepts of leisure are beginning to change from an absence of work, with its connotations of idleness and guilt, to a more positive perception of leisure as time to be used for enjoyment and self-development.
- The activities of leisure are increasingly complex, and people take their leisure pursuits more seriously today. Whereas

water sports, for example, used to be fairly simple and limited to the few who lived near the water, such sports now have wide appeal and frequently require complicated equipment and instruction in water safety. Furthermore, people are less likely to be satisfied with "amateur" instruction and performance. Instead of learning sailing from family and friends, they are likely to sign up for a tutor or a class in order to "learn how to do it right."

• There is an emerging leadership with respect to leisure studies in the recreation profession. The American Association for Leisure and Recreation advertises itself as an "action-oriented organization dedicated to improving the quality of American life through the development of school, community, and national programs of leisure services and recreation education."

Changing Roles for Women

Women constitute the fastest-growing segment of the lifelong learning movement, with a 45 percent increase in participation rate between 1969 and 1975, compared to 18 percent for men (Boaz, 1978, p. 6). Moreover, since 1969 (when the National Center for Education Statistics began conducting its triennial surveys of participation in adult education) women's participation in part-time adult learning activities has increased almost four times as fast as their numbers in the population.

The reasons for this rapid increase in women's participation in educational activities are obviously complex, a mixture of the decline of traditional female roles and a rise of new ones. Women's roles in the society were changing long before the women's movement attained the high visibility that it has today. At the beginning of this century, women not only spent all their waking hours on various household chores; they spent virtually all the years of their lives raising a family. That factor alone would dictate dramatic change in the roles of women, but all sorts of social and technological changes have steadily added to the decreased family responsibilities of women.

Children are entering school earlier and staying longer. In 1964 only about one fourth of the children between the ages of 3 and 5 were enrolled in school, but by 1975 almost half were in school (Golladay, 1977, p. 163). At the same time, the proportion of 17 year olds staying in school long enough to graduate from high school has increased steadily and markedly, from 6 percent in 1900 to 59 percent in 1950 to 74 percent in 1975 (Golladay, 1977, p. 174). Thus, even if the family and women's traditional role for child care had remained unchanged, the actual time spent caring for children would still have decreased. The fact is, of course, that "the family" has not remained constant. Divorces, for example, have shown a steady increase for the past fifty years, going from ten per thousand married women between the ages of 14 and 44 in 1920 to thirty-two in 1974 (U.S. Bureau of the Census, 1977c, p. 66), but the rise in the divorce rate has been especially marked over the last decade. In 1960 forty-one women out of a thousand between the ages of 30 and 44 were divorced; by 1975 ninety-three were.

Social change and technological change are intertwined in their impact on the family and on women's roles. To a large extent, technology has reduced the time needed for family care, making social change both necessary and desirable. The revolution in food preparation alone has changed the lives of women in the home dramatically, but automatic washers and dryers, drip-dry fabrics, dishwashers, and a host of other labor-saving devices have continued to make a dramatic impact on household chores. In 1965 full-time urban housewives reported spending 50 percent of their time on family care, and married employed women spent 29 percent; one decade later, the average housewife spent 44 percent of her time in family care, and employed wives spent one fourth of their time on domestic chores (U.S. Bureau of the Census, 1977c, p. 509).

Despite dramatic changes in the American home, the traditional roles of women as wives and mothers have not changed nearly as rapidly as their new roles as workers in the labor force. The trend toward women working outside the home began building in the 1950s and exploded in the 1970s. By September 1977, 49 percent of women over the age of 16 were in the labor force, and they constituted 41 percent of the total work force (National Commission on the Observance of International Women's Year, 1978, p. 43). For the generation of women

young enough to have children between the ages of 6 and 17,
the common pattern now is for wives and mothers to work outside the home; over half (55 percent) do so (U.S. Bureau of the
Census, 1977c, p. 375).

Thus, the revolution in women's roles is the result of two
complementary forces. On the one hand, social and technological changes push women out of the home; on the other hand,
new opportunities in education and the labor market pull
women into the new worlds of work and education. "Displaced
homemakers" and "reentry women" are a social phenomenon
of considerable importance to the learning society. Research on
educational brokering indicates that women—many of them displaced homemakers—constitute 50 to 70 percent of the clients
seeking counseling and information regarding educational and
career opportunities (National Center for Educational Brokering, 1979). Arbeiter and associates (1978, p. 18) also found a
substantial number of displaced homemakers among their sample of adults making career transitions. Women were about
equally split between those who were changing jobs (46 percent) and those who were reentering the work force (48 percent), whereas most men (88 percent) were job changers. Education undoubtedly will continue to play a major role for
women making the transition from home to workplace for at
least the next two decades. For these women, self-assessment,
career planning, brush-up courses, and new learning related to
careers will continue to be a high-priority need.

Equal Opportunity

If educational opportunity were ever to be fully realized,
it would overshadow all other growth factors of the learning
society. The present talk about eliminating age discrimination in
educational opportunities, coming as it does on the heels of the
egalitarian thrust in higher education and the community college movement, has much of the rhetoric of the equal opportunity movement about it. As is evident in the data of Chapter
Three, however, American adults currently constitute the most
unequally educated segment of society. There is considerably
more opportunity now for young people to gain access to post-

secondary education than for older people to gain access to the kind of education that would benefit them. If words and intentions predict, in any way, the actions to follow, the drive for equal educational opportunity in adult education should be a major factor in the future growth of the learning society.

Recommendations by state and national commissions usually start with the declaration that educational opportunity is the top priority. The Lifelong Learning Act (Public Law 94-482, 1976) is typical. It states that "American society should have as a goal the availability of appropriate opportunities for lifelong learning for all its citizens without regard to restrictions of previous education or training, sex, age, handicapping condition, social or ethnic background, or economic circumstance" (Section 131). The 1979 assembly of the American Association of Community and Junior Colleges proclaimed in a Bill of Rights for the lifelong learner: "Every American has the right to continue to learn throughout life. Every adult American has the right to equal opportunity for access to relevant learning opportunities at each stage of life" (Gilder, 1979, p. 113). So far, virtually every policy statement made by local, state, national, or international commissions recommends the identification of target groups of adults who are currently underserved by educational providers (Cross, 1978b; Gilder, 1979; Lifelong Learning and Public Policy, 1978; UNESCO, 1976). The target groups are almost always the same—consisting largely of the "educationally disadvantaged," which by definition means those not well served by educational providers. The recommendations for action run the gamut from educational programs that are suited to the needs of the target group to equity in financial aid to better counseling and advising systems. New adult learners will be brought into the learning society to the extent that these recommendations are perceptive about needs and realistic about implementation. Sweden has done more than any other nation to reconcile the rhetoric and the reality with respect to age discrimination. Its educational policy is clearly designed to reduce the educational opportunity gap between the generations. Today almost two thirds of all newly enrolled students in institutions of postsecondary education in

Sweden are over 25 years of age (Abrahamsson, 1980). Such social policy has immediate and widespread ramifications for the learning society.

I will not dwell further here on the role of equal opportunity as a force in the growth of the learning society because the current discrepancy between the ideal and the reality is treated in some detail in Chapter Three.

Technological Change

In industrialized nations we tend to think of change as largely the result of scientific and technological progress, because such change is so spectacular. Technological advances occur in quantum leaps that result not in just "more" or "better" but in radically "different" ways of doing things. The transportation industry serves as a good illustration. For thousands of years, man walked from place to place. With the taming of the horse, the distance traveled and the loads transported became a different order of magnitude. With the invention of trains and cars, another quantum leap occurred. Then air travel increased the speed of travel, not just from twenty to eighty miles per hour, as improvements in the car had done, but from eighty to eight hundred miles per hour. Astronauts now move through space, not just ten times faster than airplanes but at the rate of 25,000 miles per hour.

Once the quantum leap occurs, the "old" transportation method may still exist, but trying to improve it to compete with the new proves frustrating and futile. No amount of careful breeding, attention to diet, or training can make the greatest horse even approach in efficiency the "transportation work" done by the most mediocre car. Technological advance in the transportation industry has resulted not just in greater speed but in a fundamentally different mode of transportation. Moreover, the time elapsing between inventions has grown shorter and shorter. Walking, as a means of transportation, served generation after generation; jet airplanes and space travel occurred within the time span of a single generation.

The speed of change affects not only the lives of individuals but also the way in which society handles education. Instead of parents' passing what they have learned to their children, children today must learn lessons never known by their parents. It is the rare child who learns the skills for his or her livelihood from parents. There is, for example, nothing that the horse breeder, as transportation magnate of his generation, can teach his son about horses that is at all relevant to the transportation industry once the quantum leap of the invention of the internal-combustion engine has been made. If the son is 25 years old, is preparing to take over his father's business, and has "finished" his education when the gasoline engine appears on the scene, he has some decisions to make about his occupation: he can preside over a dying industry, convert from breeding horses for transportation to breeding them for pleasure or racing, or learn about cars and trucks as the transportation vehicles of the future—until another quantum leap occurs.

People living in the United States can, with only a few minutes' reflection, think of a great many technological changes that have made their lives totally different in some way from the lives of their parents—television, commercial air travel, frozen foods, credit cards, superhighways, permanent press fabrics, to mention only a few. These wonders of technology have created and wiped out entire industries and occupations in the space of a decade, and they have forced individuals to cope with change both as producers and as consumers. There is, however, a subtle change in the workplace that has even more impact on the need for lifelong learning than the changes in materials and products wrought by technology. That is the shift of American workers from people who produce things to people who produce information. Today, about half of the American payroll goes for the manipulation of symbols rather than the production of things, according to Douglass Cater, of the Aspen Institute for Humanistic Studies (in Magarrell, 1980).

This production of information, always a characteristic of academic life, has escalated so sharply in many academic disciplines that information "explosion" is not too strong an image. In the single decade between 1961 and 1970, published abstracts in psychology increased threefold—from 7,353 to 21,722 documents included in *Psychological Abstracts* (Dubin, 1972). Academics are borrowing the concept of half-life from nuclear physics to measure obsolescence in professional specialties. The half-life of a professional's competency is defined as the time after completion of professional training when, because of new developments, practicing professionals become roughly half as competent as they were upon graduation (Dubin, 1972). The half-life in medicine is estimated to be about five years; in psychology it is ten to twelve years. Chapanis (1971) estimates that a compulsive engineering psychologist would have to read thirty or forty articles and books a day to keep abreast of current literature. But even for the average well-informed professional, the estimate is that 20 percent of work time should be spent learning about recent developments (George and Dubin, 1972).

The explosion of knowledge means that almost all professionals are self-directed learners; but most are also spending increasing amounts of time in a wide variety of organized learning activities. At professional meetings tens of thousands of people converge in the hotels of a city for a week each year to get the latest information in their field. Professional associations conduct workshops throughout the country and prepare self-instructional materials so that their members can keep abreast of new developments. Large numbers of people in professional-technical-managerial careers are returning to the campus to change or upgrade their careers. Paltridge and Regan (1978) found that over three quarters of the adults who were back in formal education and training programs after an interruption of five years or more were changing careers, thinking about doing so, or upgrading present careers. Over 40 percent of these mid-career learners were in income brackets of over $20,000, most engaged in management/professional information industries.

If technological change and the knowledge explosion make lifelong learning increasingly necessary, they also make it increasingly possible. Audiotapes that can be played by commuters on the way to work are only the beginnings of a revolution in educational delivery systems. Stanford University's school of engineering uses "talk-back" television to communicate with engineers in some thirty firms located on the San Francisco peninsula. In cooperation with three other universities, the "Stanford Network" enrolled over 3,600 students during a recent twelve-month period (California Postsecondary Education Commission, 1979). The 1978 catalog of the California Continuing Education of the Bar lists forty-five video cassette titles and forty-four locations where attorneys may view the tapes. Many of the locations are private law offices. Some large companies are beginning to develop their own graduate-level courses on video in order to keep their professional staff up to date, but they are also utilizing media educational delivery systems for a wide variety of employee education, training, and communication functions. The number of things that can be done and the number of people who can be reached through distance delivery systems of education are virtually unlimited today. Within the last few years, a large number of reports, studies, and recommendations for educational uses of the media have been issued—so many, in fact, that that literature in itself constitutes a knowledge explosion about which professionals in education must now inform themselves. (For a small sample of recent literature on the uses of media in education, see Atkinson, 1978; Bretz, Rutledge, and Richards, 1978; California Postsecondary Education Commission, 1979; Carlisle, 1978; Chamberlain, 1980; Dede, 1979; Dirr and Pedone, 1979; Forman and Brown, 1978; Hargreaves, 1980; Kelly and Anandam, 1977-78; McMahon, Anderson, and Anderson, 1978; Nickerson and Teachman, 1979; Rothstein, 1978; UNESCO, 1977; Wilson and Goerke, 1978-79.)

CHAPTER 2

Issues in Recruiting Adult Learners

Most of the literature on adult education and learning begins with the assumption that education is good and that the goal is to get as many people as possible to participate. Thus, it comes as something of a shock to find that not everyone agrees that the goal of the learning society is to maximize educational participation. Historically, adult learning has been largely voluntary, and many are concerned that the lifelong learning movement may lead to some form of coercion on adults to participate in educational activities, with pressure exerted from various sources. First, there is pressure from traditional colleges and universities interested in enticing adults into educational programs as a cushion against predicted enrollment losses among younger students. The second pressure arises from consumer protection groups, professional associations, and licensing boards. It involves the hotly controversial issue of "mandated" adult education; the question is whether profes-

32

sionals and occupational groups serving the public should be required to keep up with new developments in their fields through mandated continuing education. The third pressure is a more subtle policy issue arising from society's general concern about equal opportunity. Every time a new educational opportunity presents itself, it is the already well educated who rush to take advantage of it. This has the effect of increasing the gap between the educational "haves" and "have nots" and may well result in increased pressure on the less privileged members of society to participate in educational activities "for their own good." All three issues are complex, and I see no way to provide simple answers to the dilemmas posed. Some airing of the pros and cons of these issues may prove helpful, however.

"Recruitment"

Criticism over the aggressive "recruitment" of adult learners is directed almost solely at traditional higher education, which represents only one small part of lifelong learning. But it is an important part. Some critics believe that the recruitment of adults into traditional educational programs will result ultimately in the spread of lockstep schooling and an overcredentialed society. Instead of lifelong learning, they say, we will find adults coerced into lifelong *schooling*. Warren Ziegler (1977, pp. 15-16), a futurist at Syracuse University, objects to what he sees as "a strong trend toward getting more and more citizens to conduct their learning activities within the organizational framework of the formal educational system." He recommends a "radical conservative stance" that would leave "adult learners alone to conduct their learning in ways and about concerns which meet their own criteria and standards." It should be made clear that Ziegler is an advocate of adult learning; what he is opposed to is any policy that would facilitate the extension of formal education into the adult years. He contends that "the history of public educational policy leads to the conclusion that to support means to define, curtail, render accountable, and ultimately govern. Lifelong learning should not be governed. It just should be" (p. 17). In a background paper prepared for the

Lifelong Learning Project, Green, Ericson, and Seidman (1977, p. ii) also recommend a "hands-off" public policy regarding adult education: "Any effort to produce a large-scale expansion of lifelong learning, through beginning in an effort to provide *alternatives* to existing arrangements, will end simply by creating an *expansion* of existing arrangements." Other critics are less concerned about nontraditional alternatives being absorbed by traditional education than about the erosion of traditional academic standards. Writing for the *New York Times* (Aug. 21, 1979), Frank Wolf of Columbia University charges that, in their eagerness to recruit adult learners, colleges and universities are engaging in "academic hucksterism," are "selling credentials" through liberal policies on conferring credit, and are compromising academic standards by offering programs designed by "marketing-oriented academic bureaucrats" instead of faculty committees.

The yearning for control by faculty committees is not shared by many adult educators, who believe that adults are better served by programs that meet learner standards rather than the standards of faculty committees. There is a big difference, they contend, between "serving" adults (that is, finding out what adults want and providing it) and "recruiting" them (offering predetermined programs and getting students to enroll in them). Until recently, when traditional college programs became interested in the "recruitment" of adults, adult learners were "served" by extension divisions and any number of community agencies that, by and large, offered whatever classes and other activities adult learners seemed to want. Adult educators frequently saw themselves in a subservient role, complying with the wishes of learners and making minimal demands on adults to conform to any set criteria of attendance or performance. The subservient role, idealized if not always practiced by adult educators, is a different tradition from the "authority role" practiced in most colleges, where the curriculum is determined by the faculty, the teacher is the authority, and grades and credits are used to assure conformance to certain standards set by the institution.

The issue at stake is the ultimate freedom of adults to determine their own learning programs. Some programs, of course, "recruit" adults precisely on the grounds that their program does offer more freedom than traditional educational programs. But many college personnel now talk openly of recruiting adults into regular programs to fill the seats left vacant by a diminishing number of 18 year olds. The suspicion is that colleges are more interested in meeting their own needs for survival than in serving the learning needs of adults. Rockhill (1976, p. 204) is sharply critical of the educational establishment's interest in lifelong learning. She charges that even the federal "lifelong learning bill . . . appears aimed at promoting the survival of institutions rather than the improvement of adult learning opportunities." Hilton (1979), in a survey of the responses of state planning agencies to lifelong learning, also observed a "proinstitutional stance" among agencies eager to help campuses solve enrollment problems through the recruitment of adult learners. (It is also true that he found a counterforce of state legislators and planners who took an antiinstitutional stance, contending that "institutions which have experienced poor planning and management should not expect to be rescued through public support for a new clientele.")

Perhaps these examples will serve to illustrate the emotionalism rampant in the professional literature as well as in the popular press over the issues of "recruiting" adults or indeed even encouraging them, through government policy, to join the educational mainstream. Most critics interpret "educational mainstream" to mean degree-credit programs sponsored by traditional colleges and universities, even programs labeled "nontraditional." As in most highly charged issues, critics and advocates tend to overgeneralize, but there is probably some truth in the allegations of the critics that some colleges are compromising standards in order to attract adult learners; that some colleges are more interested in meeting their needs to protect faculty jobs than in serving adult learners; and that the opportunity for lifelong learning might be turned into the threat of lifelong schooling. What, then, is the role of traditional colleges and universities in the lifelong learning movement? Let us look first at what has been happening in colleges with respect to adult learners.

There is not much doubt that hundreds of traditional col-

leges and universities have been working hard since about 1970
to attract—recruit, if you will—adult learners. A national survey
of institutional practices has not been conducted since 1972,
when the Commission on Non-traditional Study commissioned
the Center for Research and Development in Higher Education
at the University of California at Berkeley to survey two- and
four-year colleges and universities for their responses to the lifelong learning movement (Ruyle and Geiselman, 1974). At that
time, between 1,000 and 1,400 American colleges and universities offered degree programs that were considered "nontraditional" in the sense that they served nontraditional learners or
were free of the time or place requirements of traditional classroom instruction. The overwhelming majority (86 percent) of
the programs were less than five years old in 1972; only 7 percent were more than ten years old—fairly clear evidence of the
"sudden" entrance of colleges and universities into the business
of making program modifications in order to attract and serve
adult learners. Although the rate of growth of nontraditional
programs in higher education may have slowed somewhat since
those heady years of the expansion of nontraditional programs,
I suspect that a national survey today would show that a substantial majority of colleges and universities have designed programs or modified procedures specifically to attract adult
learners.

Research suggests, however, that changes in traditional
programs have been rather modest. The commission's survey
showed that 67 percent of the programs classified as "nontraditional" were nontraditional in the sense that they utilized off-
campus locations; 57 percent used nontraditional methods; and
48 percent offered nontraditional content. In the words of the
investigators (Ruyle and Geiselman, 1974, p. 71), the nontraditional programs in existence in 1972 "more often constituted
new ways of teaching old subjects to new students rather than
new subjects as such."

It is probably not unfair to conclude that around 1970
hundreds of colleges made rather minor concessions to accommodate adult learners in regular degree programs. During this
same period, however, a variety of bold, innovative degree pro-

grams for adults attracted considerable national and international attention. British Open University and the University of Mid-America are examples of experimentation with new methods for instructional delivery. Empire State College in New York and Metropolitan State College in Minnesota are examples of totally new educational programs, specifically designed for mature learners. And many colleges launched external degree programs for adults; by 1976 more than 54,000 adults were enrolled in almost 250 external degree programs in the United States (Sosdian, 1978).

Degree programs for adults represent only the tip of the iceberg of the response of traditional colleges and universities to adult learners. Noncredit programs are the most rapidly growing programs in all higher education. Between the late 1960s and the mid 1970s, both two- and four-year colleges doubled their noncredit offerings; but four-year colleges, where the decline in youth enrollments hits most heavily, now represent the fastest-growing segment for noncredit activities. Table 3 shows the trends between 1968 and 1978.

Table 3. Institutions Offering Noncredit Adult and
Continuing Education Activities

	1967-68	1975-76	1977-78
Universities	146	157	160
Other four-year colleges	534	1,076	1,236
Two-year colleges	422	992	979
Total	1,102	2,225	2,375

Source: National Center for Education Statistics, 1979.

Colleges clearly are giving a great deal of attention to adults, and the pattern of their timing casts some doubt on the altruism of their motives. At the same time, traditional colleges *are* being responsive to adult needs and interests. That is evident from the number of adults seeking the educational services of colleges and universities. The number of adults 35 years of age and older enrolled in degree programs increased by 66 percent between 1972 and 1978 (U.S. Bureau of the Census, 1979b), and registrants in noncredit courses offered by institutions of higher education swelled to over ten million in 1978, almost double what it was a decade earlier (National Center for Education Statistics, 1979).

The best answer to the charge that institutions of higher education are opportunists, looking for a new clientele to replace the old, is that with the notable exception of evening colleges and extension divisions, traditional colleges paid little attention to lifelong learning until quite recently. In the 1940s and 1950s, colleges had more young, full-time students than they could serve. The new fascination of colleges with adult learners is in large measure attributable to the demographics of the birthrate. The fact that the lifelong learning movement is of considerable financial importance to colleges does not in itself, however, constitute a valid criticism.

Most colleges are seriously interested in serving adult learning needs, and many are working hard to conduct "needs assessments" in order to determine what programs are of interest to the potential adult clientele (Cross, 1979c). Many adults do seem to be finding what they want in both credit and noncredit programs offered by colleges, and it is fairly clear that, in the highly competitive buyer's market of the 1980s, colleges that place institutional needs above those of the adults they are trying to attract will probably lose out in the long run.

Critics who fear the "control" of adult learning programs by bureaucracies of one sort or another—institutional, governmental, or professional—can perhaps take modest comfort in the fact that adult enrollments in noncredit activities are growing considerably faster than degree-credit enrollments. Critics on the other side of the fence, who deplore "hucksterism" and the erosion of academic standards, can, ironically, also find comfort in the trend toward noncredit adult learning. Since noncredit activities are openly market oriented and not subject to the usual academic regulation, they are less likely to be associated with control or regulation—at least not on the part of institutional education. The irony here, however, is that professional associations may assume ever greater control over much noncredit learning that is absolutely critical to professional advancement (see Stern, 1976). More attention will be given to the issue of "mandatory" continuing education in the section to follow.

As to the charges that alternative forms of adult education and traditional education will ruin each other, it is true that there is some blurring of the borderlines between traditional and nontraditional education. And it is possible for everyone to be unhappy about that. Traditionalists will see the absorption of nontraditional practices into regular programs as an erosion of academic standards, while nontraditionalists will see the same trends as "bureaucratic control" and the erosion of acceptable alternatives to traditional education.

For better or worse, many institutions are approving and absorbing nontraditional practices into their standard degree programs. The most "conservative" of the nontraditional practices is probably the creation of degree-credit "off-campus" offerings now practiced by the overwhelming majority of traditional institutions. There is nothing very alarming about transporting the professor and his notes five miles or even fifty miles to an off-campus location and scheduling classes when working adults can attend. A more controversial nontraditional practice is the granting of academic credit for work not accomplished through standard classroom procedures, but it too is practiced by a majority of traditional institutions today. The survey of nontraditional collegiate practices sponsored by the Commission on Non-traditional Study (Ruyle and Geiselman, 1974) showed that, as early as 1972, 80 percent of the surveyed institutions grant academic credit by examination, and a recent College Board survey ("Colleges Expect Increased Commitment," 1979) found that admissions officers expect increasing institutional support for credit-by-examination policies over the next three to five years. More controversial than credit by examination are the programs of the Council for the Advancement of Experiential Learning (CAEL), which promotes the assessment of prior learning for academic credit, and the Office on Educational Credit (OEC) of the American Council on Education (ACE), which promotes the granting of credit for noncollegiate-sponsored learning. Both expanded during the 1970s. People who want to make sharp distinctions between "traditional" and "nontraditional" learning at the collegiate level will have considerable difficulty in the years ahead. Whether that means that the educational establishment has, as the critics predicted, gained control over nontraditional alternatives or whether colleges are "selling out" to the necessities for keeping their faculties employed is subject to interpretation.

There is, I hasten to point out, also the straightforward interpretation that education is a product of the collective society and that historically it has responded to changing needs. For all the reasons discussed in Chapter One, there is a need now for attention to lifelong learning; and, fortunately, educational institutions are free to shift their efforts to this new priority. Given the speed of institutional response right now, it is undeniably important to give serious attention to the concerns expressed by the critics. Either the spread of the overcredentialed society or the compromise of the standards of the educational system would defeat the goals of the lifelong learning movement. It is hard to see, however, how responding sincerely to adult interests in continued learning will do anything but benefit learners, institutions, and society.

"Mandated" Continuing Education

The term *mandated continuing education* (MCE) came into being to describe the tendency of states and professional associations to require the members of certain vocations and professions to fulfill educational obligations in order to retain or renew their licenses to practice. Stern (1976, p. 361) calls mandated continuing education "the most vexatious issue confronting adult educators and society." Forty-five states now require continuing education for optometrists, and forty-two have continuing education requirements for nursing home administrators. In Iowa legislators recently passed an omnibus bill requiring all twenty-three professional licensing boards in the state to establish continuing education requirements for relicensure (Watkins, 1979). While most people believe that continuing education is a good way for professionals who serve the public to keep up with new developments in the field, there is rising concern about blanket legislation that would require continuing education in the professions. Interestingly enough, the organized opposition comes largely from adult educators, who presumably have the most to gain from such legislation. The controversy over mandated continuing education emerged dramatically at the 1977 National Adult Education Conference, when a rump session of adult educators convened at a YMCA down the street from the convention hotel. The issue reached the convention floor when Roby Kidd, secretary general of the International Council for Adult Education, warned in an address summarizing the conference, "This is not only a matter of great social importance, but one on which we would expect adult educators to make a great contribution. [But] instead of careful review of what is happening, some adult educators have accepted the legislation with approval or with glee. It seems that we are pathetically pleased to be wanted, to be recognized even for the wrong reasons, and we have been quick to see that in the short run there may be money to be made by offering programs to people who are legally compelled to attend some activities" (*Adult and Continuing Education Today*, July 2, 1979, p. 61). A newsletter entitled *Second Thoughts* was one of the outcomes of that rump session. It is dedicated to tracking trends and raising questions about mandated continuing. education and related issues. The primary objection is the extension of "schooling" into the adult years, with its emphasis on formal, competitive, credentialed education. A new association, the National Alliance for Voluntary Learning (NAVL), has also been established to develop an action program to promote *voluntary* learning.

So far, most of the protest over MCE has taken the form of raising questions that reveal quite clearly the position of the questioner. "Is lifelong education a guarantee of permanent inadequacy?" or "Is there school after death?" (Lister, 1975). In an article entitled "Must We All Go Back to School?" Lisman and Ohliger (1978, p. 35) complain that "for many millions of adults, continuing education is compulsory. And it is not an opportunity but a threat. . . . [Soon] the middle-aged dropout may find himself running from a truant officer." Mandatory education, in the eyes of its critics, extends even beyond the understandable desire to provide the public with well-qualified, up-to-date professional services. Traffic offenders are frequently *required* to take a course as an alternative to paying a fine or going to jail. Welfare recipients are sometimes coerced into educational programs thought to be in their best interests. These trends illustrate the enormous regard in which people hold education as the solution to a variety of social problems, but they also pose a threat to individual choice and substitute a negative image of education as punishment or threat for a positive image of education as an opportunity for personal growth and human fulfillment.

The questions about MCE are complex, centering around three basic issues: (1) To what extent should free American citizens be coerced into education? (2) Is compulsory education effective; that is, do people who are required to attend continuing education classes necessarily become more competent? (3) Who should be charged with developing and enforcing standards for professional accountability? The difficulties in arriving at a straightforward solution to these dilemmas was captured by a teacher of adult educators, who confessed "I find myself in the odd position of making it mandatory that my students move toward more self-directed, voluntary, autonomous learning" (*Adult and Continuing Education Today,* July 2, 1979, p. 60). Paradoxically, if we could only require that people be motivated to learn voluntarily, most of our problems would be solved.

The first question is basically a values question and probably will not be resolved easily. The group of adult educators organized to oppose MCE vow that they will continue to oppose its spread, but they favor working positively to get more adults into programs of voluntary education. They plan to form alliances among like-minded groups in order to seek new ways to encourage and validate learning without use of established credentialing institutions or coercion (*Adult and Continuing Education Today,* July 2, 1979). Others are inclined to accept MCE as a fact of life and bend their efforts toward making it as good as possible. If we accept compulsory education for children, Stern (1976) argues, we might just as well accept it for adults, unless we believe that children have fewer individual rights than adults. In any event, he says, compulsory education is with us, and we cannot ignore it. The professional in today's world must engage in continuing education in order to continue in his profession—or in order to change careers.

Leaving aside for a moment the unresolved issue of whether society has a right to compel professionals to continue learning, let us look at the second concern. Presumably, the question of whether MCE results in greater professional competency could be answered through research, but the answers to date remain inconclusive. That seems to leave us, for the present at least, relying on the following commonsense conclusions: (1) As a group, people who are required to learn are more likely to have up-to-date information than people who are not so required. (2) People who are motivated to learn are more likely to be better informed than people who are merely serving time in class. (3) Voluntary learning is most effective, but compulsory learning is better than nothing.

Even if research could be marshaled to validate these conclusions, such "evidence" would not really answer the ultimate question of whether MCE protects consumers from incompetent practice. The major problem, says Cyril Houle (in Vogel, 1979), is not ensuring that a professional has the competence to do something but that he or she is actually doing it. The professional must be able not only to absorb the evolving knowledge and theoretical concepts of a field but also learn the skills for implementing that knowledge; such education cannot be obtained from simply attending a class or seminar.

Regarding the third question debated in the literature without any apparent resolution—Who or what organizations should be charged with developing and enforcing the standards for professional competency on behalf of the consumer?—there seems to be general agreement that the beleaguered consumer has almost no voice and there are critics of other potential "watchdogs" or professional standards. There is rising opposition to bureaucratic governmental regulation; professional societies are accused of admitting only "their own kind"; and the universities and professional schools and the entire credentialing process are under attack for perpetuating class status. Rockhill (1977-78, p. 367) claims that historically in the United States certification has served to "(1) define social class status; (2) sort and select out people for jobs or to join the ranks of the unemployed; (3) determine who will have access to knowledge; (4) increase public dependence upon the services of experts; (5) perpetuate a vast educational enterprise directed at turning out certificate holders rather than educated individuals; and (6) limit our civil liberties as we are forced to submit to certain rituals or professional services which may not be of our choosing." While she grants that certification has had positive effects as well, she concludes that MCE will lead to "compulsory life-long education and with it the demise of adult education as a fluid, open, voluntary field of educational endeavor."

It is unlikely that the issue of MCE will be resolved to everyone's satisfaction within the next decade. Louis Phillips, who has been monitoring the issue, feels that the trend is toward professional societies' policing themselves. He notes that the idea of societies becoming the watchdogs of the professions follows the "desire of most professionals to protect the integrity of their fields from the lazy or complacent few who represent potential embarrassment and harm" (in Vogel, 1979). The idea of professions' policing themselves is all to the good, but it does not solve the problem of coerced education for professionals, nor does it address the question of the growing competition among the providers of MCE. In California there are already some 600,000 adults under statutory requirements to keep abreast of their fields through continuing education. For educational providers that represents a "gold mine" of potential students, especially since the requirements are for periodic updating throughout the entire career of the licensed professional. Colleges and universities are quite likely to see continuing education in the professions as a lucrative and logical extension of their educational responsibilities. Stern, however, believes that they may be too late, since the universities have already been "largely outflanked by what has already happened." He illustrates his point by citing the present situation in accounting.

In California, the Board of Accounting requires that to maintain status as a certified public accountant, the CPA must complete eighty hours of continuing education in every two-year period, and this parallels provisions in some twenty-seven other states at the present time. Nationally, the American Institute of Certified Public Accountants (AICPA) has organized a neat and tidy package, not only with state accounting associations, but also presently with some twenty-eight state accounting (licensing) boards to codify their provision of continuing education. In their arrangement, they have considered only a limited role for university providers and less for private entrepreneurs, with a predominant role for the professional association. The national office of the AICPA has a continuing education branch which in the current year has budgeted some 7 million dollars for its activity. Some of this is for seminars and workshops throughout the country, but most is for the provision of materials, books, programmed instruction, and so on, to be used to a limited extent by individual accountants, and more broadly by the state associations as materials for classroom instruction throughout the country [Stern, 1979, pp. 6-7].

This vigorous activity raises a number of questions. Should professional associations control continuing education in the professions? Arguments in favor concern the presumed relevance of the learning to practical problems; the arguments against concern the ultimate control by the profession of entry and continuation in the profession. What is to prevent professional associations from offering instructional packages for bachelor's degrees, asks Stern. And what is to prevent them from controlling both the number and the type of people practicing the profession? On the other side of the issue, professional associations charge that much of university professional education is irrelevant and that practicing professionals know better than university professors what kinds of learning experiences to provide. Furthermore, there is ample evidence that professional schools too practice their own form of social class bias.

Houle (1980), who has conducted the most extensive study to date of the demand for continuous learning in the professions, acknowledges that the present situation is "filled with jurisdictional conflicts and tensions" (p. 312). If the field had matured, he says, it might be worthwhile to try to resolve the allocations of function. But the field is still growing and changing so fast that "it seems likely that the number and kind of providers and the designs for learning that they offer will continue to grow in size, proliferate in form, and ceaselessly combine and recombine" (pp. 310-311). Among his policy recommendations are the following: "The primary responsibility for learning should rest on the individual" and "The processes of recredentialing should be thoroughly rethought and redeveloped to determine the appropriate role of continuing education" (pp. 305, 314). That is probably the best advice that can be given at the present time with respect to MCE.

Equal Opportunity

In national as well as international reports and recommendations, the issue of equal opportunity is a major concern and is featured prominently. The UNESCO (1976) recommendations, for example, are unequivocal in stating that "the most educationally underprivileged groups should be given the highest priority" (p. 2). Equity, defined as the accessibility and availability of learning opportunities for all citizens, is also the first recommendation in a report prepared by the Lifelong Learning Project (*Lifelong Learning and Public Policy,* 1978).

Recommending equal opportunity, however, is considerably easier than attaining it. At the present time, the gap between the well educated and the poorly educated is growing rather than narrowing. The first two issues discussed in this chapter, the growth in the recruitment of adult learners by colleges and the increase in legislation mandating continuing education for professionals, will accelerate the widening of that gap. With the new active and aggressive interest of colleges and the professions in the continuing education of adults, opportunities for lifelong learning are even more likely to tilt in the direction of relatively well-educated young professionals. Best and Stern (1976) have advanced the interesting notion that the type of job one holds is a better predictor of educational opportunity than vice versa. Young professionals, in fact, will probably have more trouble escaping continuing education than gaining entrance to it. Not so for high school dropouts and unskilled laborers.

Adults with less than a high school education constitute 40 percent of the adult population, and 23 million adults were judged to "lack important functional competencies" on the Adult Performance Level Survey sponsored by the federal government in 1975; a recent report issued by the Ford Foundation calls for the creation of a network of community-based programs in the neighborhoods of the poor in an attempt to increase the functional skills of adults (Hunter and Harman, 1979). As the report points out, adults with the reading and writing skills learned in the first four grades of school would be considered educated in India or Indonesia, but they are functionally illiterate in the United States because they are unable to address a letter, interpret a bus schedule, or understand a printed explanation of finance charges. True, considerable effort is going into addressing the problem. In 1976 the nation's largest antiliteracy project, the Adult Basic Education Program, enrolled almost two million adults and was receiving approximately $68 million in federal assistance and $184 million in local and state funds. Even so, only 2 to 4 percent of American illiterates enter such programs, and one third drop out before completion of the courses, which last the equivalent of about one semester (Hunter and Harman, 1979).

The problems of functionally illiterate adults are extremely serious and stubborn, but at least they are generally recognized by legislators as a public responsibility. Less readily recognized are responsibilities to adults whose lives are seriously limited by lack of education. According to statistics from the National Center for Education Statistics, fifty-three million adults had less than a high school education in 1975, and only 3 percent were participating in adult education programs. At the same time, 28 percent of the eighteen million college graduates were participating in adult education programs. This means that adults with less than four years of high school constitute 36 per-

cent of the out-of-school adult population but only 10 percent
of adult learners, while college graduates constitute 13 percent
of the population and 31 percent of the adult learners (Boaz,
1978).

As everyone knows by now, these problems cannot be
easily solved. Since 1970 more than fifty sets of recommendations have been issued by assorted commissions, state planning
offices, and federal agencies (see Cross, 1978b, for references to
reports issued between 1970 and 1976). Almost without exception, these agencies recommend increased efforts to reach and
serve the undereducated. There appears to be widespread agreement that governmental intervention will be necessary and that
it must tread the middle ground between laissez-faire policies,
which permit maximum individual freedom but result in a society where the educationally rich get richer and the poor get
poorer, and "compulsory adult education" policies, which curtail individual freedoms by compelling the poor to "become
more equal." Yet the middle road in governmental policy is difficult to follow. Widespread indifference to the Lifelong Learning Act (Hartle and Kutner, 1979) is an example of laissez-faire
federal policy, while compulsory education for the poor is occasionally practiced when mothers receiving food stamps are pres-
sured to take classes in nutrition or illiterates on welfare are
ordered to enroll in adult basic education classes (Lisman and
Ohliger, 1978).

Future Directions

This airing of issues in lifelong learning has raised some
questions about future directions for the learning society. A
society in which lifelong learning is a nearly universal activity is
apparently not an unmitigated blessing. Much depends on the
circumstances under which people are learning. My assumptions
about who will need to be learning under what circumstances
are as follows:

1. Lifelong learning will be increasingly necessary for everyone,
   and those who lack basic skills and the motivation for life-

long learning will be severely handicapped in obtaining the necessities of life and in adding any measure of personal satisfaction and enjoyment to the quality of their lives.

2. Voluntary learning for adult learners is the appropriate goal for the learning society. However, since we know that learning is habit forming and that the more people practice it, the more adept and motivated they become, society has an obligation to provide all citizens with the basic tools for lifelong learning and with an appropriate introduction to the satisfactions to be obtained from learning.

3. Diversity of educational opportunity through multiple providers is a proper goal of the learning society, and all citizens should be guaranteed access to the learning opportunities most relevant to their needs at any stage of life.

These assumptions involve issues of implementation beyond working with adult learners. For example, how can we prepare future generations of young people for their role as lifelong learners, and how can we encourage diversity of function among the providers of educational services? Since the focus of this book is on adults as learners, however, I shall simply recognize the importance of these broader tasks in implementing the learning society but will limit the presentation to research and theory bearing on the motivations of adult learners for voluntary participation in lifelong learning.

CHAPTER 3

Who Participates in Adult Learning

There is no lack of research on adult participation in various kinds of learning activities. The problem comes not in finding and reporting data but in synthesizing across studies to present a meaningful picture of how many adults are participating in what kinds of learning activities. To say that somewhere between 12 percent and 98 percent of all American adults over the age of 17 are currently engaged in learning activities is not a helpful conclusion, despite its derivation from competently conducted, data-based research studies. The wide discrepancies in participation rates arise from differences in the definition of "learning activities," from methodological differences, and, to a lesser extent, from differences in the populations surveyed.

When he defined learning broadly as "sustained, highly deliberate efforts to learn knowledge or a skill," Tough (1971) found that 98 percent of the adults in his research sample were

50

active learners. He further maximized the count of "lifelong learners" through his use of a methodology that consisted of conducting probing interviews designed to help people recall *all* of the intentional efforts they had made during the year to learn. Hence, if "learner" is defined broadly, and if the methodology is designed to maximize the report of learning projects, almost every adult can be considered a learner. If a more limited definition of learning is used, and the probing is less intensive, the participation rate may be much less. The 12 percent participation rate, for example, comes from the most recent of the triennial surveys of adult education conducted by the U.S. Bureau of the Census. In 1978, 12 percent of the adults over the age of 17 were reported to be engaged in "some type of organized adult education" (National Center for Education Statistics, 1980). "Adult education," the respondents were told, "consists of courses and other educational activities, organized by a teacher or sponsoring agency, and taken by persons beyond compulsory school age. Excluded is full-time attendance in a program leading toward a high school diploma or an academic degree" (National Center for Education Statistics, 1980). Thus, in the official tabulations of the Census Bureau, the learning activity is much more narrowly defined, and the survey is conducted via mailed questionnaire, with examples of adult education courses given as reminders (driver education, natural childbirth, foreign languages, electronics, tennis).

Between these extremes of definitions and methodologies are national and statewide surveys, which typically follow the definition and procedures used by Carp, Peterson, and Roelfs (1974), who conducted the 1972 national survey of adult education for the Commission on Non-traditional Study. They used brief questionnaires to inquire whether the respondent had "received instruction" in any of seventeen learning activities presented on a checklist, which served to remind people of instruction in hobbies, home repair, physical fitness, on-the-job training, managerial and professional skills, and the like. The investigators concluded that approximately one third of American adults had "received instruction" in one or more of the varied topics mentioned on the checklist. A decade earlier, Johnstone and Rivera (1965) concluded, on the basis of hour-long interviews, that approximately one fifth of the adults in the United States had received instruction, including "self-instruction, systematically organized and pursued for a period of not less than one month."

If there is some basic agreement on what type of learning constitutes "participation" in adult education, then moderate agreement can be obtained on participation rates. When the broadest definition—"sustained deliberate efforts to learn"—is used, investigators generally agree that virtually everyone can be classified as a participant (Coolican, 1974, 1975; Penland, 1977; Tough, 1971, 1978). When the definition is limited to "receipt of instruction" or "organized learning," participation rates vary from roughly 12 to 30 percent of the adult population (Carp, Peterson, and Roelfs, 1974; Johnstone and Rivera, 1965; National Center for Education Statistics, 1980). Most researchers consider the 12 percent participation rate reported by the National Center of Education Statistics low. Figures from numerous state studies conducted in the early 1970s suggest that a more realistic estimate would be one of three adults participating in some form of organized learning activity. If one were to take a highly restricted meaning of adult learning and count only those registered for credit or certificates, then the participation rate is usually less than 10 percent (Penland, 1977; Tough, 1978).

Since research studies seem to cluster themselves into three definitions of adult learners, let us discuss the characteristics of adult learners under three separate headings descriptive of the type of learning activity undertaken. The first will be "organized learning activities," the definition that conforms most closely to the common perception of adult education. About one third of all adults participate in "organized learning" or "organized instruction." The second category will be "self-directed learning," which includes just about everyone. The third category consists of that small group (less than 10 percent) of adults pursuing formal learning for credit.

Participants in Organized Learning Activities[1]

There is, by this time, a very adequate research base for describing adults who participate as part-time learners in "organized instruction." These learning activities are sometimes for credit but usually not; they are offered by continuing education and extension divisions, as well as by industry, community agencies, and labor unions; and they are usually but not always offered in classlike formats to groups of learners. Research definitions generally exclude worship services and completely self-directed learning projects, but they generally do include tutorials and independent pursuit of a course of instruction that has been prepared by a professional (for example, television and correspondence study).

The descriptions of the characteristics of these learners are amazingly consistent across research studies and over the years. The general conclusion arrived at by Johnstone and Rivera after their comprehensive national study in 1965 is as true today as it was fifteen years ago: "One of the most persistent findings emerging from this inquiry is that a great disparity exists in the involvement in continuing education of segments of the population situated at different levels of the social hierarchy" (p. 231). Table 4 presents the data from the most recent triennial survey conducted by the Census Bureau in 1978. These figures document the socioeconomic elitism of adult education. Since the overall rate of participation in adult education in the data base used was 12 percent in 1978, any group with a participation rate below that can be considered underrepresented. The following groups are seriously underrepresented in organized learning activities today: the elderly, blacks, those who failed to graduate from high school, and

[1]Earlier publications (Cross, 1978b; Cross, 1979a; Cross and Zusman, 1979) synthesized findings across more than thirty large state and national surveys of adult participation and interest in adult education. Some of the material presented here is taken from the conclusions of these earlier works, where details and citations to original data sources may be found.

Table 4. Participation Rates in Organized Instruction in 1978

	Participation Rate[a] (Percentages)
Age	
17-34	15.7
35-54	13.0
55 and over	4.5
Sex	
Male	10.7
Female	12.7
Race	
Black	5.8
White	12.5
Educational Attainment	
Less than four years of high school	3.5
Four years of high school	10.7
One to three years of college	18.1
Four or more years of college	27.6
Annual Family Income (dollars)	
Under 5,000	4.9
5,000-7,499	6.3
7,500-9,999	9.7
10,000-14,999	11.3
15,000-24,999	15.1
25,000 and over	18.3
Employment Status	
Employed	15.2
Looking for work	10.3
Keeping house	8.0

[a]NCES made substantial changes in the 1978 survey. The figures cited here are calculated by the "new method," which, unfortunately, is not directly comparable to data from previous triennial surveys.

Source: National Center for Education Statistics, 1980.

those with annual incomes under $10,000. Even those who are looking for work, who presumably have the time and the need for further education, are less likely to be participating in educational activities than those with jobs.

Of all the variables that have been related to educational interest and participation, amount of formal schooling has more influence than any other. Young people who advance furthest in the formal educational system are the most active learners as adults. Virtually all surveys, past and present, show that the more education people have, the more interested they will be in further education, the more they will know about available opportunities, and the more they will participate. In short, learning is addictive; the more education people have, the more they want, and the more they will get. A college graduate is more than twice as likely to be engaged in adult education as a high school graduate, and a high school graduate is more than twice as likely as a nongraduate to be a participant (Boaz, 1978; Carp, Peterson, and Roelfs, 1974; Johnstone and Rivera, 1965; National Center for Education Statistics, 1980; Okes, 1976).

There have been numerous attempts to explain the low participation rates of the lower socioeconomic classes. Frequently the explanations touch on the obvious—less money for fees, transportation, and books; jobs that do not require (or encourage) further education; less information about educational opportunity. The complex statistical analysis by Anderson and Darkenwald (1979), however, shows that educational attainment exerts its powerful impact on adult educational participation relatively independently of other components of socioeconomic status, such as income and occupation. The active participation of well-educated adults apparently cannot be explained solely by the fact that they have more money for fees or that education is more important in their jobs and more likely to be supported by their employers. As a matter of fact, Johnstone and Rivera (1965) found that the gap between well-educated and poorly educated adults was greater when *interest* in further education was measured than when participation was the measure. This finding, which has been consistently replicated in more recent studies, suggests that the initial barrier to adult education for the poorly educated is lack of interest. Some scholars—among them Frank Riessman, who has worked extensively with cultural deprivation—have offered explanations for this lack of interest. Riessman (1962, p. 12) is convinced that education is perceived differently by the poorly educated: "There is practically no interest in knowledge for its own sake; quite the contrary, a pragmatic antiintellectualism prevails. Nor is education seen as an opportunity for the development of self-expression, self-realization, growth, and the like. The average deprived person is interested in education in terms of how useful and practical it can be to him."

This interpretation is documented in the survey data. As one proceeds up the educational and socioeconomic scale, the dominant orientation changes from a strictly utilitarian emphasis to a greater stress on knowledge as having value in its own right. Whereas fewer than one third of those from the lowest socioeconomic third of the population cite any nonmaterial benefits of education, over two thirds of those from the highest socioeconomic third mention benefits such as adding to the enjoyment of life or having the potential to make one a better person (Johnstone and Rivera, 1965, p. 250). Johnstone and Rivera (1965, p. 263) offer an excellent summary of the data from their national survey, and it also serves as a good summary of all of the data collected since: "To sum up, the evidence . . . quite strongly supports the proposition that the lower classes do not think of learning as an experience which is rewarding in its own right. The value of education, rather, is perceived strictly in terms of tangible gains, and learning pursuits are not associated with pleasurable life experiences."

High school graduation seems to hold special significance. According to the statistical analysis conducted by Anderson and Darkenwald (1979), the adult learning participation rate for those completing two years of high school is 4.1 percent; for those with three years of high school, it is 5.9 percent; for high school graduates, it surges ahead to 10.9 percent. One possible explanation is that dropping out of high school is generally considered failure in our society, and high school dropouts, having experienced educational failure once, are not eager to try again. Therefore, if the poorly educated are to be attracted into learning activities as adults, the major problem may be to overcome their childhood experiences with school and their doubts about their ability to succeed there. If the reward is great enough (a better job or more money, but rarely the enjoyment of learning), they may enter into education as adults. Contrast that scenario with the one for well-educated adults, and it is easy to understand the great differences in educational participation between well-educated and poorly educated adults. Because the well educated have experienced success in school, they find few barriers to their participation. Indeed, because learning itself is likely to be pleasant and successful, promises of material rewards need not be especially great.

After educational attainment, the most powerful predictor of participation in adult education is age. As seen in Table 4, the participation rate for adults 55 and older is only 4.5 percent, compared with 12 percent participation for all adults. In almost all surveys, both interest and participation in education start to decline in the early 30s, continue to decline gradually through the 40s, but then drop precipitously for those 55 and older. Age, like educational attainment, seems to operate relatively independently of related variables, such as income and occupation (Anderson and Darkenwald, 1979). The generally lower level of formal education among older generations, however, accounts for part of the difference in participation rates. In 1940, when most 55 year olds would have been graduating from high school, only half of the age group were completing high school, whereas today three quarters of the population graduate from high school. But other factors that appear to have some bearing on the declining participation of older people are lack of interest in career success (which dominates the motivations of young people) and declining energy and mobility.

Age is an especially interesting characteristic because it reveals so clearly certain socialized perceptions about the role of education at various life stages. Younger people tend to be pursuing credentials and laying the groundwork for later career specialization; those in the age ranges of 25 to 45 are concentrating largely on occupational and professional training for career advancement; and those 50 and older are beginning to prepare for the use of leisure time. Sadly, the data also reveal the socialized perception that learning is for young people. The feeling of being too old to learn increases steadily with age until it becomes a common barrier to education for older people. In most state studies, the proportion of people 55 and older who state that their age is a deterrent to learning runs around 15 to 25 percent. In Iowa (Hamilton, 1976), however, a majority (59

percent) of those over 64 said that they were too old to go back
to school. Similarly, the age factor is more likely to be perceived as a barrier by those who have never participated in continuing education than by those who have.

Lack of mobility also presents a barrier to education for
many older people. About one fourth of Kansas adults over 60
years of age said they could not easily get out of the house once
a week, and many are reluctant to travel for long times or long
distances (Hoyt, 1975). Thus, it is not surprising to find the
elderly overrepresented in most forms of "lonely learning."
They tend to learn via television, radio, and tutors more often
than people in other age groups. Yet almost half of those over
60 in a California study (Hefferlin, Peterson, and Roelfs, 1975)
said that a primary motivation for their participation in learning
programs was to meet new people.

While the elderly remain among the most underrepresented of all subgroups in adult educational activities, there has
been growth in recent years. For those 55 and older, participation has grown from 2.9 percent of the age cohort in 1969 to
4.6 percent in 1978 (Boaz, 1978; National Center for Education
Statistics, 1980). We can probably expect participation by the
elderly to continue to grow as new opportunities appear and as
older people, through their very participation, legitimate learning as an appropriate activity for the elderly.

Two variables that appear closely related to educational
participation in Table 4, race and family income, are apparently
reflecting the influence of other variables. In a carefully controlled statistical analysis of data from the 1975 triennial survey, Anderson and Darkenwald (1979) found that blackness
and/or low family income, in and of themselves, have little
direct effect on participation. The severe underrepresentation of
these groups in adult education is due largely to other factors
associated with poverty, especially low educational attainment.
Black college graduates, for example, are as likely to participate
in adult education as white college graduates, and, at the other
end of the scale, white high school dropouts are no more likely
to be participants than black high school dropouts—only 4 percent of either group were participating in 1972 (Okes, 1976).

Adult education serves middle- and upper-class blacks in much the same way that it serves whites from the same classes. Black participants in adult education, like white participants, are considerably higher on the socioeconomic scale than nonparticipants—better educated, making higher salaries, and holding better jobs (Cross and Zusman, 1979).

Table 4 shows that being female is no disadvantage when it comes to adult education. In most surveys women express more interest in learning than men do, and in recent years they have closed the gap in participation rates—no doubt due to increasing opportunities in both education and careers. Recent growth in participation by women has been spectacular, rising from a little over six million in 1969 to nine million in 1975; men went from almost seven million to eight and a half million in the same period (Boaz, 1978). Thus, the rate of increase for men is less than half that for women. While changes in data collection and analysis in the 1978 survey make comparisons with previous triennial surveys difficult, it looks as though women are continuing their rapid climb; there were almost eleven million female participants in 1978, while the number of men dropped slightly, to a little over eight million. Thus, in the three years between the most recent triennial surveys, 1975 to 1978, women's participation increased by 15 percent, whereas men, for the first time since the start of the surveys, showed a drop of 2 percent (National Center for Education Statistics, 1980).

The rapid and substantial increase in women's participation is especially noteworthy given the somewhat lower educational attainment of women and the fact that women consistently report more concern over the cost of education than men. Women are more likely to be paying for their own educations, but the principal disparity occurs in employer-funded programs, where men are about twice as likely to obtain funding as women. Employers' funds are, of course, unavailable to the women who are entering or reentering the labor market and are seeking education for new jobs, whereas men are more interested in promotion in present jobs; but it is also true that employer-funded programs are more likely to be available to executives and managers (who are predominantly men) than to clerical workers (predominantly women) (Cross and Zusman, 1979). There are not large disparities between men and women in public financing, despite veterans' benefits, or in funding from private organizations. (The regression analysis conducted by Anderson and Darkenwald, 1979, showed a slight positive relationship between eligibility for veterans' benefits and participation in adult education.) Black women are especially likely to obtain financial help from public funding—35 percent, compared to 18 percent for white women (Boaz, 1978, p. 61).

At the time of this writing, statistics on the relationship between geographical access and participation in education were not yet available from the 1978 NCES survey. But data from previous surveys show a significantly higher participation rate for the western states. In 1975, for example, 16.6 percent of the eligible adults in the West were engaged in some form of organized instruction, whereas only 10 percent of those in the Northeast were so engaged (Boaz, 1978). Since research is unanimous in documenting the importance of proximity and access to educational services (Bashaw, 1965; Bishop and Van Dyk, 1977; Koos, 1944; Trent and Medsker, 1965), much of the regional differences can be attributed to the greater accessibility of free education in the West (Willingham, 1970). Since there are even greater differences in interest than in participation, however, a more subtle factor may be involved—the general atmosphere of acceptability and prestige for continuing education. Interest in participating in adult education is considerably greater in California (Hefferlin, Peterson, and Roelfs, 1975), for example, than in Iowa (Hamilton, 1976). Since the California and the Iowa studies were done at about the same time and used essentially the same methods and interview questions, they offer an unusual opportunity for a comparative study. The explanations underlying differences between California and Iowa in adult interest and participation may well have implications beyond the two states studied. Thus, it will be instructive to take a closer look at the climate for adult education in two quite different states.

In California 59 percent of the adults interviewed said that they were interested in participating in further learning beyond high school within the next two years. In Iowa only 36 percent indicated similar interests. The difference showed up again when prospective learners were asked which of twelve noninstructional services (such as counseling, assessment, and credit registry) would interest them. Fifty percent of Iowans, compared with 15 percent of Californians, said that they were not interested in any of them. Similarly, 31 percent of Iowans but only 5 percent of Californians said that they were "no longer interested in formal schooling." We can conclude from these figures that California presents a more positive climate for adult learning than Iowa does.

The climate may consist of numerous contributory factors—access to appropriate programs, educational attainment of the populace, and the participation rate itself. That is, the more adults participate in adult education, the more visible and legitimate it becomes; thus, California's higher participation rate, in and of itself, may be a stimulant to higher interest and participation. But it is also true that the educational level of the populace is higher in California than in Iowa. Thirty percent of the adults in California have had some college, compared with only 20 percent in Iowa (Grant and Lind, 1978). Moreover, Californians are apparently more likely to study part time. Hamilton (1976) reported huge differences in part-time college study —53 percent for California compared with 17 percent for Iowa. The difference probably reflects the profusion of community colleges in California, which provide commuting working adult students with ample opportunity for part-time study. There is not much question that Californians have easier access to postsecondary opportunities than Iowans have. Willingham (1970) showed that 60 percent of Californians but only 39 percent of Iowans live within a forty-five-minute commute of a free-access college. Since the Iowa study of educational resources (Hamilton, 1976) found that 82 percent of the programs for adult learners used traditional classroom lectures as their principal mode of learning, commuting distance is a matter of considerable significance.

The variable of population density can be analyzed in much the same manner as regional differences. Data from the

1975 survey (Boaz, 1978) show that people living in suburban areas are more likely to participate in educational activities than those living in areas of sparse population or in the dense populations of central cities. Farm areas were clearly disadvantaged in 1975, with a participation rate of only 6.7 percent, compared with 11.6 percent nationally (Boaz, 1978). Willingham's (1970) analysis of access to college showed that 63 percent of the people residing in small cities (population 50,000 to 250,000)—compared with 24 percent of rural residents and 38 percent of central-city residents—lived within a forty-five-minute commute of a free-access college. While access to colleges is only part of the adult education picture, the existence of colleges in communities tends to reflect educational interest, and it also seems to stimulate other providers of educational services rather than to supplant them.

An important policy issue shows up in this brief comparative analysis: without federal intervention, the rich get richer while the poor get poorer. States or population areas with the best-educated adults already are likely to pull further and further ahead of those lagging in the current educational race,[2] because well-educated adults will demand more educational services, will support such service through their attendance, and will legitimate adult education through their participation—all of which creates a positive climate for the growth of the learning society.

To date, most research has been directed toward sociodemographic analysis; that is, the study of participation as a function of race, sex, age, income, education, place of residence, and so on. However, Anderson and Darkenwald (1979) found that such variables account for only 10 percent of the variance associated with adult participation in organized learning activities. Thus, the real explanations for participation and support in the learning society lie elsewhere. Demographic de-

---

[2] It should be explicitly stated that Iowa is *not* one of most educationally deprived states. Iowa adults have a median educational level of 12.2 years (compared to 12.1 nationally), and 9.1 percent of Iowa adults 25 or older have a bachelor's degree or more (compared to 10.7 percent nationally) (Grant and Lind, 1978, pp. 15-16).

scriptors are useful primarily in the policy issues concerning equal educational opportunity. They shed relatively little light on our understanding of the motivations for adult learning. (Motivations will be addressed in detail in Chapters Five and Six.)

Participants in Self-Directed Learning

When Johnstone and Rivera (1965) conducted their national survey of adult learning, they defined learning broadly as including all "systematically organized" learning activities, but they regarded self-instruction as a residual category and therefore failed to collect detailed information about it. However, during the course of their study, they discovered that the incidence of self-education was much greater than they had anticipated and suggested that it "is probably the most overlooked avenue of activity in the whole field of adult education" (p. 37). In the early 1970s Allen Tough, of the Ontario Institute for Studies in Education, and other researchers began to correct this oversight. Most researchers studying the phenomenon have followed Tough's definition of self-directed learning. The "learning project" is the measuring unit, and it is defined as "a series of related episodes, adding up to at least seven hours. In each episode more than half of a person's total motivation is to gain and retain certain fairly clear knowledge and skill, or to produce some other lasting change in himself" (Tough, 1971, p. 6). A learning project can be planned by others but is usually self-planned and self-directed. Although our knowledge of self-directed or self-planned study is still incomplete, there is sufficiently high agreement among studies to draw the following general conclusions:

• Participation in self-directed learning is almost universal. Studies report that from 79 percent (Penland, 1977) to 100 percent (Coolican, 1974, 1975) of all adults conduct at least one learning project each year.
• The typical adult spends about one hundred hours on each learning project, conducting five projects per year, for a total

of five hundred hours per year. This means that self-directed projects are, on the average, of longer duration than the typical college course bearing three credit hours.

• Almost three fourths of the learning projects of adults are completely self-directed; about 15 percent involve group learning, 10 percent are one-to-one learning situations, and 3 percent utilize completely preprogrammed, nonhuman resources such as tapes, programmed instruction, and television. Only 20 percent of all learning projects are planned by a professional who is paid or institutionally designated to facilitate the learning (Tough, 1978).

One of the frequently touted advantages of self-directed learning is that, since almost everyone does it, it is free of the socioeconomic bias shown in "organized instruction," which serves the already well educated out of proportion to their numbers in the population. While the sheer prevalence of self-directed learning projects does reduce the social class bias, evidence suggests that there is such a thing as propensity for adult learning and that it is associated to some extent with social class. Hiemstra (1975), for example, found that among the elderly the usual class bias showed up when the hours spent on learning projects were computed. Nonwhites averaged 256 hours per year on learning projects, versus 325 for whites; those with more than a high school education spent 397 hours, compared with 261 hours for those with a high school education or less; blue-collar workers spent less time than white-collar workers; unskilled laborers and housewives spent less time than clerical, administrative, executive, and professional workers. Hiemstra also found some tendency for the better-educated upper classes to complete more learning projects than the lower classes, and it was fairly clear that the small group of "nonlearners" identified by Hiemstra was composed largely of poorly educated, low-income, elderly people living in rural areas. Similar findings were reported in a study of 466 adults in Tennessee. Adults who were not involved in learning projects were likely to be poorly educated, poorly paid, older rural residents (Coolican, 1975).

Penland's (1977) study on self-planned learning, one of the few to present comparative data for formal versus self-directed learning, probably contains the most representative sample of United States adults studied to date. His figures sustain the argument that self-planned learning is only *relatively* free of class bias; that is, it shows less class bias than formal classwork. In his sample of 1,501 adults 18 years of age or older, 79 percent were engaged in learning efforts of some kind; 16 percent of these learners were taking formal courses in addition to engaging in self-directed learning projects, 60 percent were engaged in self-directed learning projects only, and 3 percent were involved in formal classes only. Younger, better-educated adults from white-collar occupations were over-represented among formal learners, whereas the group of self-directed learners showed less class bias. Nevertheless, Penland found variables such as education, age, and income slightly related to involvement in self-directed learning (generally accounting for less than 15 percent of the variance), and he found low positive correlations between social class indicators and quantitative measures such as number of projects and number of hours spent.

Class bias might show up more strongly in self-directed learning projects if the quality and type of project were evaluated. To date, few researchers have made any effort to evaluate the quality of the learning projects. Given their nonevaluative orientation, most of those studying self-directed learning would probably be reluctant to "evaluate" the quality of projects, since the whole point of self-directed learning is to satisfy the learner, not some external authority. Even with the rough quantitative measures used to describe learning projects, however, it appears that some people spend more time learning than others and that the propensity to learn is related, albeit weakly, to social class.

Armstrong (1971) explored the possible existence of what might be termed "learning-prone" personalities. Using adults of low educational attainment who were enrolled in an academic upgrading program at a college in metropolitan Toronto, he found significant differences between "high-learning" adults, who had averaged 1,121 hours of independent learning projects during the previous year, and "low-learning" adults, who had averaged only 100 hours. Although there were no differences between the two groups in the nature and extent of learning undertaken for the purpose of gaining academic credit, the independent learning projects initiated by the two groups were quite different. Armstrong describes high-learner projects as enduring over a long period of time, motivated by high-level psychological needs, inner-directed, systematically planned, and generally closely related to the learner's self-concept; low-learning adult noncredit projects usually were stimulated by crisis or chance, poorly planned, designed to fulfill low-level needs, and unrelated to the learner's self-concept. In addition to differences in the learning projects undertaken by high and low learners, Armstrong found two distinct personality profiles. High learners saw themselves as reliable, tenacious, independent, with broad interests, high achievement motivation, and openness to new experience. Low learners perceived themselves as warm and friendly, masculine, conformist, and either complacently satisfied with or angrily resigned to their current life situations. Armstrong's study is unique and important because it attempts to answer the question of *who* participates in adult learning by looking at personality characteristics and attitudes. Few studies, of either self-directed learning or surveys of participation in organized instruction, have done that. The opportunities are wide open, and the need is great for further research on "learning-prone personalities."

The approach of those investigating self-directed learning is more attuned to answering questions about *how* adults learn than about *who* participates, and we shall return to studies of self-directed learning in Chapter Eight. Suffice it to say here that since almost everyone in American society carries out self-directed learning projects, the profile of learners under this definition is not as sharply differentiated from the profile of nonlearners as when learning is defined as participation in organized instruction, which engages a smaller segment of the population.

Participants in Adult Learning for Academic Credit

Since the attention of colleges and universities turned to adult learners about a decade ago, a number of research studies have been launched to describe the "nontraditional student"— variously defined as part time (Committee on the Financing of Higher Education for Adult Students, 1974), over the age of 20 (Holmstrom, 1973), over 21 (Solmon, Gordon, and Ochsner, 1979), over 22 (Roelfs, 1975), registered in external degree programs (Medsker and others, 1975; Sharp and Sosdian, 1979; Sosdian, 1978; Sosdian and Sharp, 1978), registered in continuing education programs (Nolfi and Nelson, 1973), or participating in free-standing nontraditional colleges especially designed for older students (Empire State College, n.d.; Lehman, 1975; McIntosh and Woodley, 1975; Minnesota Metropolitan State College, 1975). The search for a meaningful profile of the adult student pursuing college credit at the undergraduate level is further complicated by the multiplicity of comparison groups. It appears that degree-seeking adults are a privileged group of people when compared with the general population and a disadvantaged population relative to younger, full-time college students. This suggests that degree programs for adults are at least partially successful in fulfilling their mission as "second-chance" programs for people who missed the opportunity for a college education when they were younger or who dropped out of college earlier. It also suggests that the so-called nontraditional opportunities for adults do represent the continuing spread of egalitarianism in higher education. The great majority of degree-seeking adults come from working-class backgrounds; most are first-generation college students whose parents did not attend college. At the same time, the students themselves tend to be better educated and to hold better jobs than their age counterparts in the general population. The one phrase that might describe them better than any other is "upwardly mobile." They seem determined to rise above the socioeconomic level of their parents, largely through the route of advanced education.

Aside from the general picture of adult degree seekers as

serious, upwardly mobile people from working-class backgrounds, few generalizations can be made. At least five different
groups of adults are pursuing academic credit. First, there are
the adults—usually young adults—registered as full-time students
in rather traditional colleges. A good profile of this group comes
from the data collected on some 60,000 adults who entered college as full-time freshmen between 1967 and 1971. Holmstrom
(1973) compared the characteristics of those 20 years of age
and older (5 percent of the freshmen in 1967) with the characteristics of 16- to 19-year-old freshmen. She concluded that the
older students were more likely to come from socioeconomically disadvantaged backgrounds; were more concerned about
financing their education; made lower high school grades and,
except in community colleges, lower college grades in their
major fields; perceived the major benefit of a college education
as monetary; and had lower educational aspirations than
younger college students. The differences between younger and
older full-time freshmen in traditional colleges are greatest in
universities and much less significant in community colleges.

Holmstrom's 1973 analysis was updated by Solmon, Gordon, and Ochsner in 1979. They used data from the Cooperative Institutional Research Program (CIRP), and their analysis
covered 172,400 adults over the age of 21 who entered college
between 1966 and 1978. Their results confirmed and expanded
Holmstrom's earlier findings but had the added advantage of
showing trends. One such trend reflects a tenet of the learning
society—namely, that adults should be able to drop in and out
of college. In the late 1960s two thirds of the students over 21
were in college for the first time; by 1971 only 50 percent had
not had some college work elsewhere, and by 1978 only 28 percent were first timers. Thus, in the short space of a decade, the
proportion of adults returning to college after a period of absence had done an about-face, from a small minority to a substantial majority. Much of this change may be attributable to
the large influx of women who dropped out of college to get
married and raise children and then returned to college as good
jobs began to open for educated women. In 1966 only 29 per-

cent of the college entrants over the age of 21 were women; by 1978 women constituted 57 percent of the older freshmen.

Another tenet of the learning society, equal opportunity, also appears encouraging in these trend data. Ethnic minorities are far better represented among adult full-time students than among younger students. Whereas whites constitute 90 percent of the college students of traditional age, they now make up only about 70 percent of those over 21. Growth for ethnic minorities has been especially rapid in recent years. This finding may provide a partial explanation for the alarming figures showing that blacks are falling further and further behind whites in their participation in adult education (Boaz, 1978). It now looks as though increased financial aid and emphasis on college educations may have encouraged some blacks to shift out of part-time, noncredit adult education courses into full-time degree programs.

It is also clear from these data (Solmon, Gordon, and Ochsner, 1979) that adults over the age of 21 who enter college full time are considerably more representative of the general population than are traditional college students. Relative to traditional college students, however, the new adult students are disadvantaged educationally as well as economically. Adult college entrants made lower high school grades (probably only partly attributable to grade inflation) and were less likely to pursue college preparatory programs in high school than their younger colleagues. Adults are far more likely to enroll in community colleges than traditional-aged students; the majority of adults over 21 attend two-year colleges while the majority of traditional-aged students enroll in four-year colleges. Finally, adults are heavily career oriented, with business an especially popular curriculum.

Although these data are extensive and certainly the best available on the older students who are attending traditional colleges and universities, there are severe problems in generalizing from data collected in and interpreted from the perspective of traditional colleges and universities. Problems in the original sample arise because CIRP questionnaires are usually distributed

during freshman orientation or registration for traditional daytime students, thereby underrepresenting part-time and evening
degree students, probably by great amounts. Solmon, Gordon,
and Ochsner are well aware of their sampling problems and carefully caution readers about generalizing from what is undoubtedly a biased sample of even that small minority of adult
learners who are college freshmen.

   Some corrective perspective is available from a study conducted by Roelfs (1975) comparing older (22 and over) with
younger students in community colleges. In this comparison,
both younger and older students come from part-time and full-
time, evening and daytime, career and transfer populations in
twenty-seven diverse community colleges. Of the 6,500 students
surveyed, 1,403 (22 percent) were between 22 and 29 years of
age, and 616 (9 percent) were 30 or older. This is an older
group than those students studied by CIRP, and its members
constitute a much larger proportion of the survey population—
almost one third of the community college students, as compared with only 5 percent of the freshman population across
the predominantly four-year colleges and universities participating in CIRP. Also this is a commuting population, many of
whom are enrolled as part-time students.

   Compared with younger students in community colleges,
the older students in Roelf's analysis are more likely to know
what they want out of college, to be challenged rather than
bored with their classes, to feel self-confident about their ability
to keep up with their studies and to understand what is being
taught, to spend more time studying, and to express satisfaction
with their classes and their instructors. In the light of such an
academically self-confident profile, it seems surprising that this
group of older students in community colleges—especially those
over 30—were more likely than younger students to want instructor-centered classes as opposed to student-centered classes.
(Student-centered classes are defined in Roelf's study as classes
in which instructors work out course content with students,
organize classes around informal discussion rather than tests or
assignments, and follow topics of student interests even if
planned content is not covered.) Some 42 percent of those over

30, compared with only 20 percent of those between the ages of 18 and 21, wanted the instructor to assume primary responsibility for determining course content and learning activities. These findings, suggesting greater dependence on the instructor by adult learners in community colleges, contrast so sharply with most writing on adult education (see Chapter Nine and Knowles, 1978) that further study seems indicated.

Brecht (1978) found a similar profile among part-time evening school liberal arts majors at Villanova University, 75 percent of whom were over 25 years of age. Compared with full-time seniors at the university, the evening students were less critical of the curriculum and instruction than day students and also apparently more supportive of instructor-centered teaching. Although data are not presented, Brecht interprets his study as indicating that "evening students want a tightly structured traditional program" (p. 373). While Brecht appears delighted with the "nonvocational" interests of the older learners, that may be more a function of their major—liberal arts—than of their age. Certainly, most research on continuing education students—shows a strong vocational emphasis.

Nolfi and Nelson (1973) studied 6,000 students enrolled in continuing education and extension divisions in Massachusetts. They characterized these students as "young, affluent, upwardly mobile from their parents' level of education and jobs, and already employed in professional or managerial jobs. Two thirds of the students are men, one third women. The primary reason for enrolling in continuing education is job advancement" (p. 60). Relative to the general population of Massachusetts, these students were middle and upper-middle class themselves, although most came from families in which neither parent attended college. Their motivation for job advancement, although strong (83 percent of the men and 70 percent of the women mentioned career goals as their primary motivation for study), was largely internal; 67 percent of the men said that education is necessary for their own job advancement, but only 12 percent said that their employer requires it or that it is necessary for a licensing examination. Finances constituted a major reason for their dropping out of school earlier, although cost did not appear to be much of a problem at the time of the study; students were paying an average of $80 per course, with 59 percent of the men and 24 percent of the women reporting that they were being reimbursed in part or in full. Convenience of scheduling was rated very important by most of these students (72 percent), and the choice of one school over another had more to do with closeness to home or office (34 percent) than to quality considerations (11 percent). The general picture that emerges from this profile of continuing education students is one of stable, responsible citizens of the community, spending what might otherwise be leisure time to improve their socioeconomic position through further education.

A fourth profile emerges from a number of studies of adults enrolled in "nontraditional" degree programs especially designed for adult learners. These students have been studied frequently, and descriptions are reasonably consistent across studies. Perhaps the most significant characteristic of these students is that they are considerably older than the three groups profiled so far. Sosdian and Sharp (1978) studied 1,486 graduates from thirty-two undergraduate external degree programs, which were selected from 244 such programs offered in the United States in 1976-77. The median age of the group was 36 but more than one third were over 40 when they completed their external degrees. This national sample of external degree graduates consisted mostly of men (71 percent) and mostly of people employed in professional, subprofessional, and technical jobs (54 percent). They were rather well educated before they embarked on their external degrees; 82 percent had previously attended college, and 27 percent already had college degrees. Primary reasons for not going further with their education earlier were family responsibilities (47 percent for the sample; 70 percent for women); lack of clarity of educational goals (37 percent); and, for men, military service (47 percent). Students considered two things very important about their external degree program: it permitted them to maintain their regular work schedule, and it granted recognition and credit for previous college course work. While most students rated independence and an individualized approach to studies as important, they regarded the minimal residential requirements as somewhat more important. The personal satisfaction of having pursued and completed their college degrees was far and away the most important goal for adults pursuing external degrees, followed by having the credential as a prerequisite to further study and to job advancement.

The self-studies of two of the best-known adult degree programs in the United States support this general profile of external degree graduates (Empire State College, n.d.; Lehman, 1975; Minnesota Metropolitan State College, 1975). Students at Minnesota Metropolitan State College rate themselves particularly high on traits such as "independence, persistence, self-motivation, and drive to achieve." Students at Empire State College are similar. Their average age is 37; almost 60 percent are between the ages of 30 and 55. The great majority (80 percent) have had previous college experience. Women are better represented at both Empire State and Minnesota Metropolitan than in other adult degree programs, constituting approximately half of the student bodies.

Like continuing education students, students at Empire State College present a general picture of successful, working adults; only 8 percent classify themselves primarily as students and only 9 percent as housewives. They come predominantly from professional and semiprofessional jobs, and two thirds describe their present occupation as rewarding. They are interested in a college degree primarily because it opens the way to upward mobility through advanced education or job advancement; almost one third plan to go on to graduate school. Students at Empire State College place high value on the opportunity to work and study simultaneously and on the chance to receive credit for prior learning. Since the learning contract is a feature of Empire State, it is not surprising that students should rate the independence and flexibility allowed by the college as important in their decision to enroll (Lehman, 1975). The Empire State self-evaluation concluded that its program works best for students who have clear goals, are self-directed, and have adequate learning resources to draw on. To date, Empire State has not proved very attractive to the young, the old, minorities, the unemployed, the occupationally disenchanted, or people with only a high school or trade school background (Lehman, 1975, p. 3).

The Bachelor of Liberal Studies program at the University of Oklahoma is another program specifically designed for mature adult learners. According to data supplied by William H. Maehl, Jr., director of the BLS program, the students in the program are similar to those at Empire State and Metropolitan State, although most people would classify the BLS program as somewhat more academically conservative. The Oklahoma students are the oldest we have discussed so far, with an average age of 49. Overall, these students are highly successful people, both as workers and as students. Unlike ESC and MSC, men predominate (74 percent). Over half (55 percent) of the students were given released time by their employers to attend the summer seminars, but only 29 percent got any form of financial assistance from employers. Most are state or federal government employees (55 percent), and almost one third of them make $30,000 or more per year. In a tie for first place among the reasons for returning to college are to gain the satisfaction of having the degree (49 percent) and to obtain the credentials for advanced education or career advancement (50 percent). Half of the graduates of the BLS program do go on for master's or other advanced degrees—perhaps because most of the participants (61 percent) find that the program stimulates their interest in further learning. Other outcomes mentioned by students are the attainment of specific competencies such as improving communication skills (30 percent) and helping the individual think more clearly (46 percent). Major attractions of the BLS program include the ease of fulfilling the requirements of a specially designed adult degree program (72 percent), the fact that the program is new and interesting (53 percent), and its good reputation (32 percent).

Finally, there may be a fifth adult learner profile revealed in "distance learners": those who pursue college credit through programs such as British Open University and the University of Mid-America, which emphasize the delivery of education through television, correspondence, radio, and the like. The "media-oriented" university was a bold new venture of the early 1970s, and we now have a decade of experience with the type of student attracted to programs that seem to call for considerable self-discipline in learning.

The demographic profiles of students at British Open University (BOU) and the University of Mid-America (UMA) differ to some extent, partly because of the nature of the curriculum and partly because of the different role played by BOU and UMA in the higher education opportunities in Great Britain and the United States. Like most of the adult programs in the United States, BOU appeals primarily to upwardly mobile young adults who hold good jobs in professional and technical occupations but who are far more likely than full-time college students to be from working-class backgrounds. Whereas 29 percent of the students entering conventional institutions in Great Britain come from the homes of manual workers, 52 percent of BOU students have such backgrounds. Despite evidence that BOU is more egalitarian with respect to family background than most higher education in Great Britain, BOU is still accused of having a middle-class bias because the laboring classes remain underrepresented. Much of BOU's defense of its difficulty in reaching manual and clerical workers rests on data showing that information channels have a social class bias. Better-educated people with better jobs are simply more likely to have heard of BOU and also to have more accurate information about it.

As BOU becomes better known, it is becoming more broadly representative. The university was established in 1969. By 1971 one third of the adult population had heard of it, and by 1975 over half knew of its existence. Between 1971 and 1975, the following groups increased their proportionate share in the student body: women (from 26 percent to 42 percent), manual workers (from 9 percent to 14 percent), clerical workers (from 21 percent to 30 percent), and people lacking formal university requirements (from 29 percent to 43 percent). Although it is clear that BOU has made progress in reducing its middle-class bias, McIntosh and Woodley (1975, p. 16) conclude that Open University "is still far from being truly open. At every stage, from actually hearing of the [university] to accepting the

offer of a place, barriers exist which discriminate against certain
types of people, many of whom have been deprived of educational opportunity in the past." In an interesting analysis,
McIntosh and Woodley identify some of the features of the
Open University system itself that will continue to discriminate
against applicants from educationally deprived groups. They
mention, for example, the requirement of a one-week residential summer school, which is difficult for women with young
children and manual workers with only two weeks of vacation
per year, and the need for television and radio receivers and a
quiet place to study, which is less likely for low-income adults.
(See Chapter Four for a more complete enumeration of the barriers of BOU.)

Students of the University of Mid-America (UMA) are
not unlike those at BOU. UMA students show the typical
middle-class bias, with half of the students having had previous
college experience. The profile of the UMA students in Nebraska, who are enrolled in the State University of Nebraska
(SUN), is presented by Bryan and Forman (1977, p. 6) as
follows:

> The average age of the learner is 37 years, and ap-
> proximately 75 percent are women. The median income
> of learners is approximately $11,000. The percent of
> learners who live on farms, ranches, in small towns, and
> cities follow the general population pattern. About half
> of the learners have taken some college course work and
> half have not. Approximately 50 percent of the learners
> have not participated in a formal educational experience
> during the five years previous to SUN enrollment. Career
> improvement and personal satisfaction goals are most
> often cited by learners as the most important reasons for
> enrolling. Approximately two thirds of all enrollees hope
> to eventually obtain an academic degree at the undergrad-
> uate or graduate level.

UMA, like BOU, is now old enough for us to observe
some trends in student characteristics. One of those trends is
that people who reenroll in UMA courses are older, have less

formal education, and are more likely to live on a farm or ranch than people who use UMA for one course only—probably because it fills a particular course need rather than because it represents a unique educational opportunity. Both UMA and BOU can claim that, as they mature, they are reaching broader segments of the population; more important, both systems are constantly analyzing their programs, structure, and delivery systems and changing to meet the needs of a constituency without other options (McIntosh and Woodley, 1975; McNeil, 1978).

Obviously, no single profile can be regarded as representative of the adult learner, even when one looks at that small group of adults who choose to pursue academic credit. In the first place, almost any group of adults is more heterogeneous than a comparable group of 18 year olds. Their experiences are more extensive and more varied; they usually have somewhat more individualized perceptions of themselves and where they are going; and they are pursuing education for a greater variety of reasons. Moreover, as we have seen, there is already a considerable variety of options open to part-time students, and students with different needs and circumstances tend to select programs suited to their needs. Although all the studies cited described the characteristics of the students, the methods used, the questions asked, and the interpretations made are not really comparable across studies. Therefore, it is risky to make comparisons among the profiles of students pursuing different degree-credit options. Nevertheless, from the limited profiles presented above, an interesting hypothesis is suggested for further study.

Older and more mature learners are somewhat more likely than younger, less well-established adults to select a program that departs from the traditional. To put the hypothesis baldly, the more successful and established the individual is *as an adult,* the less satisfactory traditional college degree programs are going to be. The youngest group of learners profiled here were full-time college freshmen enrolled in standard undergraduate colleges in programs where 95 percent of the students were of traditional college age. The group profile of these older college freshmen suggested a general picture of lack of stability and success as adults. They were less successful as students and had lower educational aspirations than younger students and apparently had not yet established themselves in jobs that they wished to maintain while studying part time. The next group, those enrolled full time and part time in community colleges, were still a minority (31 percent) registered in programs serving predominantly younger students, but older students constitute a much more significant portion of the community college student bodies than they do in four-year freshman programs, and it is reasonable to assume that instruction and curriculum are more likely to take account of adult needs and interests. While the community college adults in Roelf's (1975) study appear generally self-confident and successful, they expressed a somewhat surprising dependence in wanting the instructor to take primary responsibility for the direction of their learning activities.

The next group of people in this hypothetical hierarchy are those enrolled in continuing education classes. These classes are designed totally for the working student. Since working adults constitute virtually 100 percent of the student population in continuing education and extension classes, these programs must necessarily be more sensitive than either two-year or four-year colleges to the special learning needs of adults. Nevertheless, most continuing education programs and courses follow rather traditional classroom formats, although the attitudes and methods of the instructors are probably responsive to the adults who enroll. Students electing part-time study in continuing education programs are characterized in the research as upwardly mobile adults, holding responsible jobs which they want to keep while pursuing additional study that will make them even more promotable.

Finally, there is the suggestion that the oldest and most self-directed learners are to be found in new programs designed specifically for adult learners. Students in external degree programs not only have the strongest educational backgrounds, at least as measured by more college work and more degrees, but they are also more likely to express intrinsic satisfactions in education and to have high aspirations for continued study.

That general profile of older men and women, well established and presumably secure in their adult roles, seems to apply also to adults pursuing college credit through special colleges designed for adults, such as Empire State and Metropolitan State, and to open learning universities, such as UMA and BOU.

At this point, the hypothesis of an existing hierarchy of adult programming for maturity is purely speculative. The research merely suggests the possibility; the methods and comparison groups available now are not comparable, and any test of the hypothesis awaits further research. Since some will interpret the hypothesis as pejorative—in the sense that traditional college programs attract people who are less adequate as adults —let me hasten to say that no value judgment is intended. All the programs profiled undoubtedly serve a needed function in the diverse world of adult learners. The programs should be evaluated not on the characteristics of the students they attract but on how well they serve those who come. At the same time, if the hypothesis holds up in future research, "nontraditional" programs—far from giving away credits and compromising academic standards, as some of their critics charge—may attract some of the best and most serious students in all higher education.

Summary and Commentary

The adult learning force can be pictured as a pyramid of learners. Its broad base consists of self-directed learners, a category that includes just about everyone. A smaller group, estimated at one third or more of the population, participate in some form of organized instruction each year, and the tip of the pyramid consists of that very small proportion of adult learners who pursue college credit in a wide variety of traditional and nontraditional programs.

The pyramid of learners can be superimposed on a pyramid of social class. The broad base of self-directed learners are representative of the population as a whole. The participants in organized instruction show consistent social class bias, especially through indicators such as educational attainment, age, and place of residence. At the top of the pyramid are those adults pursuing college degrees, who come from lower socio-economic backgrounds than younger college students but are among the socioeconomically privileged in the pyramid of adult learners.

Social class indicators are used to describe adult learners, but they fall far short of explaining adult participation. Because most research addressing the question of *who* participates uses easily measurable demographic descriptors, we fall into the trap of thinking that we must find the answers to equal educational opportunity and adult motivation for learning in variables which are at best only indirectly and remotely related to educational interests and aspirations. It should surprise no one to learn that educational attainment, which is the most educationally relevant variable included in most descriptive studies, is more closely related to educational participation than are race, sex, income, and many other variables used to describe adult learners. Although it is easy to obtain consistent demographic profiles of groups of adults participating in various types of learning activities, such descriptions explain only 10 percent of the variance associated with educational participation (Anderson and Darkenwald, 1979).

It should be almost as easy for researchers to describe adult learners in more educationally relevant terms. What have been their past experiences in school? How do they think about school? How do they think about their nonschool learning experiences? What is their present life situation, and how can education help them? There is a suggestion in some of the research that active adult learners possess "learning-prone personalities." How can we describe the learning-prone personality? Some of these questions await further research, but Chapters Four and Five attempt to shed light on what is currently known through research and theory about the motivations of adult learners.

CHAPTER 4

Why Adults Participate— and Why Not

We have reviewed the research on *who* participates in various kinds of adult learning experiences. Let us move now to what research says about *why* people participate and why they do not participate.

Research on Motivation

The research methods for seeking answers to the motivation of adult learners fall into four basic designs: (1) depth interviews, (2) statistical analysis of motivational scales, (3) survey questionnaires, and (4) hypothesis testing. While the conclusions emerging from these four methodologies differ in details, there is enough consistency to enable us to identify the major incentives for adult learning.

81

Depth Interviews. Although Houle's (1961) sensitive study of the motivations for adult learning was done twenty years ago, his three-way typology remains the single most influential motivational study today. He limited his inquiry to twenty-two case studies of men and women who were exceptionally active adult learners. In Houle's words, they were "so conspicuously engaged in various forms of continuing learning that they could be readily identified" (p. 13). Amount of motivation was not the variable under study—all were very active learners. Rather, Houle was interested in explaining *why* these learners were so active. He studied extensive holistic interviews to see whether he could find common threads running through the activities and motivations of the learners. Three subgroups emerged. The first, *goal-oriented* learners, use learning to gain specific objectives, such as learning to speak before an audience, learning to deal with particular family problems, learning better business practices, and similar concrete objectives. For the goal oriented, says Houle, learning is a series of episodes, each beginning with the identification of a need or an interest. Such learners do not restrict their learning activities to any one institution or method but select whatever method will best achieve their purpose—taking a course, joining a group, reading a book, taking a trip.

The second subgroup, *activity-oriented* learners, participate primarily for the sake of the activity itself rather than to develop a skill or learn subject matter. They may take a course or join a group to escape loneliness or boredom or an unhappy home or job situation, to find a husband or a wife, to amass credits or degrees, or to uphold family tradition. Most of the activity-oriented learners in Houle's sample said that they did almost no reading. Houle suggests, however, that if the sample had been larger, it might have included activity-oriented people who used reading for purposes other than to learn the content. There may be people, for example, who escape into the relative solitude of a library or who immerse themselves in reading in order to avoid real-life problems.

In sharp contrast to the activity oriented, the third group identified by Houle consists of those who are *learning oriented*;

that is, those who pursue learning for its own sake. They seem to possess a fundamental desire to know and to grow through learning, and their activities are constant and lifelong. Most are avid readers; they join groups, and even choose jobs, for the learning potential offered; they watch serious programs on television and make extensive background preparations when traveling in order to appreciate what they see.

Houle does not claim that his typology is a complete or final description of adult motivations, but it has been highly productive in stimulating research. Boshier (1976), after a careful review of the methodology and findings of fourteen research studies attempting in various ways to test the Houle typology, concludes that "Houle's typology is elegant and makes subjective sense, but until motivational orientation researchers develop a suitable psychometric procedure to test its validity, it cannot be accepted or rejected as an accurate description of adult learners" (pp. 42-43). Nevertheless, the Houle typology offers a useful framework for thinking about multiple motives for adult learning.

Like Houle, Tough (1968) used interviews as a methodology to try to understand what motivates people to undertake and continue self-directed learning projects. In his study, interviewers asked adults to think of something that they had spent at least seven hours trying to learn and then to state their reasons for learning it. The learning project could involve learning information, skills, or knowledge, but learning motivated primarily by the desire to obtain academic credit was excluded because Tough was interested in self-directed learning projects. It should be noted that Tough, consciously or not, was excluding activity-oriented learning by his instruction to identify an effort to learn something specific and concrete. Table 5 shows the number of learners (out of thirty-five in the study) who indicated that the reason listed was a "very strong" or "fairly strong" motivator in beginning or continuing a specific learning project.

A number of conclusions can be drawn from the study. In the first place, almost every learner has more than one reason for engaging in learning. The average number of reasons rated

Table 5. Reasons for Starting and Continuing Learning Projects

	No. Checking "Very Strong" or "Fairly Strong"	
	For Beginning	For Continuing
Reasons	*Project*	*Project*
1. Use in order to understand	11	11
2. Use in an examination	2	2
3. Use in order to impart	12	15
4. Use for taking action	29	33
5. Someone noticing the learning efforts	7	9
6. Puzzlement, curiosity, or a question	22	15
7. Satisfaction from possession	13	15
8. Enjoyment from receiving the content	14	20
9. Enjoyment from practicing the skill	8	10
10. Feeling of learning successfully	6	18
11. Pleasure from the activity of learning	18	17
12. Completing unfinished learning	3	3
13. Unconnected benefits	5	10

$N = 35$.
Source: Tough, 1968, p. 10.

"fairly" or "very" important was 5.4, and the lowest number of reasons given for any project was 3. This finding, common to most studies of adult reasons for learning, points up the inappropriateness of trying to find a single reason for adult learning.

A second finding from Tough's interviews is also common to other studies. Adult learners are most frequently motivated by the pragmatic desire to *use* or apply the knowledge or skill. Most often, they hope to take action—do something, produce something, or decide something. Table 5 shows that twenty-nine people (83 percent) started their learning project because they wanted to use the knowledge or skill in order to take action, and thirty-three (94 percent) continued their project in anticipation of using the learning in a concrete and pragmatic way.

A third finding concerns learning patterns. Tough identified three patterns in starting learning projects. Some people start with an awareness that they want to do something—or per-

haps they are assigned a task by others—that requires new learning. They then seek out learning activities that will provide the
necessary knowledge and skills. A second pattern starts with
puzzlement or curiosity, usually about controversial issues or
things that are especially important in the life of the learner.
Learning more about the topic satisfies the desire to inform
oneself on the topic. The third pattern, which Tough is less
certain of, starts with the decision to spend some extra time
learning, followed by a decision about what to learn during that
time.

Finally, the figures in Table 5 suggest that most participants *enjoy* learning, and this enjoyment plays an especially important role in the continuation of learning projects. Among the
top-rated reasons for continuing learning are pleasure from receiving the content, feelings of being a successful learner, and
satisfaction or happiness from the activity of learning. These
reasons look much like the goals of Houle's learning-oriented
people, and it is significant that enjoyment is judged especially
important in continuing the learning projects, since the ongoing
process of learning is a prime characteristic of Houle's learning-
oriented adults.

Statistical Analysis of Motivational Scales. Houle's typology, in particular, has stimulated some complex statistical
analyses over the past decade. Most of these studies begin with
psychometrically constructed instruments and then subject the
responses to factor analysis, cluster analysis, or some other technique aimed at reducing a large number of item responses to
meaningful clusters or subgroups. Typically, these studies use
some variant of the Educational Participation Scale (Boshier,
1971) or the Reasons for Educational Participation Scale
(Burgess, 1971) and, after grouping similar item responses together, come up with between five and eight factors.

The factor analysis of the Educational Participation Scale
(EPS) by Morstain and Smart (1974) illustrates the types of
conclusions derived from these methods. Morstain and Smart
found six factors. They are presented below, along with the
three items from the Educational Participation Scale that seem
most central to the cluster:

Factor I. Social Relationships

- To fulfill a need for personal associations and friendships
- To make new friends
- To meet members of the opposite sex

Factor II. External Expectations

- To comply with instructions from someone else
- To carry out the expectations of someone with formal authority
- To carry out the recommendation of some authority

Factor III. Social Welfare

- To improve my ability to serve mankind
- To prepare for service to the community
- To improve my ability to participate in community work

Factor IV. Professional Advancement

- To give me higher status in my job
- To secure professional advancement
- To keep up with competition

Factor V. Escape/Stimulation

- To get relief from boredom
- To get a break in the routine of home or work
- To provide a contrast to the rest of my life

Factor VI. Cognitive Interest

- To learn just for the sake of learning
- To seek knowledge for its own sake
- To satisfy an inquiring mind

It is easy to see Houle's three subgroups in the six factors of Morstain and Smart. Factor IV, Professional Advancement, and Factor II, External Expectations, both appear to be heavily goal oriented, and, as a matter of fact, Morstain and Smart did report a rather high correlation ($r = .41$) between these two factors. Hence, it appears that Houle's goal-oriented learner could be of two types: (1) the self-motivated individual who sets a goal and pursues it because of a personal desire to attain the goal—job advancement, personal improvement, or whatever; (2) the individual who pursues the goal at the suggestion of someone else, frequently an employer who may suggest or require job-related learning.

Similarly, Morstain and Smart's factors Escape/Stimulation and Social Relationships appear similar in intent to Houle's activity-oriented subgroup, and Morstain and Smart also found a high correlation ($r = .56$) between Escape/Stimulation and Social Relationships. Thus, one might make a distinction between two types of activity-oriented people: those who participate in learning activities in order to escape from something boring or unpleasant, as opposed to those who participate for more positive reasons of seeking social relationships. In either case, it is the activity itself that is sought rather than learning or what it might lead to.

Morstain and Smart's Factor VI, Cognitive Interest, looks much like Houle's description of the learning-oriented adult. Factor III, however, Social Welfare, seems not to have a direct relationship to Houle's three-way typology, but analysis of this factor shows it related to Social Relationships ($r = .46$) and to Cognitive Interest ($r = .40$). One thinks, in this context, of social activists who are frequently highly educated and intellectual people interested in organizing groups of people who share their intellectual and ideological views of social and humanitarian reform.

The Morstain and Smart analysis extends and, to some extent, validates Houle's more subjective observations, but there is an important difference between the two approaches. Houle was classifying groups of people, whereas Morstain and Smart were identifying clusters of reasons. The implication from Houle's typology is that people are consistently motivated by characteristic orientations to learning throughout their lives, whereas the Morstain and Smart approach makes more room for multiple reasons to exist within the same individual and for motivations to change from time to time. The Morstain and Smart data fit Tough's finding of multiple motivations, but it would be interesting to test Houle's assumption that people have characteristic orientations to learning that remain fairly consistent over time and across learning activities. Armstrong's (1971) identification of learning-prone personalities would support the assumption of some consistency in orientation (see Chapter Three).

Survey Questionnaires. In recent years, the use of survey questionnaires has been far and away the most popular method for studying adult motives for learning. While many of the survey questions were presented in a face-to-face or telephone interview, they differ from the studies I have labeled "depth interviews" because the methods of the surveys involved asking respondents to choose from a list of predetermined alternatives rather than exploring respondents' free-ranging thoughts about learning. The surveys are typically reported in numerical frequencies, whereas the depth interviews are usually narrated as subjective impressions.[1]

The format of the survey method is fairly standard: present a checklist of possible reasons for learning and ask people to indicate which ones motivate their learning or desire to learn. The options in the checklist frequently are derived from interview and factor analytic studies, and the survey questionnaires are intended to provide an easy way to study priorities and intergroup differences. The items used in the Commission on Non-traditional Study (CNS) national survey (Carp, Peterson, and Roelfs, 1974) are typical of the surveys. The checklist responses shown in Table 6 were chosen to represent the seven

---

[1] The recent tendency of researchers to depart from qualitative analyses of interview profiles in favor of quantitative presentation of data should be viewed, I think, as a dubious contribution to research. Our understandings are enhanced by variety in research methodology. The subjective insights possible in depth interviews contribute something *different* from the quantification of data, which is a primary strength of survey research.

Table 6. Reasons for Learning

Reasons	Percent of Would-Be Learners Checking "Very Important"	Percent of Learners Checking Why They Participated
Knowledge Goals		
Become better informed	56	55
Satisfy curiosity	35	32
Personal Goals		
Get new job	25	18
Advance in present job	17	25
Get certificate or license	27	14
Attain degree	21	9
Community Goals		
Understand community problems	17	9
Become better citizen	26	11
Work for solutions to problems	16	9
Religious Goals		
Serve church	12	10
Further spiritual well-being	19	13
Social Goals		
Meet new people	19	18
Feel sense of belonging	20	9
Escape Goals		
Get away from routine	19	19
Get away from personal problems	11	7
Obligation fulfillment		
Meet educational standards	13	4
Satisfy employer	24	27
Personal Fulfillment		
Be better parent, spouse	30	19
Become happier person	37	26
Cultural Knowledge		
Study own culture	14	8
Other reasons	4	2
No response or other response	14	3

Note: Columns do not total 100 because respondents gave multiple reasons.
Source: Carp, Peterson, and Roelfs, 1974, p. 42.

motivational factors derived by Burgess (1971). Burgess hypothesized eight preliminary motivation clusters, screened a list of 5,773 reasons, and came up with seventy items representative of the initial eight clusters. A factor analysis of the responses of 1,046 adults to a questionnaire employing the seventy items revealed seven interpretable factors: (1) desire to know, (2) desire to reach a personal goal, (3) desire to reach a social goal, (4) desire to reach a religious goal, (5) desire to escape, (6) desire to take part in a social activity, and (7) desire to comply with formal requirements. Two additional factors, judged by the CNS investigators to be important, were added: desire for personal fulfillment and desire for cultural knowledge.

Because these nine goals were specifically selected to conform to factors identified earlier by factor analysis, it is fairly easy to relate these goals to those we have been discussing and to go on to assess the relative importance of the learning goals to adults in general and to particular subgroups. A number of observations can be made about the data shown in Table 6.

First, there is a clear tendency for people to acquiesce to broad, socially desirable reasons for learning. It is easy to conclude from the data in Table 6 that adults are an enlightened group of learners, eager to pursue knowledge for its own sake, to become better citizens and happier people through education. These idealistic goals seem, at first blush, to contrast sharply with the pragmatic goals of Tough's learners. Before that conclusion is accepted, however, let us probe further. One probe requires taking into consideration the fact that almost all respondents give multiple reasons for learning. Would-be learners in Table 6 checked an average of 4.6 reasons as "very important." The broader and more widely applicable the item, the more chance it has of being selected as important by large numbers of people. For example, the item "to become better informed" is so broad that it could apply to almost everyone, whereas "to get a new job" is much more limited in applicability. Thus, the general applicability of an item determines to a large extent its position in the hierarchy of learning reasons.

A second probe requires looking at *what* people learn in conjunction with *why*. When subject matter interests are tallied, practical how-to-do-it courses rank far above subjects that might be pursued because they satisfy intellectual curiosity—a finding that is not obvious from the high ratings given global idealistic reasons in Table 6. Survey research almost always shows high interest in learning for immediate use. Most adults are not much interested in storing knowledge for later use or in locating answers to questions they do not have. The authors of the pioneer of survey research studies on adult learning, *Volunteers for Learning,* concluded in 1965: "It was quite clear from the results of our study that the major emphasis in adult learning is on the practical rather than the academic; on the applied rather than the theoretical; and on skills rather than on knowledge or information" (Johnstone and Rivera, 1965, p. 3). Nothing in the myriad of surveys since has changed that general conclusion.

One of the purposes of the survey methodology is to identify the learning needs of subgroups in the population— ethnic minorities, women, the elderly, those with low income and low educational attainment, and those who live in the inner city or in rural areas. In the early 1970s, a great deal of energy and effort went into conducting statewide "needs assessments" of adult learners and potential learners. These studies were usually modeled after the national studies of Johnstone and Rivera (1965) and Carp, Peterson, and Roelfs (1974) and were intended to serve as planning documents. (See Cross, 1979a, for an evaluation of this approach.) In earlier reports, I synthesized the findings across more than thirty such studies, and the highlights of those findings are presented here, roughly categorized under the motivational dimensions already discussed. (For documentation and citations of specific studies, see Cross, 1978b; Cross, 1979a; or Cross and Zusman, 1979.)

There are not many surprises in the findings. The reasons people give for learning correspond consistently and logically to the life situations of the respondents. People who do not have good jobs are interested in further education to get better jobs, and those who have good jobs would like to advance in them. Women, factory workers, and the poorly educated, for example, are more likely to be pursuing education in order to prepare for new jobs, whereas men, professionals, and college graduates are more likely to be seeking advancement in present jobs. Men are more interested in job-related learning than women are, and young people are far more interested in it than older people are. Interest in job-related goals begins to decline at age 50 and drops off sharply after age 60. Those who are not currently participating in learning activities (most often the economically disadvantaged and poorly educated) are even more likely to express an interest in job-related education than are their more advantaged peers, who can afford the luxury of education for recreation and personal satisfaction.

Typically, about one third of potential learners give personal satisfaction as their main reason for learning, but in most studies half or more of the potential learners mention personal satisfaction as *one* of their reasons for learning. Learning activities most likely to be pursued for personal satisfaction are often considered luxury items, and it is frequently adults who have no particular desire for economic or career advancement—unemployed women, older and retired persons, and the privileged classes—who cite personal satisfaction as a *major* motive.

The percent of potential learners seeking knowledge for its own sake as their *primary* motivation varies from study to study—from a low of 10 percent to a high of 39 percent across the various state studies. Percentages are much higher (around 50 percent), but variation is also considerable for those citing the possession of knowledge as one among other reasons for learning. The average adult learner apparently does not regard traditional liberal arts courses as the foundation subjects that will satisfy his or her need for new knowledge. Only small minorities of adults express a strong interest in traditional, discipline-based subjects, and these learners, predictably, are those with high levels of educational attainment.

To work to obtain a degree or certificate is given as a reason (but not usually the main reason) by 8 to 28 percent of potential learners across the various state studies. The pursuit of degrees is strongly associated with level of educational attainment and with desire for job advancement. Younger persons and those with one to three years of college are most likely to be degree oriented, and the desire for credit or certification declines steadily with increasing age. While the number of adults wanting formal academic credentials (degree or diploma) is ordinarily quite small, most studies show that about two thirds of adult learners want some kind of recognition (skill certificate, certificate of course completion, or degree) for their learning.

A surprising number of adults (over one third) are frank to admit that escape is, for them, one reason for pursuing education. It is rarely, however, offered as the primary motivation. Nevertheless, there are certain groups of people for whom education serves as an escape and an opportunity to meet new people. Such learners are likely to be interested in hobbies and recreational subjects, and they are likely to be people who lack other social outlets—the elderly, women confined to home and family, people geographically isolated on farm or ranch. For example, in the Iowa statewide study (Hamilton, 1976), 90 percent of those interested in crafts (mostly older people, 70 percent female from middle- and lower-income levels, and 40 percent farm residents) said that meeting new people and getting away from daily routine were reasons for their learning interests. Unfortunately, many of those most eager for social contact may live in isolated regions of the country and lack the mobility to participate in group learning activities. Whether home-delivered education to socially isolated learners can be designed in a way that is satisfying to them remains to be seen.

The desire to learn to be a better citizen is not a strong reason for learning, although about one fourth of the potential adult learners cite it as one reason among others. Adult educators having some experience with the market fluctuations for extension and noncredit courses have observed, however, apparent societal motivations when there is a surge of demand for courses on energy or ecology, for example.

These general conclusions about which groups of people are motivated by which reasons seem to hold across studies and over the years for which we have data—not much more than a decade or so. One senses, however, that adults' ideas about education are changing as education becomes a necessary lifetime activity. It is thus important to have a data base that permits analysis of trends. The logical candidates for trend analysis are the triennial surveys of participation in adult education, conducted every three years since 1969 by the U.S. Bureau of the Census. Unfortunately, in the most recent survey (1978) the definition of "adult education" was changed enough to make comparisons across the years hazardous. While the new definitions may be more in tune with current thought about what constitutes "adult education," they destroy the only data source we have for observing trends in adult learning activities from year to year.

Despite the difficulties in interpretation, there seems to be only one consistent trend in the reasons people have given for taking courses over the past decade: a steady increase in the proportion taking courses for personal or recreational reasons—a category that includes education for participation in community activities, for personal and family interests, and for social and recreational interests. For the four collection years of the triennial surveys, 1969, 1972, 1975, and 1978, the percent of courses taken for personal or recreational reasons rose from 22.6 to 25.1 to 30.2 to 31.2 percent (National Center for Education Statistics, 1980). The only reasons given more frequently are job related. In the 1978 survey, 38.9 percent of the courses were taken for job improvement or advancement, 10.5 percent in order to get a new job, and 3.3 percent for other job-related reasons (National Center for Education Statistics, 1980).

Hypothesis Testing. So far in this chapter, we have reported on research methodologies where the primary purpose is to describe rather than explain. We have described types of learners (as in Houle's interview study), clusters of learning motives (as in Morstain and Smart's multivariate analysis), and the prevalence of various reasons for learning among population subgroups (as in survey research). Such descriptions are not really explanations, although they can lead to increased understanding. The search for explanations is more avidly pursued by theoreticians than by researchers, and we shall review some of the theories of adult participation and learning in Chapter Five. But the study conducted by Aslanian and Brickell (1980) illustrates a type of effort that falls somewhere between descriptive research and theoretical explanation, in that they hypothesized an explanation which they wished to test through the collection of data. Their hypothesis was that transitions—such as job changes, marriage, the arrival of children, and retirement—require adults to seek new learning. They found that 83 percent of 744 adult learners interviewed by telephone named some transition in their lives as the motivating factor that caused them to start learning. Changes in jobs or careers were the most common causes for learning, mentioned by more than half (56 percent) of the respondents. Some adults were learning new job skills just in order to keep up with their present jobs. Others were learning new skills in order to advance or change careers. For some, a job change such as retirement or reduced job responsibilities allowed them, rather than required them, to learn.

The second, although distant, transition leading to learning was a change in family life—getting married, becoming pregnant, having children, buying a house, moving, divorce, death of a family member. Sixteen percent of the respondents said that their learning activities were caused by these family changes. Almost as many—13 percent of the respondents—pointed to transitions in their leisure lives, such as making constructive use of free time, as requiring them to learn something new. Other changes played minor roles in triggering learning. A change in health was mentioned by only 5 percent, and changes in religion, citizenship, art, and leisure were mentioned by fewer than 2 percent.

While Aslanian and Brickell found that 83 percent of all adult learners asserted that a change in their lives was responsible for starting them on a learning project, Tough (1968) found that life transitions or the anticipation of them accounted for the initiation of only one third of the learning projects in his study. The differences between the two figures are substantial and do not appear to be explained by a difference in the definition of learning. Aslanian and Brickell, like Tough, included informal as well as formal learning and classes as well as self-taught subjects. Aslanian and Brickell, however, knew at the start of their study that they wished to test a hypothesis about the importance of transitions as reasons for learning. They went to considerable effort to "develop questions and techniques to *elicit* 'trigger events' that have caused learning" (p. 162, emphasis mine). This illustrates one of the problems in field research designed to test hypotheses: that investigators are likely to find what they are looking for, especially when they are in a position to influence the response—as is the case in most studies using interviews.

Summary of Research on Motivation. The question of

why adults choose to participate in various kinds of learning activities has not been answered definitively by any of the four major research methods discussed. Each method, however, has shed a little light on the topic, and the following overall conclusions seem warranted:

- Although Houle's three-way typology of adult learners has been neither proved nor disproved by subsequent and sophisticated statistical studies, it appears to provide a reasonably good practitioner's handle for thinking about individual motivations for learning. Some people may engage in continuous lifelong learning simply because they have an itch to learn; others may participate when they have a need to know or when a specific reward for the learning effort is clear to them. These two motivations account for what might be termed "intrinsic" and "extrinsic" rewards for learning. Houle's third motivation appears unrelated to the reward for learning subject matter but is related to the activity involved—getting out of the house, meeting other people, and so forth. The more sophisticated statistical studies purporting to test Houle's three-way typology have illuminated rather than changed Houle's basic conclusions. Typically, they include Houle's categories but add between two and five factors, often subdividing one of Houle's categories but rarely adding a completely new dimension.
- Most adults give practical, pragmatic reasons for learning. Most are what Houle would call "goal oriented." They have a problem to solve, which may be as broad as the desire for a better job or as narrow as learning to raise better begonias. Many goal-oriented learners are apparently responding to transitions in which needs for new job skills or for knowledge pertaining to family life serve as "triggers" to initiate learning activity.
- Broad-scale surveys of adult learning interests and needs contain no real surprises. Learning that will improve one's position in life is a major motivation. Just what will "improve life" varies with age, sex, occupation, and life stage in rather predictable ways. Young people are primarily interested in

education for upward career mobility; adults with a good job want a better one, and those without a good job want new career options. Older people and those reaching career levels where additional education promises few extrinsic rewards are often interested in learning that will enhance the quality of life and leisure.

The answer to the question of why adults participate in learning activities will probably never be answered by any simple formula. Motives differ for different groups of learners, at different stages of life, and most individuals have not one but multiple reasons for learning. Whether there is a general tendency for people to have a characteristic stance toward learning —that is, a learning orientation compelling them to seek learning opportunities to grow personally and vocationally—is a question worth further study.

Research on Barriers to Learning

It is just as important to know why adults do not participate as why they do. Indeed, since it is usually the people who "need" education most—the poorly educated—who fail to participate, understanding the barriers to participation has been a subject of special interest to researchers and policymakers. Unfortunately, it is usually even harder to find out why people do not do something than why they do.

Several research methods have been used to study barriers to adult learning. The most common method is to ask people directly through interviews or questionnaires to identify barriers to learning. A second method is to study what people do rather than what they say. If, for example, we wish to know how important cost is as a barrier, we might observe the impact of raising or lowering fees or of negotiating educational benefits into union contracts for workers. A third method might consist of advancing hypotheses about barriers and testing the hypothesis through experimental design. For example, we might advance the hypothesis that unpleasant early school experiences are a major deterrent to adult participation in learning activities. An experimental design to test the hypothesis would involve devising a measure of "unpleasant school experiences" and a measure of "adult participation" and determining the relationship between the two.

It is possible to shed modest light on why certain adults fail to participate in learning activities by combining knowledge from all three approaches. Let us look first at the data from surveys and questionnaires. Admittedly, the variety of items and reporting formats across numerous state and national studies makes precision in conclusions difficult. Respondents can be asked to name all obstacles or only the major one. Percentages can be computed by using people or number of mentions as a base. Lack of time can be considered one barrier or divided into home responsibilities and job responsibilities. Cost can be one variable or separated into tuition costs, books and transportation, lost time from work, and so on. However, although percentage figures are not comparable, there is enough consistency in the findings to give a generalized picture of what people *say* deters them from participating in adult learning activities.

Obstacles can be classified under three headings: situational, institutional, and dispositional barriers. *Situational barriers* are those arising from one's situation in life at a given time. Lack of time due to job and home responsibilities, for example, deters large numbers of potential learners in the 25- to 45-year-old age group. Lack of money is a problem for young people and others of low income. Lack of child care is a problem for young parents; transportation is a situational barrier for geographically isolated and physically handicapped learners. *Institutional barriers* consist of all those practices and procedures that exclude or discourage working adults from participating in educational activities—inconvenient schedules or locations, fulltime fees for part-time study, inappropriate courses of study, and so forth. *Dispositional barriers* are those related to attitudes and self-perceptions about oneself as a learner. Many older citizens, for example, feel that they are too old to learn. Adults with poor educational backgrounds frequently lack interest in learning or confidence in their ability to learn.

Table 7 presents data from the national survey conducted for the Commission on Non-traditional Study (Carp, Peterson,

Table 7. Perceived Barriers to Learning

Barriers	Percent of Potential Learners[a]
Situational Barriers	
Cost, including tuition, books, child care, and so on	53
Not enough time	46
Home responsibilities	32
Job responsibilities	28
No child care	11
No transportation	8
No place to study or practice	7
Friends or family don't like the idea	3
Institutional Barriers	
Don't want to go to school full time	35
Amount of time required to complete program	21
Courses aren't scheduled when I can attend	16
No information about offerings	16
Strict attendance requirements	15
Courses I want don't seem to be available	12
Too much red tape in getting enrolled	10
Don't meet requirements to begin program	6
No way to get credit or a degree	5
Dispositional Barriers	
Afraid that I'm too old to begin	17
Low grades in past, not confident of my ability	12
Not enough energy and stamina	9
Don't enjoy studying	9
Tired of school, tired of classrooms	6
Don't know what to learn or what it would lead to	5
Hesitate to seem too ambitious	3

[a]Potential learners are those who indicated a desire to learn but who are not currently engaged in organized instruction.
    Source: Adapted from Carp, Peterson, and Roelfs, 1974, p. 46.

and Roelfs, 1974). Respondents were asked to "circle *all* those [items listed] that you feel are important in keeping you from learning what you want to learn." I have grouped the twenty-four items into situational, institutional, and dispositional barriers in order to illustrate the relative importance of the three types of barriers. Some items can, of course, be included in more than one category. Lack of information, for example, could be an institutional barrier if one assumes that institutions should assume the responsibility for making their offerings known; it could be a situational barrier if one assumes that residents of a low-cost housing development rarely receive information about adult education courses, or a dispositional barrier under the assumption that adults who are not favorably disposed toward learning will make little effort to inform themselves about opportunities. In such cases, assignments of items to categories may be rather arbitrary, but I have tried to place the item in the category that seems most direct and straightforward. The percentages in this particular table are reasonably representative of the data from other surveys, but the range is considerable, and it is not wise to attach too much significance to any one set of figures. In my discussion of the barriers, I have attempted to cite percentages that reflect the center of the range across studies. (The data for much of this discussion come from two earlier efforts to synthesize findings across thirty state and national surveys. For details and citations see Cross, 1979a; Cross and Zusman, 1979.)

Situational Barriers. In all survey research, situational barriers lead the list, ranging from roughly 10 percent citing situational factors such as lack of child care or transportation to about 50 percent mentioning cost or lack of time. The cost of education and lack of time lead all other barriers of any sort by substantial margins. Ironically, the people who have the time for learning frequently lack the money, and the people who have the money often lack the time. Low-income groups are *far* more likely to mention cost as a barrier than middle- and upper-income groups (Johnstone and Rivera, 1965). Among actual learners, however, public funding is supporting adult education for about one third of the black learners, while employers are supporting educational costs for about a third of the white males. This leaves white females the only population subgroup presented in NCES data in which a *majority* of learners (66 percent) are supporting educational costs from their own or family funds (Boaz, 1978, p. 73). No doubt that is one reason why, in almost all surveys, women are more likely than men to cite the cost of education as a barrier.

Although there is a general trend now toward granting tuition-free opportunities to the elderly on a space-available basis, young people are actually more likely than old people to mention cost as a problem. This may be due to competing demands on the income of young people just starting homes and families, but there is also the fact that younger people often aspire to relatively high-cost degree programs, whereas the majority of older people express more interest in noncredit, low-cost community education programs. Cost, however, is an exceptionally difficult barrier to study via the survey method. In the first place, many adults who cite cost as a barrier probably have no idea of the cost of the various options. This speculation is reinforced by the exceptional number of survey respondents (between 20 and 40 percent) who fail to answer questions about what they would be willing to pay. Moreover, there is evidence that willingness to pay is not the same thing as ability to pay. Wilcox, Saltford, and Veres (1975) found, for example, that people are willing to pay more money for courses that advance their careers than for learning activities that add to their personal satisfaction, provide an escape from boredom, or help them to become better parents or better citizens. Men from a given socioeconomic level are ordinarily willing to pay more money for education than women from the same socioeconomic level, and older people, despite fixed incomes, are more willing to pay than younger people. These differences probably arise from complex cultural mores and expectations. Older people grew up in times when education did not receive the extensive public support that it does today, and they may expect to pay for the "privilege" of education, whereas younger people may question why they should have to pay for the "right" to an education. Women, as a group, may be less willing to pay for education than men because to date, at least, they are less likely to express an interest in education as an investment in their careers, because social mores make them feel guilty about spending "family" funds for their own education, or simply because they receive less financial support from government and business and are more likely to have to pay out of their own funds.

A second problem in attempting to determine the real

impact of cost on participation in adult education from survey research is that, in our society, to say that something costs too much is a socially acceptable reason for not doing it. When Johnstone and Rivera (1965) did their national study, they found that one out of five men and women from high socioeconomic levels said that they could not afford adult education. It might be more accurate to say that education was not as high in their priorities as something else, or that they never really thought much about education or investigated costs. When "costs too much" was presented in the survey as a possible excuse for not doing something they thought they should be doing, they may have accepted it as an easy answer. This interpretation is given some support by Penland's (1979) interesting finding that when people were not defensive (that is, they had an opportunity to identify themselves to the interviewer as active self-directed learners), the cost of courses was mentioned by only 5 percent as an important reason for learning on their own instead of taking a class. Thus, we can conclude that the context in which a respondent is asked about the barriers to learning plays an important and frequently unrecognized role in structuring the answer.

While there are all kinds of problems in interpreting the data from self-report surveys, when these data are interpreted in conjunction with other research, we can put somewhat more confidence in common findings that the cost of education probably deters some from participating in adult learning. Let us turn now to results derived from research measuring what people *do,* as opposed to what they *say.*

Bishop and Van Dyk (1977) found that Vietnam War veterans were three times more likely to attend college than other males were, and lowering tuition from $400 to zero doubled the college attendance rates for local adults. An unplanned experiment that shed some light on the role of veterans' benefits came about as a result of the termination of benefits in 1976. In the fall of 1976, enrollments in televised courses sponsored by TELECON, a consortium of thirty-five community colleges in the Los Angeles area, plummeted 43 percent—from 61,680 students in 1975 to 35,517 in 1976 (Carlisle, 1978, p. 68). How much of that enormous drop of enrollments in off-campus learning options was due to the fact that without veterans' benefits people could no longer afford to take a course they really wanted to take and how much was due to the removal of what some thought of as "an appealing giveaway" is anyone's guess. But the fact is that the loss of financial benefits had a very significant impact on participation.

Another bit of knowledge about cost barriers can be gleaned from the California experience with Proposition 13. In this case, the sudden withdrawal of public funds from a large segment of adult education offered an unusual opportunity to determine its significance. Follow-up studies of the impact of Proposition 13 on California community colleges leave little doubt that the dramatic reduction in public funding for education made a highly significant difference to adult education in California in the fall of 1979. The greatest immediate impact was on part-time students enrolled only in noncredit courses (down 40 percent from the previous fall). What is not yet clear is how much of the loss in registration was due to cancelation of courses (20 percent of the noncredit courses were dropped), how much to the initiation of fees (10 percent of the courses were shifted to fee-supported status), how much to the "nonessential" nature of many of the courses most seriously affected (most were recreation and crafts courses and offerings for senior citizens), and how much to general uncertainty and confusion. The loss of financial support did make a difference in California, and it probably constitutes a significant barrier for precisely those population subgroups who could profit most from adult learning—the young, ethnic minorities, and the educationally and economically disadvantaged.

In most surveys, lack of time vies with cost for first place among the obstacles to education. It is mentioned more often by people in their 30s and 40s than by those younger or older, more often by the highly educated than by the poorly educated, and more often by those in high-income occupations than by those in low-paying jobs (Cross and Zusman, 1979). Other situational barriers, such as lack of child care and lack of transportation, are situation specific. Child care presents a significant problem to women between the ages of 18 and 39 (and to few other population subgroups), and transportation is a significant problem to the elderly and the poor but rarely to the middle class or middle aged.

Institutional Barriers. Institutional barriers, usually subconsciously erected by providers of educational services, rank second in importance to situational barriers, affecting between 10 and 25 percent of the potential learners in most surveys. Institutional barriers exist primarily in that segment of adult education that was originally devised for full-time learners—that is, in colleges and universities; but barriers are rapidly being lowered by colleges seeking to attract the adult market. The survey of higher education sponsored by the Commission on Non-traditional Study (Ruyle and Geiselman, 1974) showed that making college programs accessible to working adult students through devices such as scheduling classes when and where working adults can attend, granting credit by examination for noncollegiate learning, and creating more flexible admissions procedures are common ways to reduce institutional barriers to learning. Indeed, so much has been done in recent years to lower institutional barriers that many providers will be mildly annoyed that the average adult is not more aware of recent changes than their responses seem to indicate. But surveys are intended to tell us what people *perceive* to be obstacles—which may have as much to do with lack of participation as actual barriers. If an individual thinks that courses would not be of interest or that they are scheduled only during the individual's working day, then the perception itself acts as a barrier, whether it actually exists or not.

Institutional barriers can generally be grouped into five areas: scheduling problems; problems with location or transportation; lack of courses that are interesting, practical, or relevant; procedural problems and time requirements; and lack of information about programs and procedures. Of these, potential learners complain most about inconvenient locations and schedules and about the lack of interesting or relevant courses. Relatively few respondents cite lack of information as an obstacle to learning—although there is good evidence that adults do lack information about the opportunities available. In the data shown in Table 7, for example, 35 percent of those interested in further learning said that they were deterred from participation because they did not want to go to school full time, yet only 16 percent complained about a lack of information. If respondents had had accurate information, they surely would have been aware that there are undoubtedly many opportunities for part-time adult study in their home communities. While procedural requirements may bother adults who have made the decision to enroll, few survey respondents, usually less than 10 percent, anticipate problems in these areas. Data on adult perceptions of the institutional barriers to learning stand as vivid testimony to the amount of work that remains to be done, both in informing adults about realistic learning opportunities and in removing obstacles that unnecessarily deter people from participating.

Familiarity with the survey data on barriers should enable planners of courses and programs to predict which groups of potential learners will be deterred by which barriers. McIntosh and Woodley (1975) did an interesting self-assessment of British Open University, in which they simply looked at the various features of their program and made some observations about barriers that still existed in a program designed from the very beginning for working adults. The following examples from their analysis of British Open University illustrate a sound way of going about identifying institutional barriers, while also providing some good insight into how difficult it is to eliminate all such barriers.

1. Students taking each foundation course must attend a one-week summer school. For manual workers this will generally mean that they have to sacrifice one of their two or three weeks' annual holiday. Attendance is also especially difficult for women with young children.

2. To obtain an ordinary degree six credits are needed, but students are awarded up to three credit exemptions depending upon how much higher education they have already received. The majority of manual workers, and all of those without experience of higher education, receive no credit exemptions. As most of these can

only cope with studying for one credit each year, this means that it will take them at least six years to obtain a degree, whereas many others may graduate in two or three years.

3. Local authorities generally only pay the student's summer school fees. The expense of course tuition fees, textbooks, traveling to study centers, and the like, must be met by the student. This is more of a problem for those in manual and routine nonmanual occupations, where earnings may be less and their employers are less likely to sponsor them or to give them paid leave. Many people who may well be studying out of interest, rather than to further their career prospects, feel guilty about using the family income for a "selfish indulgence." This is especially true for housewives who are currently without an income of their own.

4. For a good home-study environment the student requires a BBC2 television receiver, a VHF receiver, and a quiet place to study. Those with low incomes are less likely to have, or to be able to afford, the necessary receivers, and they are also less likely to have a room which they can set aside for their studies.

5. For those with a limited education, correspondence study, with its reliance on a high degree of literacy, is probably the most arduous and least accessible method for making up the deficiency.

6. Open University courses, being largely nonvocational, offer little short-term prospects of advancement compared with other, more vocational courses.

The elimination of institutional barriers is seemingly a never ending task. Even Open University, which was specially designed to serve adult students, still has institutional barriers for groups that they are desirous of serving.

Dispositional Barriers. The "real" importance of dispositional barriers is probably underestimated in survey data; such barriers are mentioned by only 5 to 15 percent of the survey respondents. But there are several methodological problems in understanding the actual role of dispositional barriers. One problem lies in the social desirability issue; it is far more acceptable to say that one is too busy to participate in learning activities or that they cost too much than it is to say that one is not interested in learning, is too old, or lacks ability. One of the more interesting findings to emerge from studies of the barriers to adult learning comes from a study done in New York (Wilcox, Saltford, and Veres, 1975), where respondents were asked not only to cite barriers to their own learning but also to speculate on why other adults of their acquaintance did not take part in educational activities. Lack of interest was a leading barrier (26 percent) attributed to others, but fewer than 2 percent were willing to admit that lack of interest deterred their own participation. Similar findings were reported in the community studies conducted by a California research team (Peterson and others, 1975). When community leaders were asked to estimate what the people in their communities would perceive as barriers to their continued learning, the leaders consistently assigned more importance to dispositional barriers than did survey respondents. For example, 18 percent of the leaders but fewer than 5 percent of the adult respondents said that "inability to do the work" would constitute a barrier to continued learning. Findings such as these highlight the problem of social desirability as a response bias in survey research.

In addition to the social desirability issue, which depresses the count in dispositional barriers, there is the methodological problem that respondents who said they were not interested in further education were frequently dropped from further analysis. We would almost certainly get higher counts for dispositional barriers if we asked those who said they were not interested in further learning the reasons for their lack of interest than if we ask those who want to learn to indicate what obstacles might prevent them. In the Commission on Nontraditional Study survey (Carp, Peterson, and Roelfs, 1974), for example, 25 percent of those with nine to eleven years of formal schooling said that they were not interested in further learning. Having received that answer, the interviewer could scarcely ask what barriers prevented further education, but it would be interesting to know what factors contributed to their lack of interest.

Summary of Research on Barriers. The list of possible explanations for nonparticipation in adult learning activities could be extended, but this brief enumeration illustrates the complementarity of different methods of analyzing the barriers to lifelong learning. One gets slightly different answers and certainly different perspectives depending on the method of study used. All of the methods discussed here aid understanding. The survey method, whether by interview or questionnaire, gives broad coverage, shows a certain faith in the capacity of people to analyze their own behavior, and is highly useful in identifying different barriers for the various population subgroups. Surveys, however, probably underestimate the importance of dispositional barriers in adult learning. Respondents are more likely to say that the cost of education is a more formidable barrier to learning than their own disinterest. The experimental method has the advantage of studying what people actually do rather than what they say they might do. Of the "experimental" designs mentioned (loss of veterans' benefits, Proposition 13, and the 1977 Bishop and Van Dyk study), two took advantage of the withdrawal of funding to study the impact of cost on participation in adult education programs, and the other used comparative analysis of comparable programs which differed in locations, fees, and so on. Finally, the construction and testing of plausible theories for examining barriers and explaining participation is a powerful tool that has not yet been adequately utilized in adult education. It is to a more comprehensive analysis of what theory has to contribute to understanding that we turn now.

CHAPTER 5

Toward a Model of Adult Motivation for Learning

One of the most underutilized vehicles for understanding various aspects of adult learning is theory. The notable lack of theory in adult education has led to some harsh words by some of its best friends. Boshier (1971, p. 3) goes so far as to call adult education a "conceptual desert," and Mezirow (1971, p. 135) complains that the absence of theory is a "pervasively debilitating influence" in adult education. Unfortunately, they are correct in their judgment that theory is almost nonexistent. A content analysis of the 517 articles appearing in *Adult Education* between 1950 and 1970 showed that over half (54 percent) described educational programs or personal experience, 23 percent reported on empirical research, and 3 percent discussed theoretical formulations (Dickinson and Rusnell, 1971). Since

Adult Education is specifically billed as "a journal of research and theory," we can safely assume that these figures exaggerate the attention given in the past to research and theory in the total literature of adult education. Recent articles in the journal show considerably more research emphasis, but articles dealing with theory are still rare in adult education.

The pragmatism of adult education can be easily understood, and to some extent even commended for its no-nonsense practicality, but the lack of theory is easier to explain than to defend. Undoubtedly, the novice in the teaching of adults—and there are always many in this field, which is heavily populated by part-time, in-and-out educators—can benefit from the experience and accumulated wisdom of those who have worked with adults in a variety of learning situations. However, the profession of adult education cannot advance beyond its present stage of development if one generation of adult educators simply passes on what it has learned through experience to the next generation. Such an approach results in a static, if not downright stagnant, profession, because each new generation of professionals simply catches up with the preceding generation rather than forging new frontiers of knowledge. The systematic accumulation of knowledge is essential for progress in any profession. In an applied profession, however, theory and practice must be constantly interactive. Theory without practice is empty, and practice without theory is blind.

Theory building in adult education has proved difficult for a number of reasons. First, there is the marketplace orientation of most adult educators. Adult education has grown up marketing its wares to volunteer learners who can "take it or leave it." A tip from a successful entrepreneur of adult education programs may be perceived as far more useful than a bit of theory from a university professor. Furthermore, the market mentality tends to preclude the search for explanations of complex phenomena. If the task of adult educators is to provide "service" to "consumers," efficiency would seem to call for the pragmatic approach of finding out what consumers want and giving it to them. (See Monette, 1979, for a thoughtful critique of this position.)

The second obstacle to theory building is that the field of adult education has produced few scholars. Most of the people involved in adult education on college campuses have been administrators and program planners in extension divisions, where the first obligation is to serve the immediate needs of their publics. While graduate programs and funding for research in adult education has grown substantially over the past fifteen years, future growth probably will be modest, given the vigorous competition for funds in higher education.

A third stumbling block to theory building in adult education is the multidisciplinary, applied nature of the field. Would the theory come from psychology, sociology, gerontology, physiology, or all of the above? Do we need a special learning theory for adults, presumably one that will tell us how the processes of learning are different for adults than for children or rats? Do we need a theory of motivation that will tell us why some adults seek new learning experiences while others do not? Do we need a theory of instruction that will answer the questions of practitioners about how to provide effective instruction? Do we need a theory of adult development that will guide our thinking and understanding about physiological and psychological maturation?

Overwhelmed by such questions, many scholars in adult education opt for what might be called eclectic pragmatism in theory building. Broschart (1977, p. 10) says, "We might be well advised to examine 'what works' regardless of its theoretical derivation." Kidd (1977, p. 19) would also be satisfied with some sort of eclectic theory: "Some have said that there is little point in attempting to achieve an integrated theory; they argue that we should enjoy our multiplicity of concepts and practices, opt for pluralism, and practice tolerance for differences. Others believe that some integration is possible and have made some attempts to achieve it. On my own account, I have made no such effort. While I would welcome attempts at greater coherence, I would be content facing the 1970s and 1980s if we continued to observe and test all theories that seem appropriate as well as scores of fields of practice."

It is unlikely that there will ever be a single theory of

adult education. Instead, there will be many theories useful in improving our understanding of adults as learners. In this book, I have chosen to develop two conceptual frameworks. The first, developed in this chapter, is a theory of adult motivations for learning. The second, developed in Chapter Nine, is a theory of teaching or, more accurately, for facilitating learning in adults. The models I have developed have their origins in the theoretical work of the past fifteen years. The work of four scholars on the motivation for adult learning seems especially promising.

Force Field Analysis: Harry L. Miller

Harry Miller (1967) is one of the few adult educators to tackle directly the problem of explaining why socioeconomic status (SES) and participation in adult education are inevitably related. Miller's (1967) social class theory builds on the needs hierarchy of Maslow (1954) and the force-field analysis of Lewin (1947), to explain not only why people participate but also why there are large differences between social classes in what they hope to attain from participation. Maslow maintains that people cannot be concerned about higher human needs— for recognition (status), achievement, and self-realization—until the lower fundamental needs—for survival, safety, and belonging —have been met. Applied to adult education, the needs hierarchy would predict that members of the lower social classes will be interested primarily in education that meets survival needs, mostly job training and adult basic education, while the upper social classes will have fulfilled those needs and will seek education that leads to achievement and self-realization. Clearly, data showing who wants what in adult education support Miller's use of Maslow's needs hierarchy. That is, those with a high school education or less are interested primarily in job-related education, while education aimed toward self-understanding, recreation, personal development, and the like, appeals primarily to well-educated people and to others not concerned about survival in the labor market (Carp, Peterson, and Roelfs, 1974; Cross, 1979a; Johnstone and Rivera, 1965).

Miller points out that the needs hierarchy is also useful in accommodating research showing a relationship between educational interests and age and position in the life cycle. Early stages of adulthood are concerned with satisfaction of needs low in the hierarchy—getting established in a job and beginning a family. Older people, having satisfied those needs, are free to devote energy to achieving status, to enhancing achievement, and to working toward self-realization.

Miller's basic strategy is to use Lewin's concept of positive and negative forces, which, when combined, form a resultant motivational force. Figure 1 illustrates Miller's analysis

Figure 1. Education for Vocational Competence, Lower-Lower-Class Level

Positive Forces

1. Survival needs
2. Changing technology
3. Safety needs of female culture
4. Governmental attempts to change opportunity structure

Negative Forces

5. Action-excitement orientation of male culture
6. Hostility to education and to middle-class object orientation
7. Relative absence of specific, immediate job opportunities at end of training
8. Limited access through organizational ties
9. Weak family structure

Negative Forces

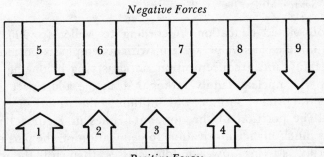

Positive Forces

Source: Miller, 1967, p. 21.

of the forces present in the motivation of the lower-lower class for education for vocational competence. The width of the arrow symbolizes the strength of the force, while the position of the horizontal line indicates the resultant force—quite low in this example, indicating little motivation for participation.

Figure 2 is presented for contrast. It represents Miller's conception of the strong motivation of the lower-middle class

Figure 2. Education for Vocational Competence, Lower-Middle-Class Level
Positive Forces

1. Satisfied survival need
2. Satisfied safety need
3. Strong status need
4. Changing technology
5. Access through organizational ties
6. Acceptance of middle-class career drives
7. Familiarity with educational processes

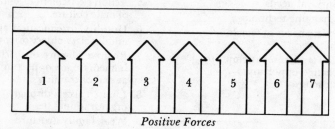

Positive Forces

Source: Miller, 1967, p. 23.

for job-related education. According to Miller (p. 11), "The lower-middle-class value system, with its emphasis on mobility and status and a concentration on satisfying belonging needs within the nuclear family rather than in the adult peer group, makes it a prime consumer of continuing education."

The position of the horizontal lines in Figures 1 and 2 shows much higher motivation for education on the part of the upwardly striving lower-middle classes than for the down-trodden lower-lower classes—which helps to explain research findings. Miller's force-field analysis also permits us to think about how forces might be modified. Miller suggests that a marketing strategy is likely to attract the lower-middle classes because positive motivational forces are already present. Presumably, if they know of appropriate opportunities, they will rush to take advantage of them. Marketing will do little, however, to attract the lower-lower classes. To do that, some modification of existing forces would be necessary. It might be possible, for example, to concentrate on modifying Arrow 8 in Figure 1 by trying to strengthen organizational ties and then working through membership groups toward appropriate forms of education. For example, a community center might strive to strengthen feelings of belonging to a group that is active in gaining access to educational opportunity. At the same time, the negative force of the action-excitement orientation of males from the lower-lower classes (Arrow 5) might be reduced through emphasizing more action-oriented forms of learning than traditional middle-class education.

Miller's force-field analysis incorporates basic sociological research in identifying positive and negative forces in the environment, and his model also accommodates the research findings on participation. The dropout rate of lower-class males from job training programs is very high, suggesting that even when they know about learning opportunities and get far enough to enroll (presumably because, momentarily at least, the positive forces overcome the negative), negative forces in the culture prevent continuation.

Figures 1 and 2, taken together, illustrate all too clearly present trends in participation. Any increase in vocational education that adheres to essentially middle-class values will attract the lower-middle classes in growing numbers, but the lower-lower classes will remain unaffected—thus the well-documented and growing gap between the social classes in adult education. In my search of the literature, I was unable to locate recent theoretical work or research building on Miller's force-field analysis. It appears, however, to be useful theory in the sense that it suggests further research as well as some possible action strategies.

Expectancy-Valence Paradigm: Kjell Rubenson

Kjell Rubenson (1977), a Swedish educator, has probably gone further than anyone else in utilizing current research findings and past theoretical models to develop a framework for understanding the competing forces at work in motivating adults to participate in organized education. In a paper prepared for the Organization for Economic Cooperation and Development (OECD), Rubenson developed a paradigm that he hopes will lead eventually to a theory of recruitment. His work is a modification and application of earlier work by Vroom (1964), in which Vroom attempted to explain the motivation and incentives of people for work. Education, like work, appears to be an achievement-oriented activity, meaning that people who want to "get ahead" will put effort into personal achievement in school or on the job. Thus, the application of Vroom's expectancy-valence theory to adult education seems fitting.

The expectancy-valence model starts with psychological theories of motivation, drawing heavily from the work of theorists such as Lewin, Tolman, McClelland, and Atkinson, who explain human behavior in terms of the interaction between the individual (with his acquired experience) and the environment (as he perceives and experiences it). The resultant strength of the individual's motivation is determined by combining positive and negative forces existing in the individual and the environment. The "expectancy" part of Rubenson's formula consists of two components: the expectation of personal success in the educational activity and the expectation that being successful in the learning activity will have positive consequences. These two components are multiplicative. If either assumes a value of zero —that is, if the individual does not perceive himself as able to participate successfully or if there seems to be no reward for doing so—the resultant force is zero, and there is no motivation to participate. The other part of the formula, valence, is concerned with affect and can be positive, indifferent, or negative. Its strength depends on the anticipated consequences of participation. For example, participation in adult education can lead to higher pay, but it can also mean seeing less of the family. The valence is the algebraic sum of the values that the individual puts on the different consequences of participation.

Rubenson precedes the expectancy-valence portion of his paradigm with what he calls an ahistorical approach. He is interested first and foremost in the present life space, but in that life space, it should be understood, are the traces left from previous experience which contribute to the person's personality, knowledge, and convictions. Rubenson's paradigm is shown in Figure 3.

Rubenson works a number of what I would call sub-hypotheses into his paradigm, so that it is difficult to be certain just how he would label the various valence and expectancy components. The following is my simplified interpretation of how he might handle the various forces contributing to the motivation of Henry, a hypothetical learner.

Henry's major decision-making activity occurs when Henry's needs interact with his perception of the environment to create the expectancy-valence forces. If Henry has a positive self-concept (usually formed, Rubenson thinks, by childhood, school, and work experiences which encourage self-direction) and is offered a job promotion for completion of a course, the expectancy force in the formula is strong, because Henry has reason to think that he will complete the course satisfactorily and will receive a promotion.

That expectancy alone, however, may not lead to course enrollment unless there is a positive valence associated with the anticipated outcomes; in this case, job promotion must be perceived as desirable. Rubenson places considerable emphasis on the role of reference groups in shaping attitudes. If, for example, Henry's fellow workers place a negative value on adult education or on Henry's possible promotion, then the valence for Henry might be negative and his participation unlikely.

Rubenson's paradigm, although complex, is helpful in shifting attention from demographic variables—such as age, sex, and race—to more individually based measures. He makes room for social class through a strong emphasis on the influence of membership groups, but his major attention is given to how an individual learner perceives his environment and what he expects to gain from participation in adult education.

Quite significantly, Rubenson's paradigm places much less emphasis on so-called external barriers to educational participation than current research investigations do. Much of the current thinking about educational participation in the United

Figure 3. Rubenson's Paradigm of Recruitment

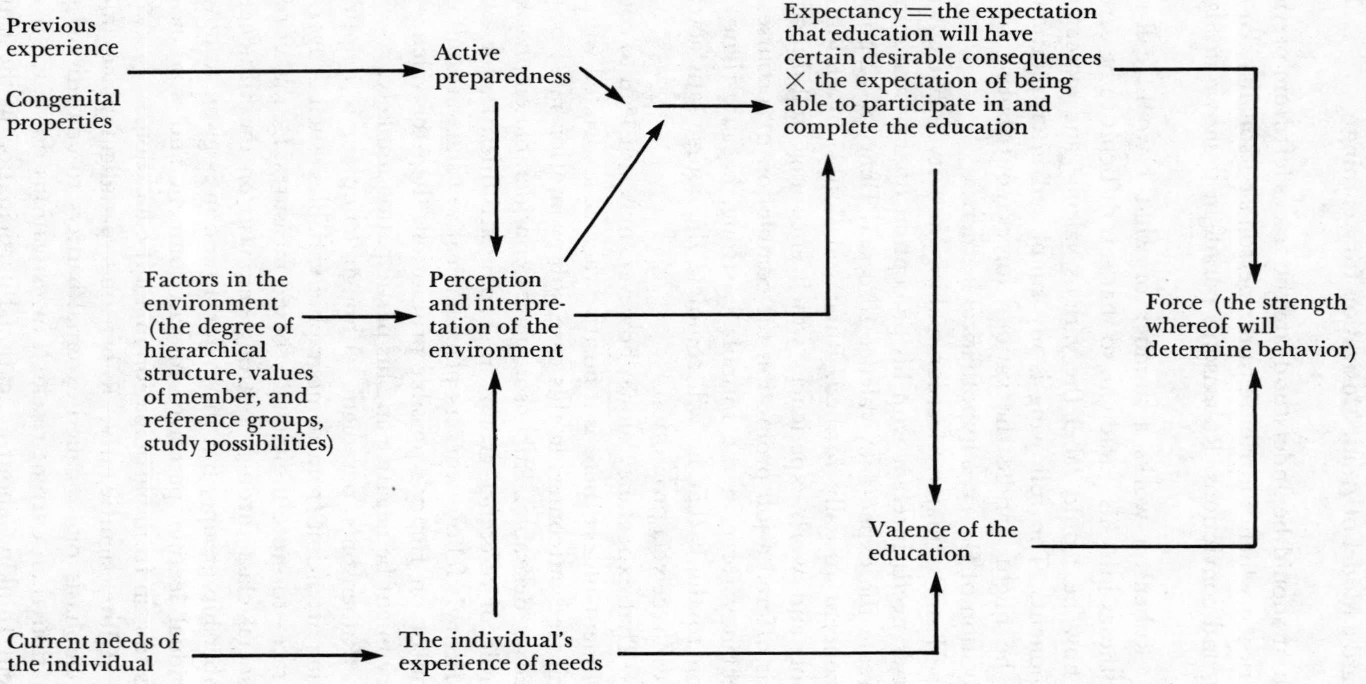

Previous
experience

Congenital
properties

Active
preparedness

Factors in the
environment
(the degree of
hierarchical
structure, values
of member, and
reference groups,
study possibilities)

Current needs of
the individual

Perception
and interpre-
tation of the
environment

The individual's
experience of needs

Expectancy = the expectation
that education will have
certain desirable consequences
× the expectation of being
able to participate in and
complete the education

Valence of the
education

Force (the strength
whereof will
determine behavior)

Source: Rubenson, 1977, p. 35.

States assumes that most people are motivated to participate in education and that the removal of external barriers will permit them to do so. I retain a considerable amount of skepticism regarding that assumption, and I believe that Rubenson's paradigm places the real role of so-called "external barriers" in a more realistic perspective. Provision for the role of external barriers is built into Rubenson's formula primarily through the perceptions of the potential learners. Motivation, according to Rubenson, is based on the "perceived" situation, which may or may not be the "real" situation. If Henry thinks he lacks the money to participate in adult education, then his expectancy is zero, and the resultant force is zero. Presumably, if someone tells an otherwise highly motivated Henry that the course he wants to take is offered at no charge, his expectancy for successful participation would become strong and the forces would add up to participation. At the same time, if Henry is convinced that he would be unsuccessful in the educational pursuit, provision of financial aid will have no effect on his participation.

A Congruence Model: Roger Boshier

Roger Boshier (1973) has much in common with Rubenson and Miller, in that all believe that motivation for learning is a function of the interaction between internal psychological factors and external environmental variables, or at least the participant's perception and interpretation of environmental factors. Boshier has studied nonparticipation and dropout in noncredit courses in continuing education in New Zealand, and his theory arises out of his research.

His theoretical conclusion is that "both adult education participation and dropout can be understood to occur as a function of the magnitude of the discrepancy between the participant's self-concept and key aspects (largely people) of the educational environment. Nonparticipants manifest self/institution incongruence and do not enroll" (1973, p. 260). Boshier seems to suggest that a number of incongruencies (between self and ideal self, self and other students, self and teacher, self and institutional environment) are additive; the greater the sum, the greater the likelihood of nonparticipation or dropout. To oversimplify a bit, if an individual feels uncomfortable with herself, her teachers, her fellow students, or the educational environment, she has high potential for dropping out. That does not seem a very startling insight, but it is a hypothesis which had not been tested until Boshier attempted to test it by correlating various measures of congruence with dropping out of classes in continuing education. He found confirmation of his hypothesis; that is, that students with high incongruence scores are significantly more likely to drop out than other people are. Boshier did not test his model with nonparticipants, but he defends his congruence model for nonparticipants, as well as for dropouts, on the grounds that dropping out is simply an extension of nonparticipation and that the low participation rate of adults from the lower socioeconomic classes is due to the lack of congruence between their lives and the essentially middle-class educational environment of continuing education.

Boshier's theory suggests that the proper matching of adults to educational environments is important. But he also suggests that certain people, especially those who show a high degree of dissatisfaction with themselves (through high discrepancy scores between self and ideal self), are likely to project their own dissatisfaction onto the environment and to drop out of almost any kind of environment; that is, they are "dropout prone." What educators can do to make what Boshier terms the "maladjusted" (in the sense that Rogers or Lecky might use the term to describe people who are far from what they would like to be) happier in the educational environment is not discussed, but the congruence between learners and their environments is a frequently ignored hypothesis that needs a research airing. Both Boshier and Rubenson suggest that one of the very important factors in educational participation is the self-esteem of the individual. Those who evaluate themselves negatively are less likely to expect success (in Rubenson's theory) and less likely to experience congruence with the educational environment (in Boshier's theory).

Anticipated Benefits: Allen Tough

Allen Tough (1979), the leading proponent of research on self-directed learning, does not have a well-developed theory about why people undertake self-directed learning projects, but a recent paper (Tough, 1979) is clearly moving toward explanation and toward the conceptual organization of data. Since those are steps in theory building, a brief summary of his recent efforts to measure multiple components of motivation is included here. In an interesting experiment, Tough and his colleagues (Tough, Abbey, and Orton, 1979) asked learners to assign weights to their reasons for learning, observing that this is a task that people can do fairly easily. Their assignment of the task and people's acceptance of it makes a basic assumption about learners that is not made by all psychologists, namely, that behavior is understood and can be articulated by the subjects of the research. This assumption, of course, underlies most of Tough's research on self-directed learning, showing a faith in adults not only to direct their own learning but also to understand why they wish to do so. Tough and his colleagues make no claim that the total picture of learning motivation can be explained by the participants, but they build their model on the belief that the anticipated benefits to be derived from learning are "present in the person's conscious mind" and constitute a "significant portion of the person's total motivation for learning." Indeed, they claim that the learner's *conscious* anticipation of reward is more important than subconscious forces or environmental forces. Their initial data suggest that their direct approach to constructing a theory of motivation based on anticipated benefits is feasible and may provide one piece of the puzzle of a theory or theories of participation in learning activities.

Their model consists of five stages at which benefits might be anticipated, moving generally through (1) *engaging* in a learning activity to (2) *retaining* the knowledge or skill to (3) *applying* the knowledge to (4) *gaining a material reward,* as in promotion, or (5) *gaining a symbolic reward,* as in credits and degrees. At each stage, anticipated benefits might be classified into three clusters of personal feelings: pleasure (happiness, satisfaction, enjoyment, feeling good), self-esteem (regarding self more highly, feeling more confident, maintaining self-images), and a category labeled "others" (others regard individual more highly, praise him, like him, feel grateful).

In a research test of the model, people were given ten "points" and asked to distribute the points among the anticipated benefits of pleasure, self-esteem, and responses from others for each of the five stages. When a research sample of one hundred people distributed 1,000 points, the stage at which benefits were most likely to be anticipated was in the application of the knowledge or skill (33 percent of all points), followed by engagement in the activity (24 percent), retaining knowledge (19 percent), material rewards (15 percent), and credit (9 percent). The most frequent anticipated benefit was in the form of pleasure (50 percent of all points), followed by self-esteem (41 percent) and reaction from others (9 percent).

While many might wish greater defense of the particular categories chosen and more explanation of the presumed interactions, Tough's work appears to be a preliminary effort that could, upon further development, provide a useful piece of the conscious forces involved in motivation for learning.

Common Elements in Existing Theories

Of the writers reviewed here, none would lay claim to a fully developed theory regarding participation in adult education. Nevertheless, all have helped to develop a preliminary framework for ordering research on who participates in adult learning and why. Although the first three models happen to deal with registrations in organized classes as the criterion for participation, there is no reason why the models should not be applicable to the kinds of self-directed learning that have been the concern of Allen Tough, and no reason why Tough's initial efforts to understand anticipated benefits cannot be applied to learners pursuing courses and class work. Agreements among these theorists are considerably greater than their differences, and it seems reasonable now to proceed to build on the base that has been suggested by their work. Since Tough's work is much more fragmentary and incomplete than the others at this time, it is presented primarily as an interesting beginning. Common elements among the other three theorists are as follows:

1. All three are interactionists, operating from the conviction that participation can be understood through an analysis of the interaction between an individual and his or her environment.

2. All use some form of field-force analysis, drawing heavily from the work of Kurt Lewin and the concept that the strength of the motivation to participate in adult education is the result of the individual's perception of positive and negative forces in the situation.

3. All might be termed "cognitivists" in the sense that they believe that the individual has some control over his destiny. They reject both the Freudian notion that human beings are the captives of subconscious forces and the Skinnerian contention that people are pawns in stimulus-response chains.

4. Rubenson and Boshier are quite explicit about the hypothesis that certain personality types will be difficult to attract to education because of their low self-esteem. The hypothesis that people wih low self-esteem do not do well in achievement-oriented situations (which education is thought to be) has been a kingpin of psychological theories of motivation for some years. The hypothesis is also implicit in Miller's social class analysis, where he considers lack of achievement motivation a deterrent to the participation of the lower-lower socioeconomic classes.

5. All make some use of reference group theory, with Miller and Rubenson explicitly recommending that undereducated adults be recruited not through market strategies but by working through membership groups.

6. All make some use of the concepts of incongruence and dissonance. Boshier refers to his work as a "congruence" model; Miller's analysis is based on the compatibility of the values of the various social classes with the values of the educational system. For Rubenson the concepts of expectancy and valence assume congruence between participation and anticipated outcomes.

7. There is strong use of Maslow's needs hierarchy in these works. All accept Maslow's basic premise that higher-order needs for achievement and self-actualization cannot be ful-

filled until lower-order needs for security and safety have
been met. (For recent questioning of the validity of the Maslow hierarchy, see Korman, Greenhaus, and Badin, 1977.)
8. Rubenson has developed the role played by "expectancy"
   more thoroughly than the other two theorists. But all
   assume that the individual's expectation of reward is an important variable in the motivation for adult learning.

Chain-of-Response (COR) Model

Figure 4 represents the rough beginnings of a conceptual
framework designed to identify the relevant variables and

**Figure 4. Chain-of-Response (COR) Model for Understanding Participation
in Adult Learning Activities**

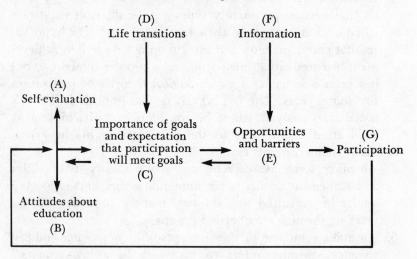

hypothesize their interrelationships. While it is still far from the
kind of theory that can be used to predict who will participate
in which adult learning activities, it may be useful in organizing
existing knowledge and in suggesting more sharply focused research projects to add to the gradual accumulation of knowledge. The framework depicted in Figure 4 may be called a

chain-of-response (COR) model. It assumes that participation in a learning activity, whether in organized classes or self-directed, is not a single act but the result of a chain of responses, each based on an evaluation of the position of the individual in his or her environment. This conception of behavior as a constantly flowing stream rather than a series of discrete events is consistent with the "radical theoretical revision" now taking place in the psychology of motivation. "The problem for motivation," say deCharms and Muir in their 1978 review of motivational psychology (p. 93), "is to understand the determinants of change in the stream of action, not to find what drives impel specific behaviors." The continuum implied in the order of the presentation in Figure 4 indicates that forces for participation in adult learning activities begin with the individual and move to increasingly external conditions—although it must be generally understood that, in any interaction situation, forces flow in both directions. Ultimately, participation in adult learning changes self-perceptions and attitudes about education. A brief discussion of each of the variables may help make the model concrete.

Regarding point A, self-evaluation, past research has shown that certain relatively stable personality characteristics play an important role in the motivation for achievement. Since education, especially any form of competitive education, is considered achievement motivated, this body of psychological research has considerable relevance for any theory of voluntary participation in adult learning. Specifically, the research suggests that persons who lack confidence in their own abilities (frequently termed failure threatened or deficiency oriented) avoid putting themselves to the test and are unlikely to volunteer for learning which might present a threat to their sense of self-esteem. Although the situation is not as linear as Figure 4 suggests, self-evaluation is where the chain of responses leading to participation begins.

Attitudes toward education (B) arise directly from the learner's own past experience and indirectly from the attitudes and experiences of friends and "significant others." Adults who hated school as children, in part at least because they were constantly placed in a competitive situation where they did not do well, are unlikely to return voluntarily to the scene of their former embarrassment. Attitudes about education also arise indirectly through the attitudes of reference groups and membership groups. The widespread failure of members of the United Auto Workers to use educational benefits, for example, is frequently attributed to indifferent or negative attitudes toward adult education on the part of fellow workers.

In linking A and B in Figure 4, I intend to suggest that there is a relatively stable and characteristic stance toward learning that makes some people eager to seek out new experiences with a potential for growth while others avoid challenges to their accustomed ways of thinking or behaving. This characteristic can be likened to Houle's (1961) learning-oriented adult, to Atkinson and Feather's (1966) achievement-motivated personality, and to Heath's (1964) reasonable adventurer. These personalities seek challenges and new opportunities for growth through learning. In Figure 4, the learning-oriented personality is represented by the interaction between A and B, which derive primarily from past experience and learning. A child who enjoys school and does well is likely to develop a positive self-evaluation, which in turn contributes to doing well in school.

Point C, the importance of goals and the expectation that goals will be met, will be recognized as the familiar expectancy-valence theory of motivation arising out of the work of Tolman, Lewin, Atkinson, Vroom, and, more recently, Rubenson. It has two components: "valence," the importance of the goal to the individual; and "expectancy," the individual's subjective judgment that pursuit of the goal will be successful and will lead to the desired reward. If a goal that is important to a person is likely to be achieved through further education, then the motivation at point C is strong. If the goal is not especially important or the likelihood of success is in doubt, motivation decreases accordingly.

Expectancy is related to self-esteem (indicated by reverse arrow), in that individuals with high self-esteem "expect" to be successful, whereas those with less self-confidence entertain doubts about their probable success. Considerable attention has been given in recent years to the relationship of valence (C) to attitudes toward adult learning (B). Sweden, in particular, has been notably successful in changing attitudes toward education (increasing positive valence) by working with membership groups such as labor unions.

In the recent literature of lifelong learning, considerable attention is given to life transitions (D) as periods of change calling for adjustment to new phases of the life cycle (see Chapter Seven). Related to the gradual transitions of life are more sudden dramatic changes, such as divorce or loss of a job, which may "trigger" a latent desire for education into action. The identification of the transitions of life as positive forces for learning is related to much of the current interest in adult phases of development and to Havighurst's (1972) identification of "the teachable moment." Havighurst's idea, which could be considered another theory of adult motivation, is that there are times of special sensitivity for learning certain things. These times depend on developmental tasks that are predictably associated with each phase of human development. The "right" time to teach a couple about child development, for example, is when they are expecting or raising children.

Once the individual is motivated to participate in some form of learning activity, barriers and special opportunities for adult learning (E) are thought to play an important role. If adults get to this point in the COR model with a strong desire to participate, it is likely that the force of their motivation will encourage them to seek out special opportunities and to overcome modest barriers. For the weakly motivated, modest barriers may preclude participation, while the awareness of special new opportunities for adults may enhance the motivational force for participation.

Point F in the COR model, accurate information, is receiving considerable attention now in the creation of education information centers and educational brokering agencies. Its role in the model is critical in that it provides the information that links motivated learners to appropriate opportunities. Without accurate information, point E in the model is weak because opportunities are not discovered and barriers loom large.

To illustrate how the COR model might work, let us trace the decisions that might be made by a hypothetical learner, whom we shall call Sally. Let us assume that Sally is a self-confident individual (positive force at point A in the COR model, indicated as +A) who liked school and was successful in it (+A and +B) but whose husband opposes her pursuit of a college degree (−B). Sally would like a bachelor's degree, partly to qualify her for a better job and partly for her own satisfaction, and she is confident that she would be a successful student (+C), but her husband's mild opposition decreases the total force of her motivation for participation. Were her husband's opposition stronger or her self-confidence less or her past experiences with education unhappy, this might be the end of the matter; her motivational force would be too weak to overcome any barriers or respond to special opportunities for adults at point E. Let us assume, however, that as Sally is subconsciously weighing the positive and negative forces at work, a friend discovers that both she and Sally can obtain credit for life experiences related to their educational goals and urges Sally to join her in taking courses at the local college (+E). This positive force at point E may activate her participation despite her anticipation of dissension at home.

In a somewhat different scenario, let us assume that Sally becomes divorced, a life transition (+D) that removes the negative force of her husband's opposition to further education (+B) at the same time that it adds a strong force for gaining the qualifications for a job that is self-supporting (+C). The force for participation at this point is quite strong, and she may take the initiative in ferreting out information about her options (+F). Her awareness then that a good opportunity exists (+E) adds to the positive forces of participation. Now let us assume that the course Sally wants to take meets from 2:00 to 4:00 on Wednesdays, leaving her with a babysitting problem for her 4-year-old child (−E). If these external barriers are extremely strong and cannot be overcome, this may terminate the force for participation. If, however, Sally finds a solution to her child care problem or finds a home study course for credit or a morning class that meets when her child is in nursery school, the cumulative total of the force is sufficient to cross the threshold to participation.

Although I have overemphasized the linearity of decision making in order to illustrate the cumulative nature of the forces for and against participation, there is an important implication in the order of the variables in the COR model. Most efforts to attract adults to learning activities start at point E in Figure 4, trying to reduce the negative forces (barriers) or enhance the positive ones (new opportunities). For people who get to point E with their positive forces intact, such actions may well encourage participation. The elimination of external barriers, however, will do nothing for the individual whose weak positive forces for participation were wiped out by the strength of negative forces encountered before he reached point E. As indicated by the reverse arrow from E to C, the creation of new opportunities (E) may add to an individual's expectation (C) of being able to participate successfully and therefore may raise the strength of the motivational force above the threshold level. In most cases, however, people will have to have some motivation for adult education before the removal of external barriers will make any difference to them. The arrow from G to AB accommodates the well-known research finding that people who have participated in adult education are more likely to do so in the future—presumably because such participation enhanced self-esteem, created positive attitudes toward education, led to increased expectation of success, and so forth.

Given this line of analysis, the removal of external barriers and the creation of new learning opportunities would be expected to benefit women more than any of the other groups underrepresented in adult education, because many women have had successful school experiences, hold positive attitudes toward schools and education, and have newly acquired aspirations regarding good job opportunities. The accuracy of that predictive analysis is supported by research on participation conducted over the past decade. It shows major advances in women's participation concurrent with major progress in the removal of external barriers. The removal of external barriers, however, has done almost nothing for blacks, whose participation in adult education has actually decreased over the past decade, and for other poorly educated segments of the population. For these groups, the incentives and rewards for adult education will have to be much greater than is currently the case. The simple creation of new opportunities is not a sufficiently strong force to overcome the negative forces built up at other points in the COR model. The creation of new opportunities has had modest influence on the participation rates of the elderly, but the self-evaluation of being "too old" to learn is still given by surprisingly large numbers of people over the age of 65, and the lifelong learning report (*Lifelong Learning and Public Policy,* 1978, p. 43) terms "lack of interest" the "most formidable" barrier to education for the elderly. In any event, the basic point remains; the COR model requires much greater attention than has heretofore been given to understanding forces generated by *internal* psychological variables affecting self-evaluation and attitudes toward education. In short, if adult educators wish to understand why some adults fail to participate in learning opportunities, they need to begin at the beginning of the COR model—with an understanding of attitudes toward self and education.

Most of the current knowledge about the role of internal variables appears in the literature of psychology, whereas the influence of external barriers is emphasized in the burgeoning literature on lifelong learning. This specialization of function has some advantages, but it also increases the difficulty in understanding human behavior as a chain or stream of responses of the individual to his environment. Phares and Lamiell (1977, p. 133) note, for example, that psychologists have been more concerned over the years with studying the factors that *lead* to low self-esteem than they have been with studying the *effects* of low self-esteem on subsequent behavior. Adult educators, on the other hand, are appropriately more interested in studying the impact of low self-esteem on participation in adult education. Cooperation between psychologists and adult educators would provide some continuity in our understandings regarding human motivation.

The purpose of a theoretical model as broad as the COR

model is not so much to explain and predict adult participation at this stage in the development of knowledge, as it is to organize thinking and research. The general usefulness of the model will be judged by its capacity to accommodate existing research and, even more important, by its ability to stimulate new research and, ultimately, to improve practice.

CHAPTER 6

Implications for Increasing Participation

There are basically two kinds of learning associated with the learning society: self-directed learning, for which the base of knowledge is the work of Allen Tough and others who have joined him more recently; and participation in organized instruction (including learning for credit and certification), for which the base of research is primarily surveys and census data. In general, educators who want to increase participation in self-directed learning concentrate mainly on individual motivations (points A through D of the COR model discussed in Chapter Five and depicted in Figure 4). In contrast, those who wish to encourage participation in organized instruction start at point E, opening up new opportunities and removing existing barriers. Educators of all persuasions, however, might well think about how lifelong learning can be improved across the full range of opportunities—from self-directed learning projects to participation in college degree programs.

Raising Self-Confidence Levels

The general hypothesis about the relationship of self-evaluation (point A of the COR model) to educational participation is that those with low self-confidence in their learning abilities will avoid the risk required in learning new things, basically because they do not expect to succeed. In their experience with education in the past, the outcome of effort is more likely to be the pain of failure than the reward of a new job, a promotion, the admiration of others, or the self-satisfaction of succeeding at the learning task. If we assume with Bloom (1976), Glaser (1977), Holt (1970), and others that early and constant failure in school leads to lowered self-esteem, then those with poor records of school achievement will be unlikely to seek education as adults, because to them school means threat of further failure. This hypothesis is confirmed by repeated findings that the unsuccessful in school leave early and avoid becoming engaged in organized instruction as adults. Self-directed learning, however, occurs almost as frequently among early school leavers as among more academically successful adults—possibly because self-directed learning projects do not carry the reminder of earlier school failure and ordinarily contain less threat than organized learning activities.

Thus, one of the things that educators can do to encourage those with low levels of self-confidence about their ability to participate successfully in adult learning is to create more educational opportunities with low levels of risk and threat. Adult learning activities can be ordered, I suggest, from low threat to high as follows:

1. *Self-directed learning projects.* Such projects are essentially nonthreatening because learners have complete control over the situation. They can gauge the learning tasks to levels of achievement with which they feel comfortable; they can

expose themselves to the queries of other people only at times and on topics of their own choosing; they can retreat or withdraw from any task at any time.

2. *Televised courses as unregistered learners.* No commitment is made, no test of ability required. The risk is slightly higher than in self-directed learning because someone else has determined the learning task; however the learner can thereby test his ability to understand subject matter proposed by others.

3. *Noncredit adult education.* There is some public commitment in joining a learning group, but no public assessment, such as grades or tests, is involved. The learner retains control over level of performance, and evaluation is self-evaluation.

4. *Competency-based learning.* A commitment is made to develop a competency; evaluation is conducted, but the situation is noncompetitive.

5. *Credit classes.* The learner enters a threatening and competitive environment in which she must pit her skills against the performance of others in the class and must be evaluated by another person, whose opinion may be critical to the learner's future.

This hypothesized continuum from low-threat to high-threat learning situations does not include all possibilities, but it establishes some points for locating the threat level inherent in various learning options. Other things being equal, we would expect adults with low self-evaluations of their learning ability to cluster in learning activities at the low end of the threat scale, whereas those with high self-confidence would feel free to utilize whatever learning options best meet their needs.

Although there is little research available to test hypotheses about the relationship of low academic self-confidence to participation in adult education, what evidence there is confirms the hypothesis. Those most likely to feel threatened in school learning situations (those who leave school early) are more likely to participate in low-threat than in high-threat learning activities (see Chapter Three). Almost everyone conducts self-directed learning projects, but credit learning is heavily biased toward those with higher levels of educational attainment—and presumably more academic self-confidence. We need more information about marker points in between. If our threat hypothesis is correct, it suggests that we might well give more attention to the role of televised courses in reaching people who would like to test their ability in the privacy of their own homes. We might, for example, present test questions, followed by answers, on the television screen, so that unregistered viewers can assess their understanding. (Usually, the only people offered the testing option are those registered for credit.) Those who have had unpleasant experiences in school and who have grown to adulthood thinking that they were "too dumb" to succeed in academic learning might receive a boost to their self-confidence and be willing to venture out of their living rooms into the higher-threat learning situations.

Most current efforts to reach the poorly educated are pitched at threat level 4 (competency-based education). The disadvantaged are usually encouraged to enroll in job training or basic skills courses, which actually have considerable threat present: public commitment to learn the competency (despite private fears that they may not be able to do it), evaluation, and the (probably accurate) perception that the evaluator has considerable power to influence the type of job they get or whether they get a job. The COR model does not imply that competency-based job training is necessarily inappropriate for those with low levels of self-confidence. For such training to be successful, however, other variables in the model depicted in Figure 4—such as transitions (D) and goals (C)—will have to generate sufficiently strong forces to overcome the negative forces generated by low self-confidence. Negative forces at A will require strong positive forces somewhere else in the COR model in order to add up to participation. In most job training programs, the positive force is high at point C. There is an expectation that participation will lead to employment. Job training programs are also usually designed to generate high positive forces at points E and F. Special efforts are made to open opportunities, to remove any barriers to participation, and to make certain that potential trainees receive information about the program. Not much attention is paid to A and B, and in those variables may lie much of the problem with dropout. The COR model suggests that we might reduce the notoriously high dropout from these programs if we lower the threat level for people with low self-confidence in their ability to learn. The level of threat in job training programs appears to lie primarily in the attitudes and techniques of the teaching personnel. If the attitude is one of collaborator expressing faith that the learner is capable of achieving the competency, and if teaching methods allow ample time to master learning tasks, the threat will be much less than if the attitude is one of evaluator and judge.

For other learning situations, there are numerous ways to build positive forces at point A in the anticipation of increasing the overall motivation at point G. Generally speaking, they involve feedback to the potential learner and the provision of positive learning experiences. Aptitude and interest tests, especially those that are self-administered and self-interpreted, may help to assure some people that they can compete easily in the classroom. Reentry women, who have been out of school for some time, may not suffer from low overall self-confidence, but they may have doubts about how much their school learning has deteriorated in years away from formal learning situations. Tests that provide objective data may reassure them and thus enhance positive forces at point A. It is also true, of course, that a low score on the test could confirm the fears of some low achievers with low self-esteem. In such instances, test scores might be accompanied by positive suggestions for an appropriate entry level—for example, a televised course, with tests on the material presented, or a noncredit class or other low-threat learning opportunities. The hypothesis of self-esteem underlying the amount of threat learners are willing and able to tolerate is a strong argument for support of the full range of learning options, emphasizing low threat options as good entry points for adults with low levels of self-esteem.

It is especially important that remedial programs, or any program designed primarily for adults who have experienced past failure in learning situations, be noncompetitive and nonthreatening. At the same time, the learning tasks should be clearly defined, and adequate feedback and instructions for improvement must be provided. Otherwise, the opportunity for new perceptions regarding learning ability is not present. The objective is to demonstrate to failure-threatened personalities that through their own efforts they can succeed. (For further discussion see Cross, 1971, 1976.)

These hypotheses about the role of self-confidence in adult learning contain some implications about competition among providers in the learning society. For example, they suggest that college degree programs are not in competition with agencies providing education at the low end of the threat scale. In fact, these agencies are more likely to bring new people into the educational system than to compete for people who might otherwise enter degree programs.[1]

Informal data verify the hypothesis that low-threat activities serve as entry points for some adult learners. We know that many adults who stick their toes in the water by taking a televised or noncredit course later enroll in on-campus courses, presumably as they become more comfortable with the situation and more confident about their ability to succeed. Among adults with low levels of self-confidence (undoubtedly over-represented among those with low levels of educational attainment), there may be a phenomenon of progressive entry into the more competitive forms of education. It is therefore important that nonthreatening learning situations be especially well publicized among those not currently participating in adult education.

Self-confidence, or any other single variable, is just one small piece of the chain of responses (COR) that go into one's decision to become an active adult learner. *Other things being equal,* however, adults with high self-evaluations are likely to participate in whatever form of education meets their needs, whereas those with low self-confidence are limited by a need to

[1]Nothing that is said here, incidentally, should be taken to suggest that most adults taking noncredit courses have low self-esteem. While fear-threatened people may prefer noncredit learning situations, it does not follow that people who want noncredit learning situations have low self-esteem or are fear threatened.

protect themselves from the threat of further failure—which too many have already experienced in the American school system.

In this analysis of the variable of self-confidence in the COR model, I have suggested a number of steps that could be implemented directly with no possible harm to anyone. But most of the suggestions are based on *assumptions,* not on confirmed research findings. There is a need for further research to test and revise the COR model. The following researchable questions are raised:

- Do adults with unsuccessful school learning experience (probably best defined by below-average grades in school) have low self-evaluations of their learning ability?
- What are the threat levels of various adult learning options? Are they ordered as hypothesized in the threat scale presented here?
- Do people with low self-confidence in their learning ability tend to engage primarily or exclusively in low-threat learning activities? (The appropriate hypothesis for those with high levels of self-confidence is that they should be unaffected by the threat level of various learning options.)
- Who are the unregistered viewers of televised courses? How often are they later attracted into other forms of education?
- Potential adult learners have expressed considerable interest in self-assessment (Hefferlin, Peterson, and Roelfs, 1975). What are the characteristics (especially level of educational attainment and self-evaluation of learning ability) of people who express such an interest? What do they want to know about themselves?
- Does successful participation in adult learning activities (point G) raise self-esteem (point A), improve attitudes toward education (point B), and therefore result in increased likelihood of future participation?

Building Positive Attitudes Toward Education

Attitudes toward education (point B of the COR model) are presumably influenced by two things: one's own experiences and the attitudes and opinions of other people. If positive forces for participation in adult learning are to be reinforced at point B, educators must try to (1) create more positive personal experiences for more people early in their learning careers and (2) tap the support of "significant others" for educational participation. It seems clear that educators need to prepare young people (through positive experiences in school) for their futures as lifelong learners and to develop low-threat learning experiences for adults with doubts about their ability to compete. Let us consider here how others influence the attitudes of potential learners toward education.

If family, friends, and co-workers think that participation in learning activities is a good thing for adults, the COR model predicts that the forces for participation at point B will be positive, resulting in a greater likelihood of participation at point G. A corollary assumption is that the more the potential learner values the opinion of those expressing positive attitudes toward education, the greater the influence for participation will be. In support of this hypothesis, Rubenson (1977) observes that Sweden has had considerably more success in recruiting adult learners from among blue-collar workers at the work site than at housing developments. His explanation is that co-workers serve as a stronger reference group (people whose opinions matter) than neighbors in the housing development do. A related finding was presented in Chapter Three, where it was shown that positive attitudes toward adult learning are more prevalent in California than in Iowa. It was suggested that this created a positive climate for adult learning in which the probability of a California adult running into positive support from friends and acquaintances was somewhat higher than for Iowans.

Positive attitudes toward education seem to be contagious; individuals catch the interest from others around them, and the closer the contagious person is to the potential learner, the greater the likelihood of his coming down with the bug for learning. At the same time, unfortunately, until exposure infiltrates geographically or culturally isolated groups of people, some immunity to adult learning may prevail. It is one more example of how the rich get richer while the poor get poorer. The greater the density of support for adult learning, the more people will demand educational opportunities, the more they will participate themselves, and the more they will encourage their friends to participate. Since we already know that participation leads to further participation, the cycle of support spirals in some communities and languishes in others. This suggests the need for governmental intervention in some areas, sufficient to introduce the bug for lifelong learning.

Since there is already a fairly adequate research base for the power of reference groups, variable B in the COR model can be discussed in terms of some practical applications of the knowledge. First, the most powerful recruiting device for any form of education is word of mouth. Building on this well-known fact, educators interested in recruiting new learners might sponsor an "each-one-bring-one" night, in which enrolled adult learners are invited to bring to class a guest not currently participating in adult education. (It goes without saying that the class itself would have to be a positive experience for the guests if this approach is to work.)

Second, a very effective way to recruit learners is through membership and reference groups: "It is not enough to try to inform and influence individual persons; . . . All experiments hitherto have served to underline the importance of outreach work operating through the medium of organizations to which the target persons belong" (Rubenson, 1977, pp. 27-28).

Third, it may be necessary to build more positive attitudes toward adult learning in certain membership groups. As mentioned, one reason why few members of the United Auto Workers use their educational benefits is perhaps that adult learning is not valued by their co-workers. Thus, there may be a need for more information about adult educational opportunities in workplaces. In addition, if some of the most influential leaders of the peer group can be given a sufficiently positive educational experience, their satisfaction may prove contagious.

Fourth, public relations programs may need to develop more effective methods for communicating a positive image of adult learning to underrepresented groups. This recommendation leads to point C in the COR model, which requires that the learning experience be perceived as worthwhile in attaining the goals of the adult learner, and to point F, which suggests that accurate information must be received by the appropriate groups.

Meeting Goals and Expectations of Learners

An example will illustrate the significance of goals and expectations (point C of the COR model) in implementation. If an activity-oriented learner whose goal is to make social contacts attends a class where the professor lectures the entire period to a group of people who then depart to go their separate ways, the probability for dropout is very high. The activity-oriented learner will realize immediately that participation in the class will not lead to expanded social opportunities. The potential for dropout will be equally high in a class where a great deal of social interaction seems to be going on but the potential learner is either too shy or too different from others in the class to participate effectively. The implication of point C in the COR model is that two conditions must be met: participation must be successful, and successful participation must accomplish the learner's goal.

The implications of point C in the COR model can be further illustrated by examples from the realm of self-directed learning. If a self-directed learner already has confidence that she can develop the knowledge or skill required for job promotion, but knows that some form of certificate is necessary for the promotion, motivation will depend on whether the competency can somehow be certified—either through participation in a credential-bearing class or through obtaining credit for self-directed learning. On the other side of the coin may be the self-directed learner who is not certain that she will be successful but knows that the desired reward would be forthcoming if she could develop the competency. In this case, the need is for a tutor or some other form of help in successfully learning the task.

The importance of designing learning experiences that meet the goals of adult learners seems clear. The problem is to determine what those goals are. On this point, greater diversity of research methods seems indicated. So far, most of the research on motivation has been done through surveys; with the possible exception of job-oriented motives, however, the goals mentioned are so broad (for example, for personal satisfaction or to expand knowledge) that they offer little insight as to how educators might design learning experiences to help people achieve such goals. More in-depth interviews, focusing on what people hope to get out of their learning, would be helpful. These might be extensions, elaborations, and updates on Houle's (1961) interview studies, described in *The Inquiring Mind.* They might also build on Tough's (1968, 1971) pioneering methodology with probing interviews. Hard data, such as those provided when respondents are asked to check options on a questionnaire, give us information about the diversity of motivations and about the relative popularity of each response for population subgroups. But there is a need now for greater depth of understanding through more insightful probing into people's expectations about various kinds of learning experiences. What, specifically, do people hope to gain—both immediately and in the future—from their participation? What problems do they think might be alleviated if they had knowledge or skills that they do not possess now? Such questions are variations on the theme of asking people about their motivations for learning. They are directed, however, at rather pragmatic questions about expected rewards.

Certain philosophical questions also might be illuminated through more insightful research. Is the desire to learn (specifically in organized groups) natural in human beings, or is it an acquired taste? If it is natural, then the documented differences in voluntary learning participation between poorly educated and well-educated adults must be attributed to earlier negative experiences or influences that stifled the natural inclination to learn. That position is taken by many educators, and it underlies much of our earlier discussion about the role of self-evaluation in motivating learning. The implications of the hypothesis are fairly clear. Learning should be a rewarding experience from a child's earliest years. Negative or punishing experiences should be avoided, and the best way to treat "lack of knowledge" is probably to regard it as a temporary state in the natural inclination for lifelong learning. Formative evaluations, suggesting diagnosis and prescription for further learning, would be preferable to summative evaluations, suggesting judgment and calling for a decision about what to do with a person with that level of knowledge—whether to admit or not, whether to graduate or not, whether to employ or not, whether to promote or not. Admittedly, those judgments must be made, but to hand out a prescription for what needs to be done to correct the lack of knowledge or skill is the more positive lifelong learning approach, whereas to merely pronounce the decision is more negative, suggesting that the level of knowledge or skill is static.

If learning is an acquired taste rather than—or perhaps in addition to—a natural human inclination, then insisting that people keep on trying, even if they are not enthusiastic at first, would be expected to result in a gradual appreciation for lifelong learning. There is ample research support for this position too. It is quite clear that the more formal education people have, the more they want. Evidence also surrounds us in our daily lives. The more people know about almost any subject— whether it be antique cars or Greek history—the greater their appreciation of good learning experiences. The implications for this assumption are also fairly clear. Requiring people to be exposed to quality learning experiences is justifiable, even if painful at first, on the grounds that they will eventually acquire the taste for lifelong learning—and not so incidentally the tools to satisfy such acquired tastes.

Whether one assumes that learning is natural and will occur unless stifled by bad experiences or that learning is an acquired taste, and bad experiences may be expected as temporary setbacks on the road to lifelong learning, there are some implications for the issues raised in Chapter Two. Do colleges have the right to aggressively recruit adults in order to expose them to the lifelong satisfaction of the type of learning offered by the college curriculum? Can society compel the undereducated to master the tools necessary to implement an acquired taste for lifelong learning—or will such compulsion simply result in greater resistance? Is mandated continuing education justified on the grounds that lifelong learning is a necessity in the professions and that prolonged exposure will eventually result in self-motivated professional learning?

As with most issues, the answers to these questions probably lie not in an either/or position but in achieving the best of both worlds. If adults who were "turned off" to education at an early age by negative experiences in school are required to participate in adult learning, they might see for themselves that learning can be a positive experience. However, the adult learning that people are compelled to participate in must in fact *be* a positive experience. It is hard to acquire a taste for a consistently distasteful experience, and until relearning occurs as a result of positive experiences, compulsion will only be followed by further resistance.

This analysis suggests that point C in the COR model is critical to the motivational force generated at point G, in that the greater the reward, the greater the force for participation. It also implies that intrinsic and extrinsic rewards are interactive. The greater the intrinsic reward for learning, the less the extrinsic reward will have to be in order to overcome the barriers at point E.

Responding to Life Transitions

The necessity to adapt to changing circumstances of life (point D of the COR model) constitutes a powerful motivating force for learning. Some changes are almost universal and represent the phases of the life cycle: first job, marriage, children, increasing responsibility on the job and in the community, retirement, and so forth. Other changes may be sudden and traumatic: loss of job, divorce, illness, death of spouse. Research on the life cycle and on life changes that "trigger" learning (see Chapter Seven) shows that at some periods in life the motivation for learning is exceptionally high. Havighurst (1972) has called these "teachable moments"; Aslanian and Brickell (1980) refer to "trigger events" as potent motivating forces, and adult learning programs today abound with programs for reentry women, new parents, midlife career changers, retirees, and so on.

The research has implications for subject matter as well as timing. It will be extremely difficult, for example, to teach new job skills to a person about to retire. The "teachable moment" for job skills has passed. This may say something about the probable success of mandatory continuing education for a professional about ready to retire but extremely out of date in his profession. What to do? Analysis using the COR model would show that the transition anticipated by the employee will generate negative forces at point D as far as job-relevant learning is concerned. Such forces will have to be offset by positive forces elsewhere. Unless some threat or reward can be devised to motivate the individual to learn (Loss of job? Admiration of fellow workers for new learning? Appeal to professional pride? Time off from work? Placement in a position of responsibility for tutoring younger workers?), mandating continuing education seems likely to fail.

Some programs—for example, those designed for reentry women—capitalize on teachable moments by gearing an entire program to a particular transition in the life cycle. Under such circumstances, the positive forces at point C-D are sufficiently strong to counter any negative forces elsewhere and carry the individual over barriers that might stop an individual with less motivation and expectation of attaining the desired reward.

Although educators cannot do much about influencing transitions directly, they can be prepared to respond to the direction of the motivational forces so generated. This takes us to point E, the creation of opportunities and the removal of barriers.

Creating Opportunities and Removing Barriers

A study done in 1972 by the Center for Research and Development in Higher Education at the University of California, Berkeley (Ruyle and Geiselman, 1974), and discussed in Chapter Three, documented the fact that colleges and universities are responding rapidly in opening new opportunities to adult learners and in removing existing barriers. Research updating that study is needed now, but it would probably show the continuing trend of colleges, as well as new semieducational agencies of society, to develop programs attractive to adult learners. The pace of change may be slowing somewhat because of the current economic situation and the fear of legislators that public support for adult education could unleash a demand that, in their opinion, a budget-conscious economy can ill afford. The probability is extremely strong, however, that adult learning programs that can be supported by nonpublic funds (primarily individual or industry) will be opening new opportunities at a rapid rate. This heightens the concern about the growing gap between the well educated and the poorly educated, and the implications for public policy are considerable and urgent. Almost every public document—state, national, or international—expresses a commitment to serve undereducated adults. If those public commitments are to be met, far more attention needs to be given to points A through D in the COR model. Nothing will happen if we open new opportunities and remove barriers for people whose motivational force to participate is low or negative at point E.

We have already given a great deal of attention in Chapter Four to the identification of barriers that potential learners say deter them. We will not repeat the details here. Educators can do little about the large numbers of people who say that they are too busy to participate—which is the single most common barrier cited by people who say that they are interested in further learning. Although we have suggested that the barriers people identify on surveys should be viewed with healthy skepticism, it may be helpful here to present a summary of the major barriers to participation (as discussed in Cross and Zusman, 1979) in descending order of mention: (1) lack of time; (2) costs; (3) scheduling problems; (4) assorted institutional requirements/red tape; (5) lack of information about appropriate opportunities; (6) problems with child care or transportation; (7) lack of confidence; (8) lack of interest.

The major barriers of lack of time and, to a lesser extent, costs are actually complex barriers in which the message is that participation in educational activities is not as high in priority as other things that adults might wish to do or to spend their money on at this stage in their lives. The COR model suggests two courses of action for educators wishing to recruit adult learners: raise the priority for educational participation and/or lower the barriers. The best approach will probably lie in a judicious combination of the two. Programs that are highly relevant and attractive to adult learners will suffer less from perceived barriers than programs that are not so appealing. The most attractive program in the world, however, will not attract working people if it is scheduled at 2 o'clock in the afternoon.

The best advice anyone can give on the removal of barriers is to look at all the characteristics of a given program carefully and to identify which groups of people are logically deterred by the provisions and requirements of the program. The analysis of remaining barriers in the Open University program, given in Chapter Four, is a good example of a workable model for identifying barriers. The implications for educators in the identification and removal of barriers seem so obvious that there is little more that can be added here. Any educator lacking ideas might benefit from rereading Chapter Four with a view to taking action on the barriers identified through research.

Opening up new opportunities for adult learners has been just as important to adult participation as removing barriers, especially over the past ten years. Numerous new programs have been established that are geared to the special needs and interests of mature learners. Open University in England, Empire State College in New York, and Metropolitan University in Minnesota are some of the better-known programmatic approaches, but more convenient schedules and locations, more efficient delivery systems, more appropriate content and teaching methods also represent a vast network of new opportunities. Perhaps the most important lesson to be learned from the success of these new opportunities is that many of the most innovative and successful of them were not established in direct response to consumer demand. The potential sponsors of new learning opportunities for adults will not find a good program design by putting together the elements that people say they want in response to a questionnaire. The assumption of market surveys and needs assessments is that consumers know what they want.

A more accurate assumption would be that consumers know what they want when they see it.

The point can be made clear through the use of an analogy. Suppose that years ago, when daily ice delivery was the primary answer to the preservation of food, General Electric had set out to respond to consumer demand by conducting a survey of what people said they wanted in the way of improved services. The majority of respondents, no doubt, would have favored cheaper ice and more frequent delivery. There would have been no demand for electric refrigerators. Even if General Electric had suggested that a plug into an electric wall socket would deliver reliable and inexpensive refrigeration, there would have been no way to explain that option to survey respondents. A few examples will make clear the problems in the too-literal interpretation of survey data and will help to emphasize the central thesis of this book; namely, that planning for the learning society requires a comprehensive understanding of adults as learners. Successful implementation of research requires far more than the application of market research.

One of the most successful programs for adults to be launched in the last decade is Elderhostel, which began with five colleges in New Hampshire in 1975 and grew rapidly to a network of more than three hundred colleges and universities in fifty states. Elderhostel offers one-week summer residential programs for people 60 years of age and older. These elders travel to campuses throughout the United States, live in college residence halls, and participate in classes taught by college professors.

The consistent finding from market surveys is that the elderly express less interest in education than almost any other identifiable group; they consider themselves "too old" to learn; they regard travel and expense as major barriers to their participation; and they do not particularly care for academic lectures given by college professors. What folly, then, to launch a program calling for extensive travel and for classroom lectures on academic subjects delivered by college professors to the least likely market identified in the needs assessments. Had the founders of Elderhostel been building a program from the elements of survey data, they never would have started the program. The lessons are that Elderhostel is more than the sum of its parts and that an insightful understanding of the needs of the elderly—informed by research—is more useful than a too-rigid interpretation of individual survey items.

• Coast Community College in California has enrolled 50,000 students in a telecourse in introductory psychology since the course was first offered in 1975 (Purdy, 1980). Although the use of new media rarely attracts more than 1 or 2 percent of the survey respondents (Carp, Peterson, and Roelfs, 1974; Cross and Zusman, 1979), people who have experienced education via television evidently find it a very acceptable method. Four out of five enrollees in telecourses in California would like to study again by that method (California Postsecondary Education Commission, 1979). The lesson in this experience is that if an educator removes barriers or opens new opportunities, people's positive experience with it will lead to acceptance—and perhaps even demand for expanded opportunities.

• Hundreds of colleges have started highly successful weekend colleges—yet surveys are unanimous in showing that very few adults (usually fewer than 5 percent) are willing to devote weekends to classes (Cross and Zusman, 1979).

There are explanations behind these apparent miscues (see Cross, 1979c), but the point is that only a dying and unimaginative industry would attempt to base its future on consumer demand. Consumers cannot respond beyond their experience; thus, responding to consumer demand usually means getting yesterday's answers to tomorrow's questions. Positive forces will be generated at point E in the COR model to the extent that imaginative educators can formulate new programs, perhaps undreamed of by potential learners, that strike people as a better way to do things.

Providing Accurate Information

Information (point F of the COR model) represents the critical link in bringing potential learners and providers together. It will not matter how motivated the learner is (points

A-D), or how great the opportunities are (point E), if accurate, up-to-date information is not received by potential learners. Notice that the operative word is not the *dissemination* of information but the *receipt* of information by potential learners.

Virtually everything that has been said up to this point about variables in the COR model has some bearing on the receipt of information. Potential learners with low self-confidence (A) and unfavorable attitudes toward education (B) will not perceive information about new opportunities as relevant to their lives and therefore will not "see" or "hear" the message. Providers interested in reaching an audience "turned off" by previous unpleasant experiences will have to either address the negative image problems at point A-B directly or compensate for those negative forces by generating highly positive forces at point C-D. Information designed to reduce negative forces at A-B would have to convince the individual that he or she is different now (able to learn successfully) or that education is. Disseminators of information to potential learners with positive forces at point A-B (favorable evaluations of themselves and education) will have an easier task. They need to emphasize the appropriateness of the education to the goals of the learners (C-D).

We have already discussed ways to increase positive forces at various points in the COR model. Because the use of supportive reference groups is likely to generate positive forces at point B, posters and information programs at the work site might be expected to have more impact than posters on the bus or in a housing development. Information presented to membership groups of the elderly or women's clubs or church groups might be expected to generate more response than posters at the supermarket or announcements in the newspaper. Announcements about education aimed at job promotion and relicensure are appropriate reinforcers of motivation at point C and might be most appropriate in trade and professional journals. If point E is thought to be the "sticking" point for well-motivated potential learners, then information should stress the removal of barriers and the creation of new opportunities. The stronger the positive forces are for a given group going into point E-F, the easier the job of the disseminator. Highly motivated people will go to considerable effort to ferret out information; unmotivated adults will not "see" information placed before their eyes everyday.

The point is that the *receipt* of information is embedded in the chain of responses that lead to participation at point G. The successful disseminator of information will estimate motivational forces all along the route of the COR model and will design the message—as well as the program—to address the problems of the desired target groups.

Conclusion

The implications of the COR model extend far beyond the illustrations of applications offered here. After all, the reason for devising some kind of conceptual framework for understanding the motivations of volunteer adult learners is that it permits us to go beyond the simple enumeration of research findings for suggestions for implementation. It permits educators to analyze their own hypotheses in the context of an explanatory model. Research has played a critical role in designing the COR model, and it will be even more important in testing and revising the model. Without the model—or a model—there is no way to add up numerous disparate research findings to contribute to our basic understanding, no way to suggest research priorities, and no way to interpret findings in the context of an action program. There is no assumption that the COR model is *the* model that should be used nor even the best model that can be devised given the present state of knowledge. It is consistent with what we know to date through research and experience, and I have tried to demonstrate its utility through exploring some of the implications that arise from it.

CHAPTER 7

Patterns of Adult Learning and Development

The question of *how* learning takes place can be approached in at least four ways. Two of those ways are discussed in this chapter; the other two, in Chapter Eight.

The first interpretation, learning as process, can be approached through the vast and constantly expanding literature of learning psychology. Typically, such literature emphasizes the measurement of mental ability, research on perception and sensation, memory and forgetting, cognitive function, and the like. Such subjects, of course, can apply to any age of the life span. Unfortunately, perhaps, psychologists interested in adult learning have been preoccupied with the fairly narrow question of changes in performance on intelligence tests as people age. There is, however, also some work on the physiological aging of

152

cells affecting the sensory functions of vision, hearing, and reaction time. And some psychologists have studied changes in personality as a function of aging.

A second source of information about how adults learn comes from the recent flood of research on adult development, a broad and ill-defined category that includes research on life cycles or life stages (Chickering and Havighurst, 1981; Gould, 1972, 1975; Levinson and others, 1974; McCoy, 1977; Sheehy, 1976; Weathersby, 1981), ego and personality development (Erikson, 1959; Loevinger, 1976), moral development (Gilligan, 1981; Kohlberg and Turiel, 1971; Rest, 1974), and cognitive or intellectual development (Perry, 1970, 1981). From this research, based largely in the theories of developmental psychology, we can ask questions about *what* adults are ready to learn at various times in their lives and *how* they can be helped to accomplish various developmental tasks. At this writing, materials are so extensive and so easily available in a wide range of treatments—ranging from workbooks for practitioners to theoretical treatises for scholars—that the discussion here can be quite limited and will be more in the nature of an introduction with examples rather than a comprehensive synthesis of current knowledge. (In addition to the sources referenced above, readers interested in pursuing research on adult development and life cycles will find an excellent up-to-date overview in Chickering and Associates, 1981.)

Learning Processes

There are many good reviews, overviews, and summaries of what is known about the learning process, beginning as early as 1885 with Ebbinghaus and his studies on memory, proceeding through the works of such famous names as William James, John Dewey, Edward Thorndike, Thomas Watson, and Kurt Lewin to modern theorists and researchers as diverse as B. F. Skinner, Robert Gagne, Jerome Bruner, and Jean Piaget. All these scholars have stimulated substantial research, and all have something to say that is relevant to adult learning. Most of these psychologists, however, have concentrated on early childhood learning, and it would serve no purpose here to present even the briefest of summaries about the current state of knowledge regarding the learning process. The interested reader can gain entry to this enormous, and still growing, body of literature by perusing recent issues of the *Annual Review of Psychology,* which presents excellent and scholarly reviews of the literature in specified fields of psychology each year. The general topic "learning and memory," for example, has been reviewed in one or more chapters of the *Annual Review* each year, and each review typically cites between one hundred and two hundred current references. For the reader who wants a more limited, but still comprehensive, list of references to learning psychology applied to the adult years, Birren and Schaie (1977), Kidd (1973), Horn (1970), and Schaie and Parr (1981) would be good places to start. In this synthesis, I shall limit discussion to what is known through research about learning ability as a function of aging.

Learning as a Function of Aging: Physical Changes

It was once thought that learning is for young people and that "you can't teach an old dog new tricks." The evidence shows, however, that aging need not be considered a major handicap in learning until quite late in life. Moreover, as research accumulates, the age at which consideration needs to be given to physiological aging seems to be moving steadily upward. It is now generally agreed that, if there is an age limit on learning performance, it is not likely to occur until around 75, when deterioration of bodily functions begins to set in (Kidd, 1973). That does not mean that aging cells in the body have no effect until age 75 but, rather, that compensations for their gradual decline can generally be easily handled via eyeglasses, hearing aids, increased illumination, increased time for learning, and so on. Although aging encompasses a wide spectrum of physical changes, reaction time, vision, and hearing are the three that are most likely to interfere with learning. A brief synopsis of current knowledge about the probable effect of these factors on learning follows.

Reaction Time. There is no question that as people grow

older, they slow down. There is more question about what effect this has or should have on learning. Typically, learning ability has been measured under time limits, and the individual who produces the largest number of correct answers in the specified time is assumed to be the most intelligent or to have the greatest capacity for learning. There is not much evidence that speed of learning—at least within fairly normal ranges—is very important in adult learning. As a matter of fact, there is growing evidence that it is overemphasized in most schools to the detriment of learners of all ages (see Bloom, 1971; Cross, 1979b).

Speed of learning involves reaction time to perceive the stimulus, transmission time to transmit the message to the brain, and response time to carry out the action. On the average, older learners perceive more slowly, think more slowly, and act more slowly than younger people. Current knowledge suggests that aging has somewhat more impact on time needed to perceive the stimulus than on time needed to react, but reaction time is related to the complexity of the task and to individual differences (Knox, 1977). Quickness or slowness seems to be a habit that becomes a general personality characteristic. Whereas in younger people speed of performance varies with the nature of the task and the individual's familiarity with it, older people tend to adopt a characteristic pace that is consistent across a wide variety of activities (Kidd, 1973).

In general, it can be concluded that the time required for learning new things increases with age. There are, however, substantial individual differences, and speed of response by itself should not prevent anyone from learning almost anything he wants to learn. "When they can control the pace," Knox (1977, p. 422) concludes, "most adults in their 40s and 50s have about the same ability to learn as they had in their 20s and 30s."

Vision. Changes in the eye are well researched and well documented. As eyes age, there is a loss of elasticity and transparency, pupils become smaller and react more feebly, and there is an increasing incidence of cataracts and defective color vision. For the general population, vision is at its best at about age 18; it then declines gradually until around age 40, at which

time there is a sharp decline for the next fifteen years. After age
55 vision continues to deteriorate, but at a slower rate than between the ages of 40 and 55. One study showed normal vision
for 77 percent of those under the age of 20, 50 percent of those
between the ages of 40 and 44, 25 percent of those between 50
and 54, and only 6 percent of those 60 and older (Kidd, 1973).
While almost everyone recognizes the need for bifocals as a sign
of aging, not everyone is aware of the need for increased illumination as people age. After age 50, the amount of illumination
becomes a critical factor. A 50 year old is likely to need 50 percent more illumination than a 20 year old.

The aging of the eyes serves as a good example of how
the effects of aging need not interfere greatly with the capacity
for learning. Clearly, there are physical changes that, if ignored,
have a detrimental effect on learning, at least through the
medium of reading. In the absence of disease or serious impairment, however, the normal physical changes of the eyes can be
accommodated easily through the use of eyeglasses and increased illumination.

Hearing. Hearing, like vision, is well researched and
charted through the life cycle. Hearing loss is the result of
changes in the sensory, mechanical, and neural processes involved in the transmission of sound. The combined effect of
these changes results in a gradual but consistent decline in hearing until about age 65 or 70, when the rate of hearing impairment increases sharply. Hearing impairment sufficient to interfere with normal conversation increases from about 5 percent in
children under 15 to about 65 percent in adults 65 or older
(Kidd, 1973).

Aging brings problems with pitch, volume, and rate of response. Not only do older people take longer to perceive the
original stimulus, especially if it is delivered in high frequencies
(10,000 cycles per second) or low frequencies (125 cycles per
second), but they also take longer to translate the meaning of
sound and to act on it. Rapid speech, for example, can result in
loss of intelligibility of up to 45 percent for older people
(Calearo and Lazzaroni, 1957). Women seem to lose acuity for
lower pitch, while men lose acuity for high pitch, making older

women able to communicate more readily with women while older men can hear men's voices better.

Of all the physical impairments accompanying aging, loss of hearing is likely to be among the most difficult, because it isolates the individual and is not usually visible to others. Thus, the psychological damage may be more serious than the actual physical impairment. People with hearing loss often withdraw into themselves, suffering a loss of confidence and a general reluctance to venture into new activities or new associations. Since learning involves not only auditory signals but also self-confidence and willingness to confront new experiences, hearing loss may be among the most serious of the handicaps faced by older learners. But, like changes in vision, changes in hearing as a function of aging can usually be treated and should not have much impact on learning capabilities until age 65 or older.

Intellectual Functioning and Aging

There is a continual tug-of-war between the "bearish" versus the "bullish" stance toward changes in adult intelligence with age (Horn, 1970). Those bullish on adults as learners contend that, insofar as intelligence is a product of learning, it should increase from infancy to old age. If tests do not show this, the argument goes, something is wrong with the tests, since abilities that represent true intelligence should improve with learning and experience. The bearish use a more biological approach, comparing intelligence to growth in stature. Intelligence, they say, should grow up to the late teens or early 20s and then remain stable until late years, when it would decline. These two positions are reflections of the age-old nature/nurture controversy, which has dominated the literature on intelligence ever since psychologists started defining it. Most investigators, however, probably agree that practical intelligence—that is, the ability to learn—is affected by both inheritance and the accumulation of experience and knowledge. Which plays the more important role at any given time probably depends on the nature of the learning task, the physical condition of the learner, and the conditions of the learning.

For better or worse—mostly worse for adult learners—

scores on intelligence tests have long been used as measures of learning capacity. In the early days of intelligence testing, investigators showed little interest in measuring adult intelligence because they thought that the IQ score measured "innate" ability, which reached maximum development at age 16 and then remained fairly constant thereafter. The first extensive study of learning ability as a function of age was published by E. L. Thorndike and his associates in 1928. Although, in Thorndike's view, the most advantageous period for learning occurred between 20 and 25 years of age, he also concluded that "In general, teachers of adults of age 25 to 45 should expect them to learn at nearly the same rate and in nearly the same manner as they would have learned the same thing at 15 to 20" (pp. 177-178). Other psychologists, using research methods similar to Thorndike's, reached similar conclusions, although they found that decline begins at a later age and that the rate of decline is not as sharp as in Thorndike's curve (Jones and Conrad, 1933; Miles and Miles, 1932; Weschler, 1955). Most cross-sectional research using omnibus measures of intelligence shows a peak in overall performance somewhere between the late teens and early 30s, followed by a gradual decline up to the early 60s, with a more rapid drop thereafter.

There are, however, methodological problems with both the conventional omnibus measures of intelligence and with the cross-sectional designs. Irving Lorge, in a series of articles in the 1940s, criticized the research on the grounds that conventional speeded intelligence tests bias the results against adults. He then demonstrated that power tests (those deemphasizing speed) do not show the same decline as speeded tests. Ghiselli (1957) supported the findings of Lorge. That is, he found no consistent trends, either up or down, when he permitted superior adults, ranging in age from 20 to 65, to work as long as necessary to complete the tests. Today's research suggests that eliminating speed requirements reduces age discrepancies but does not eliminate them completely (Botwinick, 1977).

A generalized slowing down is one of the best-documented accompaniments of aging, but adult educators need to raise two fundamental questions about the research showing some decline in "intelligence" (measured on speeded tests) with age: (1) How important to adult learning are the abilities measured by speeded intelligence tests? (2) At what age does slowing down of cognitive function have any practical effect on learning ability? The first question is coming under increased fire (see, for example, Schaie, 1978) on the grounds that adults are rarely if ever asked in real life to perform the types of intellectual tasks that appear on intelligence tests. It was one thing to use IQ tests in the 1930s, when scientists thought they were measuring "innate" ability; it is quite another to persist in their use now that we know that such tests measure schooling, acculturation, speed, practice, and a host of other "impurities" in genetic endowment. Certainly, one has to be sympathetic to the call for more relevant measures of adult learning abilities (Schaie and Willis, 1979). The second question has been answered reasonably well through research. Even if one grants that learning something quickly is better than learning it slowly, the rate of decline is gradual and makes little practical difference until ages 60 to 75 (depending on which research study is cited). One study, using Thurstone's tests of Primary Mental Abilities (PMA), showed no appreciable age decline from 20 to 50 years of age; not until age 60 were scores more than one standard deviation lower than peak performance at age 31 to 35 (Schaie, 1958).

In addition to the controversies over the appropriateness of conventional intelligence tests as measures of adult learning capacity, questions arise about the differences in results from cross-sectional versus longitudinal studies. Longitudinal studies almost always show less decline than cross-sectional research designs. Owens (1953, 1966), in follow-up studies of adults first tested at roughly age 20, found significant *gains* for the group when they were retested thirty years later and nonsignificant losses when tested again eleven years after that, at roughly age 61. His findings are confirmed in other longitudinal studies (Kangas and Bradway, 1971; Nisbet, 1957). Although longitudinal studies have methodological problems too (which we shall discuss later), they generally conclude that there is actually a rise in intelligence to the mid 40s (which is especially obvious in the verbal skills of superior adults); a high plateau into the mid 50s; and increasingly large decrements for successively older age cohorts after that (Botwinick, 1977).

There are a number of explanations for the differences between cross-sectional and longitudinal data. Ironically, the greater incidence of illness among older age groups tends to exaggerate the decline in test scores in cross-sectional data, whereas in longitudinal designs it covers up changes. The typical cross-sectional study, for example, might compare the performance of five hundred people 30 years of age with five hundred people 70 years of age and find a large drop in mean score simply because the 70-year-old group contained more people who were not in good health. In longitudinal studies there is the problem of selective dropout, with lower-ability adults tending to die off earlier or to be unavailable for retesting some years later. Schaie (1958), for example, tested five hundred subjects in 1956; he then found 302 of them for retesting in 1963 and only 161 for retesting in 1970—a loss of 65 percent of the sample in fourteen years. The problem is that the 161 adults tested in 1970 were not a representative sample of the 1956 group. Those with superior test scores in 1956 were overrepresented among the survivors.

Another problem in the interpretation of research data lies in the fact that age cohorts from different generations have had quite different experiences. This factor is especially troublesome in cross-sectional designs. The level of educational attainment in the United States, for example, has been rising rapidly over the past half century. This means that a representative group of 50 year olds have fewer years of formal schooling than a representative group of 20 year olds. Since tests of intelligence are demonstrably affected by amount of formal schooling, the sample with the least schooling (50 year olds) would be expected to make lower test scores—which is just what cross-sectional studies show. The fallacy results from treating cross-sectional data as though they were longitudinal, reasoning erroneously that the difference between a sample of 20 year olds and a sample of 50 year olds is the same thing as aging thirty years. It is as though one concluded that as people grow older they are more likely to speak Italian because cross sectional samples show that more 50 year olds than 20 year olds speak Italian. While cross-sectional studies of learning are quite likely to make the error of measuring differences between generations rather than changes in individuals over time, longitudinal studies tell us how survivors have changed, but they do not tell us what an individual may expect as he or she grows older.

Perhaps we have learned as much as we can learn about the impact of aging on performance on intelligence tests. The discrepancies between cross-sectional and longitudinal studies are more or less resolved, with the conclusion that normal, healthy adults can expect to be efficient and effective lifelong learners well into old age. Researchers are now moving away from plotting omnibus intelligence test scores against chronological age toward looking at different kinds of cognitive functions.

Cattell (1963) makes a distinction between fluid and crystallized intelligence, contending that the two types of intelligence show different patterns in aging—patterns that are complementary in terms of adaptation. As fluid intelligence declines with age, crystallized intelligence increases. Fluid intelligence has more of the characteristics that used to be equated with the old "innate" biologically determined concept of the IQ, whereas crystallized intelligence is influenced more heavily by education and experience. In the nature/nurture controversy, fluid intelligence would weigh in on the side of nature, whereas crystallized intelligence would be more subject to nurture. In Cattell's factor analytic research, fluid intelligence derives its loadings from tests that measure such abilities as memory span, spatial perception, and adaptation to new or novel situations. Culture-fair tests and speeded tests also show high loadings on the factor of fluid intelligence. Crystallized intelligence, in contrast, is more likely to have factor loadings from nonspeeded tests calling for judgment, knowledge, and experience—tests such as vocabulary, general information, and arithmetic reasoning.

Research generally confirms the notion that crystallized

intelligence increases or remains stable up to about age 60. Beyond that age, it seems to depend a great deal on what the person is doing. Those actively involved in intellectual pursuits maintain and even increase the abilities that are most clearly related to acculturation (Horn, 1970). Research on fluid intelligence shows a different trend. A study conducted by Horn and Cattell and described by Horn (1970) shows an X-shaped plot of intelligence as a function of age, with crystallized intelligence rising from age 14 to 61 and fluid intelligence starting high at age 14 and declining to age 61. If general intelligence is comprised of both fluid and crystallized intelligence, the resultant is rather stable, showing neither rise nor decline with advancing age—although one would expect to find differences in the types of tasks that are performed well at various ages.

Part of the appeal of the findings on fluid and crystallized intelligence lies in their commonsense credibility. Throughout history, societies have revered the wisdom and judgment of the aged and called on younger people for quickness in learning new skills. Today's research confirms the ancient wisdom. On the average, people seem to perform best in their youth on tasks requiring quick insight, short-term memorization, and complex interactions. As people get older, they accumulate knowledge and develop perspective and experience in the use and application of it.

In the literature of adult education, it is common to speak of older people's "compensating" for the loss of quickness in learning by substituting experience and wisdom, but Schaie and Parr (1981) advance the thesis that different stages of life actually call for different learning abilities. Youth is the time for acquisition, young adulthood the time for achievement, middle age the time for responsibility, and old age the time for reintegration. These phases of the life cycle call for different kinds of learning abilities. Most school learning, with its emphasis on acquisition rather than application or responsibility, is designed to capitalize on the learning strengths of young people. Both the methods and the content of traditional schooling are disadvantageous to older learners, who would, according to the research, perform better on tasks calling for crystallized intelligence. The educational model that would capitalize on the learning strengths of adults would deemphasize the processing and acquisition of large amounts of new information, emphasizing instead the development of cognitive functions calling for integration, interpretation, and application of knowledge. Speed and quickness in learning would also give way to emphasis on responsibility and accuracy.

Another facet of cognitive function concerns a specific mental ability that has been given considerable attention—maybe too much attention—in education. Memory, as a cognitive function, is included in the prior discussion regarding crystallized and fluid intelligence, but memory per se has been the focus of a great deal of research on learning. Both memory span and associative memory are measures of fluid intelligence and are thought to deteriorate with age, but there seems to be general agreement among researchers now that the deterioration is minor, up to old age, if the material is learned well initially and if the amount of new information to be stored is not too large or complex to scan efficiently for recall. There are few problems in aging with what has been called long-term memory. Oldsters can recall, sometimes in great detail, things that happened decades ago. The problems observed in short-term memory lead researchers to question whether the problem is not largely related to the strength of original registration and its subsequent organization. When acquisition is equated for younger and older learners, age differences in recognition memory disappear (Craik, 1977). Moreover, when material is learned well and new information is related to previously learned material, memory remains rather stable during most of adulthood (Moenster, 1972).

The greatest problems with memory for older people occur with meaningless learning, complex learning, and the learning of new things that require reassessment of old learning. Meaningless material is poorly retained, it is thought, because older learners have no reason or motivation to learn it and no way to organize it and connect it to previously stored material. Children may learn nonsense syllables to prove to themselves that they can or to please the experimenter, but older learners are less likely to be motivated by such considerations. Hence, lack of motivation may contribute in part to lowered scores on short-term memory tests. Research also suggests that complex learning and distraction during learning are especially difficult for older people because they have accumulated large stores of information and scanning the stored information for recall takes longer, especially if the new information is inadequately associated with stored information. Older people probably need to be helped in making associations, since evidence to date suggests that people, as they age, become less effective in generating their own associations between stored and incoming material (Arenberg and Robertson-Tchabo, 1977). However, adults with high verbal ability show less deterioration of short-term memory than those of low ability, probably because low-ability adults are less able to organize information during acquisition into meaningful clusters which facilitate retrieval. Overall, older learners seem to have the most difficulty with both initial learning and subsequent recall when learning tasks are fast paced, complex, or unusual. But it is important to remember that the learning performance of some 70 year olds is equal to and sometimes superior to that of some 30 year olds.

A number of steps can be taken to minimize impairment of short-term memory on the part of older learners. Interestingly, all the suggestions apply equally well to good education for young people. First, the presentation of new information should be meaningful, and it should include aids to help the learner organize it and relate it to previously stored information. Second, it should be presented at a pace that permits mastery in order to strengthen the original registration. Third, presentation of one idea at a time and minimization of competing intellectual demands should aid original comprehension. Finally, frequent summarization should facilitate retention and recall.

Personality and Aging

All the research problems previously discussed in the section on intelligence as a function of aging appear in the research on personality: resolving the differences in the findings of cross-sectional versus longitudinal designs, finding appropriate measures of "personality," and establishing relationships between behavior in experimental conditions and behavior in life. Small wonder that Neugarten (1977, p. 644) concludes that knowledge about personality and aging is in a "state of disarray" marked by "methodological flaws and conceptual impoverishment." Until someone comes along with a conceptual scheme that pulls together all the bits and pieces of research findings, we seem destined to cite the results of thousands of separate studies, finding threads of consistency where we can.

Perhaps the major conclusion that can be drawn from all the research on personality change is that people show remarkable consistency throughout life. One study, attempting to separate age changes from cohort changes, concluded that differences in personality are more a function of a changing world than of aging people (Woodruff and Birren, 1972)—meaning that 50 year olds differ from 20 year olds more because they have experienced social and industrial revolutions than because they have lived thirty years longer. After following two different groups longitudinally from age 12 to 40 and 50, Haan and Day (1974, p. 17) concluded that "the main thrust of development from early adolescence to later adulthood is the maintenance of personal continuity." Of special interest to us in this chapter is their finding that among the most stable of all characteristics is "style of cognitive engagement," a term used to encompass verbal fluency, unconventional thought, wide-ranging interests, aesthetic reaction, pride in objectivity, and intellectual level. Thus, we can assume that, in general, individuals who engaged themselves in cognitive activities with enthusiasm in junior high school will continue to stand out from the norm when they become middle-aged adults. Activity level in general —whether physical or intellectual—is a characteristic that shows considerable stability. To be sure, there is a general slowing down as people grow older, but people who are active and energetic as adolescents generally remain among the most active in their age group when they reach middle and old age.

While, for the most part, individuals maintain personal consistency, some age trends can be identified. The common stereotype of the adult moving from adolescence to old age is one of generally rising self-confidence, autonomy, and sense of self up to old age, at which time social role changes and physical changes begin to cast a shadow of doubt on self-esteem and sense of well-being. Then the characteristics most frequently associated with old age are a slowing down of responsiveness and a general withdrawal from engagement with the environment. Given the caution that people differ enormously—more and more as they grow older—the stereotype of the aging personality is not too far wrong.

Many studies have shown the growth of the positive self-concept and rise in self-esteem as people approach the "prime of life" in the 40s and 50s (Kuhlen, 1968; Neugarten, 1968). After the peak of expansiveness and "investment in life," the typical older person turns to more internal satisfactions. Neugarten (1968, p. 140) describes the changes in self-perception as adults move from age 40 to old age:

> Forty year olds, for example, seem to see the environment as one that rewards boldness and risk taking and to see themselves as possessing energy congruent with the opportunities perceived in the outer world. Sixty year olds, however, perceive the world as complex and dangerous, no longer to be reformed in line with one's wishes, and the individual as conforming and accommodating to outer-world demands.
>
> With increasing old age, ego functions are turned inward, as it were. With the change from active to passive modes of mastering the environment, there is also a movement of energy away from an outer-world to an inner-world orientation.

Against this background of changing self-perceptions, which may have a generalized effect on how adults approach the learning task, there are some specific changes that have a direct impact on learning performance. On almost any task in which speededness is a factor, older adults generally compensate for their loss of quickness by increased attention to accuracy. But the increased cautiousness that comes with age is thought to be more than compensation for lack of speed. Older people show more task orientation than younger, with a desire to "do the job right" and a reluctance to suffer a blow to self-esteem by being proved "wrong." The lowering of risk-taking behavior, which has been shown to accompany aging, has both desirable and undesirable effects. On the one hand, efficiency in work and learning may improve, because older people have an expanded repertoire and can select from the environment those things relevant to the task. Furthermore, an experienced adult can operate with greater skill and deliberation than a younger person, who may need to try out several approaches before finding one that works. Welford (1951) calls this more deliberative, experienced approach "efficient" behavior in the sense that it avoids the energy waste of trial and error. On the other hand, the superior experience and knowledge of adults may make them more reluctant to take risks and explore new approaches—older people seem to rely on strategies that have worked for them in the past, even when they are not effective in the current situation. Moreover, there is some tendency for older adults to misinterpret feedback on errors as though they confirmed their responses (Knox, 1977). Where evidences of rigidity have been demonstrated, however, it is usually limited to adults approaching old age—70 and older.

For teachers of adults, the following conclusions regarding personality change are significant. First, for most of the adult years consistency in personality is more probable than change, and individual differences become more pronounced as people accumulate different life experiences. Second, there is a general trend toward accuracy and dependence on previously learned solutions in the place of higher-risk behavior and trial-and-error solutions associated with more youthful learners. Third, whatever personality changes exist as a function of aging should have mostly positive effects on learning up until old age. Young and middle-aged adults are high in self-confidence and goal directedness. They are likely to know what they want and to be task oriented in their pursuit of learning. Finally, those working with elderly learners may need to take account of the increasing passivity and interiority of elderly learners and to make special efforts to encourage flexibility and to provide non-threatening environments.

Developmental Research

There has been an explosion of research and writing over the past decade on what has been broadly termed "adult development." There are, however, two rather different streams of study, and it will be helpful to clarify the differences in the very beginning. One, which we shall call research on the life cycle or phases of life, is interested in the responses people make to age and changing social expectations as they advance through the phases of adulthood. This line of inquiry has been likened to the seasons of life, each with its own distinctive character—the springtime of youth, the harvest of midlife, the winter of advanced age. Strictly speaking, this is not a developmental process if one regards development as a continuous flow toward growth and maturity. Rather, it represents qualitatively different phases through which people pass from birth to death. Some researchers relate the phases to age; for example, adults between the ages of 45 and 55 are in the "settling-down" phase of life. Others stress the importance of social expectations—those in positions of leadership and authority on the job, at home, and in the community are in a settling-down phase of the life cycle. Illustrative names associated with life-phase or life-cycle research are Levinson (1978; Levinson and others, 1974), Sheehy (1976), Neugarten (1968), Lowenthal (Lowenthal and others, 1975), and Weathersby (1978).

The other branch of study falling under the general rubric of adult development is represented by names such as Erikson (1950), Loevinger (1976), Perry (1970, 1981), and Kohlberg (1969). They are likely to use a biological metaphor, in which it is appropriate to speak of continuous growth from simple to higher or more complex forms of life and from immaturity to maturity. Some, such as Erikson and Loevinger, are concerned with broad-gauged personality or ego development; others, such as Perry and Kohlberg, work on the more tightly defined domains of intellectual or moral development. There is a hierarchy implied in the theories of these developmental psychologists. Most contend that it is "better" to be at a higher level or position of intellectual or moral development than at a lower level— although Loevinger and, to a lesser extent, Weathersby (1981) have some reservations about the validity of the concept of hierarchy, pointing out that higher stages do not necessarily bring about happiness or better adjustment to society.

Today's literature is strewn with loose terminology and mixed images of these two streams of research and theory. However, a helpful convention seems to be emerging, in which writers refer to the *phases* of the life cycle and to developmental *stages* of growth and maturity (Lasker and Moore, 1979). I shall follow that convention throughout the remainder of this discussion—although most of the writing of the 1970s on which I shall be drawing for this discussion does not make the distinction clear. Some may even disagree with it. For educational purposes, however, there are profoundly different implications depending on whether one is talking about developmental stages or life-cycle phases. Whereas an educator might legitimately wish to help or encourage an individual to achieve a more advanced stage of ego development, the same case cannot be made for an educational goal of phasic development. The more likely role for an educator in phasic development is to assist with transitions and to help individuals adapt to the phase of the life cycle that is appropriate for their age and social role.

Phases of the Life Cycle

The observation that there seem to be identifiable transitions and periods of change in the lives of people is not new. Shakespeare wrote, with his usual prescience, about the "seven ages" of life in the well-known "All the world's a stage" speech from the second act of *As You Like It*. More recently, another popular writer has catapulted discussion about a universal life cycle into national prominence. In 1976 Gail Sheehy's *Passages: Predictable Crises of Adult Life* became a national best seller. Her premise is that there are predictable turning points in the lives of adults and that these turning points represent an internal unfolding in a sequence of natural growth. Drawing inspiration and confidence from the research of psychiatrists Roger Gould (1972) and Daniel Levinson and colleagues (1974), Sheehy interviewed 115 adults with three goals in mind: to locate common inner changes in the way adults view themselves and their world, to compare the developmental rhythms of men and women, and to examine the predictable crises for couples.

The well-publicized work of the 1970s on life phases was not new. Research on life-phase identification began in the 1920s and has continued to the present time. The mid 1960s were especially rich years for academic research on the life cycle, with the publication of Bernice Neugarten's *Middle Age and Aging* in 1968, followed by Baltes and Shaie's *Life-Span Developmental Psychology* in 1973. In the mid 1970s the subject was popularized, and in the 1980s writers are likely to try to settle the dust and substantiate the claims.

The methods used to categorize and describe life phases have included biographical studies of the lives of well-known people; clinical studies utilizing in-depth interviews of people reflecting on their own life cycles; factor analyses of multiple variables in an effort to group related characteristics together empirically; card sorting of descriptions of hypothetical people into similar age groups; and, most recently, a raft of syntheses of past research in an effort to identify age-linked phases that seem common across studies.

All this activity seems to have resulted in at least modest agreement that there are phases in the lives of people and that these phases can be identified as common to a given age group. The number of categories identified by researchers and scholars ranges from two to ten, with a mean of five. Interestingly enough, it is about the same for laymen. When Fry (1976) asked a sample of adults to sort thirty-five brief descriptions of adults into groups with similar age characteristics, the number of categories ranged from two to fifteen, with a mean of about five. The recent tendency has been to move toward more categories, with six or seven appearing to represent common agreement. Since most of the recent categorizations of life phases have leaned rather heavily on the research of Gould and Levinson, however, the seeming agreement on seven life phases should be considered tentative.

Despite the tentativeness of the findings, however, there is a temptation to construct charts of the phases of life, assigning age boundaries and descriptive labels to each of the (usually seven) phases. The major controversy about such charts is not over the details of defining age boundaries or phasic descriptors but over the whole idea of using chronological age as the baseline. All researchers and theorists on adult life cycles provide room for individual differences, and all admit that chronological age boundaries should be considered only rough indices. But there is a continuum among researchers regarding the role of age. Levinson and associates (1974), for example, believe that there are "relatively universal, genotypic, age-linked, adult developmental periods." Lowenthal and her colleagues (1975), on the other hand, defined their research groups by social role rather than age. They grouped their subjects into four categories: high school seniors, newlyweds, middle-aged parents, and preretirement couples. Perhaps it is not surprising that Levinson came out with similarities for age-defined groups, whereas Lowenthal concluded that chronological age is generally less significant than socially defined roles.

The other split on the chronological versus sociological debate exists among those who are interested primarily in the *application* of life-cycle research and those who are interested in research as *disciplinary inquiry*. Almost universally, it seems, educators, counselors, educational researchers, and others who work directly with adult learners find the age-linked descriptions useful. Workbooks, popular writings, and adult counseling materials almost always use age guidelines to help people visualize the life cycle. The so-called "popularization" of age-linked life phases, however, upsets researchers who are interested in adult development as a disciplinary inquiry. Orval Brim (1976, p. 7) writes, "It may be that the field of adult development is similar to child development some fifty years ago in its exploration of age-linked developmental sequences. And, like child development then, it is in real danger from pop culture renderings of 'life stages,' from the public seizing on the idea of age-linked stages of development, such as the 'male midlife crisis,' just as it seizes on astrology and tea-leaf reading." Baltes and Schaie (1973, p. 367) are even more emphatic in their conviction that "it is not only shortsighted but sometimes even useless and damaging to construct age-specific developmental models that ignore interage networks and other aspects of long-term ontogenetic linkages." They resent the current popularizations on the grounds that "the optimism surrounding the increasing acceptance of a life-span view may easily outrun its scientific utility if not properly channeled and regulated on a conceptual and methodological level" (p. 366).

Some of the difficulty between researchers and practitioners may be attributable to the terminology confusion over stages of development versus phases of the life cycle. It seems alarmist to call age-specific schemes "shortsighted," "dangerous," and comparable to "astrology and tea-leaf reading." Indeed, it might be more shortsighted *not* to challenge adults to grapple with the ideas presented in the life-cycle research and to think about the relevance of such research to their own lives—as long as such schemes are presented as speculative and suggestive rather than definitive. The *New York Times* in a review of Sheehy's *Passages* advised readers, "If you read *Passages,* you will be in less danger of living the unexamined life that Socrates decried."

The enormous interest on the part of adults themselves in books such as *Passages* and in popular articles about the research (*Time,* April 28, 1975; *Psychology Today,* March 1974, Feb. 1975, Sept. 1977) indicates that there is an eagerness to learn about the seasons of life. The suggestion by researchers that this enthusiasm should be "properly channeled and regulated" seems as inappropriate as the implication that life-cycle research has the answers and that "normal" adults should grow and change along the lines indicated. All the workshop materials that I have seen, however, make clear the ambiguity of research findings and the tentativeness and flexibility of the phases identified. If the fear of the critics is that the current high interest in age-linked phases will foreclose research and theoretical work on other alternatives, then their point is well taken, but that seems improbable, since the research community is engaged in a lively debate on the issue. The debate itself is more likely to stimulate good research than to stifle it.

With these disagreements and reservations about age-linked phases as background, it seems useful to describe the phases delineated in such research as briefly yet specifically as possible. The literature abounds with various modes of description, ranging from narrative essays of the "developmental tasks" faced by each age group (Havighurst, 1972) to research graphs showing life phase as a function of questionnaire responses (Gould, 1972; Lehman and Lester, 1978). The most helpful descriptive scheme I have seen in the literature is one devised by Weathersby (1978), which describes life phases on three dimensions: major psychic tasks, marker events, and characteristic stance. McCoy, Ryan, and Lictenberg (1978, p. 229) have also developed an interesting chart for educators. They describe stages by tasks, program response, and outcomes sought. To cite an example, one task for the Leaving Home Stage (age 18-22) is to break psychological ties; the program response is help with personal development and offering of assertive training workshops; the outcome sought is strengthened autonomy.

Table 8 is my synthesis of the research, using Weathersby's work and classification scheme as the starting point but including most of the current schemes that use chronological age as a rough index to life-cycle phase.

In a very rough analogy, the psychic tasks listed in Table 9 correspond to *what* adults need to learn at each phase, while the characteristic stance contains some clues about *how* adults learn. Adults in their early 30s, who are searching for stability, have different learning tasks from those in their late 50s; but, according to Table 9, they also have a different stance. The younger learner's (age 29-34) concern about order and setting long-range goals suggests a fairly aggressive search for goal-specific education, a willingness to compete in order to "make it," and perhaps a willingness to conform to certification and degree criteria in order to advance career goals. One message contained in Table 9 is that educators would approach the young aggressive learner quite differently from the older learner in the mellowing phase, who would be expected to be turned off by competitive education, who might be more interested in analytical discussion than in acquisition of new information,

Table 8. Descriptions of Life-Cycle Phases

Phase and Age	Marker Events	Psychic Tasks	Characteristic Stance
Leaving Home 18-22	Leave home Establish new living arrangements Enter college Start first full-time job Select mate	Establish autonomy and independence from family Define identity Define sex role Establish new peer alliances	A balance between "being in" and "moving out" of the family
Moving into Adult World 23-28	Marry Establish home Become parent Get hired/fired/quit job Enter into community activities	Regard self as adult Develop capacity for intimacy Fashion initial life structure Build the dream Find a mentor	"Doing what one should" Living and building for the future Launched as an adult
Search for Stability 29-34	Establish children in school Progress in career or consider change Possible separation, divorce, remarriage Possible return to school	Reappraise relationships Reexamine life structure and present commitments Strive for success Search for stability, security, control Search for personal values Set long-range goals Accept growing children	"What is this life all about now that I am doing what I am supposed to?" Concern for order and stability and with "making it" Desire to set long-range goals and meet them
Becoming One's Own Person 37-42	Crucial promotion Break with mentor Responsibility for three-generation family; i.e., growing children and aging parents For women: empty nest; enter career and education	Face reality Confront mortality; sense of aging Prune dependent ties to boss, spouse, mentor Reassess marriage Reassess personal priorities and values	Suspended animation More nurturing stance for men; more assertive stance for women "Have I done the right thing? Is there time to change?"

Stage/Age			
Settling Down 45-55	Cap career Become mentor Launch children; become grandparents New interests and hobbies Physical limitations; menopause Active participation in community events	Increase feelings of self-awareness and competence Reestablish family relationships Enjoy one's choices and life style Reexamine the fit between life structure and self	"It is perhaps late, but there are things I would like to do in the last half of my life" Best time of life
The Mellowing 57-64	Possible loss of mate Health problems Preparation for retirement	Accomplish goals in the time left to live Accept and adjust to aging process	Mellowing of feelings and relationships Spouse increasingly important Greater comfort with self
Life Review 65 +	Retirement Physical decline Change in finances New living arrangements Death of friends/spouse Major shift in daily routine	Search for integrity versus despair Acceptance of self Disengagement Rehearsal for death of spouse	Review of accomplishments Eagerness to share everyday human joys and sorrows Family is important Death is a new presence

Sources: Chickering and Havighurst, 1981; Gould, 1972; Lehman and Lester, 1978; Levinson and others, 1974; McCoy, Ryan, and Lichtenberg, 1978; Neugarten, 1968; Sheehy, 1976; Weathersby, 1978.

and who would most likely be less interested in conforming to externally imposed regulation in the interests of having the learning accepted by others. We will return to further implications of phasic research in Chapter Nine, after we have had an opportunity to merge the more subjective, holistic research of developmental studies (whether on phases or stages) with the more objective, elemental research of quantitative methodologies reviewed in Chapter Eight.

Developmental Stages

In contrast to the age-defined horizontal progression of the phasic life cycle, developmental-stage research involves vertical progression. Here it is appropriate to speak of levels, positions, and goals. Developmental-stage research is based in stronger theory than any research we have discussed so far. Whereas phasic researchers spend more time *describing* the phase than *explaining* its origin, stage researchers are likely to give at least as much attention to explanation as to description. Indeed, it is appropriate to call most of the people interested in developmental stages theorists as well as researchers, since their research is as frequently designed to develop or test theory as to report research findings. The best known of the current stage researchers are Loevinger (1976) on ego development, Perry (1970) on intellectual development, and Kohlberg and Turiel (1971) on moral development. Description here will be brief; I urge interested readers to seek further details in the references cited.

Jane Loevinger. Loevinger (1976) uses the concept of ego development to suggest the creation of a central frame of reference through which people view themselves and their relationships with others. Her developmental stages refer to the growth of the core personality and are more inclusive than moral development or intellectual development, to which we shall turn in a moment.

Table 9 shows Loevinger's stages, which she calls milestones of ego development. The stages were developed through extensive clinical studies and the use of a thirty-six-item projective test involving sentence completion. The sentence completions are scored as indicators of the stage of ego development. For example, an individual at the Impulsive and Self-Protective stages completes the stem "Education—" with the following characteristic responses: —is fun and hard, —is good for finding a job, —is a drag but important, —and me don't get along too good (Loevinger, Wessler, and Redmore, 1970, vol. 2). According to Loevinger, people at these lower-level stages of ego development view education as a *thing* that one gets in school and then has. At the Conformist stage, responses indicating an uncritical and idealized view of education are characteristic. Responses to the stem "Education—" are as follows: —is a very important and useful thing today, —is a necessity for all U.S. citizens, —helps everyone, —is an essential requirement in acquiring a good job. Education, to the Conformist, is interpreted as school attendance and is valued primarily for its *practical usefulness.* At the Conscientious stage, people begin to view education as an experience that affects the inner life; its importance lies in its stimulation and potential for enrichment, and it has value for society as well as for individuals. Characteristic sentence completions are: Education is the standard for a strong America, —is a privilege and not a right, —is a constant process not limited to a classroom, —is essential to gaining maturity. At the Autonomous stage, education is seen as leading to creativity, self-fulfillment, and deeper values; it is viewed as an *ongoing process.* Characteristic sentence completions are these: Education seems valuable in itself, —is the development of the entire man, mental, physical, and spiritual, —is rewarding only if you learn to see things in a variety of ways and can have feelings for other people's beliefs.

As in almost all developmental-stage research, the movement is from simple stereotyped thinking and perceptions, through an awareness of multiple possibilities and differentiated views of oneself and society, to conceptual complexity, toleration of ambiguity, objectivity, and broadened vision.

William Perry (1970). The nine developmental positions identified by Perry (1970, pp. 9-10) are shown below. They were devised through close observation, intensive interviews, and measurement of Harvard undergraduates (eighty-two men

Table 9. Milestones of Ego Development

Stage	Impulse Control, Character Development	Interpersonal Style	Conscious Preoccupations	Cognitive Style
Presocial		Autistic		
Symbiotic		Symbiotic	Self vs. nonself	
Impulsive	Impulsive, fear of retaliation	Receiving, dependent, exploitative	Bodily feelings, especially sexual and aggressive	Stereotyping, conceptual confusion
Self-protective	Fear of being caught, externalizing blame, opportunistic	Wary, manipulative, exploitative	Self-protection, trouble, wishes, things, advantage, control	
Conformist	Conformity to external rules, shame, guilt for breaking rules	Belonging, superficial niceness	Appearance, social acceptability, banal feelings, behavior	Conceptual simplicity, stereotypes, clichés
Conscientious-conformist	Differentiation of norms, goals	Aware of self in relation to group, helping	Adjustment, problems, reasons, opportunities (vague)	Multiplicity
Conscientious	Self-evaluated standards, self-criticism, guilt for consequences, long-term goals and ideals	Intensive, responsible, mutual, concern for communication	Differentiated feelings, motives for behavior, self-respect, achievements, traits, expression	Conceptual complexity, idea of patterning
Individualistic	Add: Respect for individuality	Add: Dependence as an emotional problem	Add: Development, social problems, differentiation of inner life from outer	Add: Distinction of process and outcome

	Autonomous	Integrated
Impulse control, character development	Add: Coping with conflicting inner needs, toleration	Add: Reconciling inner conflicts, renunciation of unattainable
Interpersonal style	Add: Respect for autonomy, interdependence	Add: Cherishing of individuality
Conscious preoccupations	Vividly conveyed feelings, integration of physiological and psychological causation of behavior, role conception, self-fulfillment, self in social context	Add: Identity
Cognitive style	Increased conceptual complexity, complex patterns, toleration for ambiguity, broad scope, objectivity	

Note: "Add" means in addition to the description applying to the previous level.
Source: Loevinger, 1976, pp. 24-25.

and two women) as they proceeded through college in the 1950s and 1960s. Perry was specifically interested in how college students think and in the impact of education on intellectual and ethical development.

Position 1: The student sees the world in polar terms of we-right-good vs. other-wrong-bad. Right Answers for everything exist in the Absolute, known to Authority, whose role is to mediate (teach) them. Knowledge and goodness are perceived as quantitative accretions of discrete rightnesses to be collected by hard work and obedience (paradigm: a spelling test).

Position 2: The student perceives diversity of opinion, and uncertainty, and accounts for them as unwarranted confusion in poorly qualified Authorities or as mere exercises set by Authority "so we can learn to find The Answer for ourselves."

Position 3: The student accepts diversity and uncertainty as legitimate but still *temporary* in areas where Authority "hasn't found The Answer yet." He supposes Authority grades him in these areas on "good expression" but remains puzzled as to standards.

Position 4: (a) The student perceives legitimate uncertainty (and therefore diversity of opinion) to be extensive and raises it to the status of an unstructured epistemological realm of its own, in which "anyone has a right to his own opinion," a realm which he sets over against Authority's realm, where right-wrong still prevails; or (b) the student discovers qualitative contextual relativistic reasoning as a special case of "what They want" within Authority's realm.

Position 5: The student perceives all knowledge and values (including Authority's) as contextual and relativistic and subordinates dualistic right-wrong functions to the status of a special case, in context.

Position 6: The student apprehends the necessity of orienting himself in a relativistic world through some form of personal Commitment (as distinct from unquestioned or unconsidered commitment to simple belief in certainty).

Position 7: The student makes an initial Commitment in some area.

Position 8: The student experiences the implications of Commitment and explores the subjective and stylistic issues of responsibility.

Position 9: The student experiences the affirmation of identity among multiple responsibilities and realizes Commitment as an ongoing, unfolding activity through which he expresses his life style.

Perry's model moves from perceiving the world in absolutist terms (positions 1, 2, 3) to making more room for diversity and recognizing the problematic nature of life (positions 4, 5, 6) to finding one's own place through personal commitment in a relativistic world (positions 7, 8, 9). In brief, development moves through sequences—from simplicity to complexity and from differentiation to integration. In Perry's scheme, the immature person perceives the world in either-or, good-bad, permitted-not permitted terms. A child or an immature adult looks to an outside authority—parent or teacher—for the "right" answer. Gradually he begins to discover that authorities disagree and that the values of fellow students differ from his own. In an effort to resolve the differences between equally credible people, he adopts the "everyone has a right to his own opinion" stance or the "I'll do what *they* want even though I don't see why" attitude. The individual attaining more advanced levels of development begins to see that he must find integrity for himself in a relativistic world, identifying the things that are important and central to his sense of self.

In his research, Perry found that most Harvard freshmen enter college at stages 3, 4, and 5 and graduate in positions 6, 7, and 8. Position 9 was rarely observed in college students, but I would expect it to be more common among adult learners, especially those engaged in substantial intellectual work. Indeed, as research extends to the adult years, I would expect revision and extension of Perry's top three or four positions.

It is, of course, possible that the highest positions of intellectual development reported by Perry for Harvard undergraduates would also be the highest positions among adults, but that seems unlikely. As we saw in the early pages of this chapter, IQ was once thought to parallel physical growth, rising to a maximum when physical maturity is attained, declining as old age is approached. Further investigation of intellectual performance on intelligence tests revealed not so much different amounts of intelligence between youth and old age as different patterns, as represented in the concepts of fluid and crystallized intelligence. Similarly, I would expect new patterns and new developmental positions to appear among adults doing extensive intellectual work. The promise of further study of developmental theories of intellectual growth lies in their potential to illuminate the range and sequence of patterns of human learning. If we know where an adult stands in intellectual development, we are in a better position to help him or her advance to the next stage.

Lawrence Kohlberg. Another model of stage development, also arising from study at Harvard, is the one developed by Kohlberg, whose model for "moral development" has much in common with Perry's scheme. He, like Perry, arrived at his model through extensive interviews and careful study of a small group of people. Kohlberg refers to his theory as cognitive-developmental. In the choice of the name and in the structure of the theory, he follows in the path of such illustrious and respected theorists as Dewey, Piaget, and Bruner.

Kohlberg finds that the dictionary's definition of "development" makes a perfectly good starting point. To develop means "to make active; to move from the original position to one providing more opportunity for effective use; to cause to grow and differentiate along lines natural of its kind; to go through a process of natural growth, differentiation, or evolution by successive changes" (Kohlberg and Mayer, 1972, p. 483). Kohlberg, like Perry, has clearly set forth a hierarchical sequence of the stages of moral development (Kohlberg and Turiel, 1971, pp. 415-416):

I. Stage 0: Premoral Stage

Neither understands rules nor judges good or bad in terms of rules and authority. Good is what is pleasant or exciting, bad is what is painful or fearful. Has no idea of obligation, should, or have to, even in terms of external authority, but is guided only by can do and want to do.

II. Preconventional Level

At this level, the child is responsive to cultural rules and labels of good and bad, right or wrong, but interprets these labels in terms of either the physical or the hedonistic consequences of action (punishment, reward, exchange of favors) or in terms of the physical power of those who enunciate the rules and labels. The level is divided into two stages:

Stage 1: The punishment and obedience orientation. The physical consequences of action determine its goodness or badness regardless of the human meaning or value of these consequences. Avoidance of punishment and unquestioning deference to power are valued in their own right, not in terms of respect for an underlying moral order supported by punishment and authority (the latter being Stage 4).

Stage 2: The instrumental relativist orientation. Right action consists of that which instrumentally satisfies one's own needs and occasionally the needs of others. Human relations are viewed in terms like those of the marketplace. Elements of fairness, reciprocity, and equal sharing are present, but they are always interpreted in a physical or pragmatic way. Reciprocity is a matter of "you scratch my back and I'll scratch yours," not of loyalty, gratitude, or justice.

III. Conventional Level

At this level, maintaining the expectations of the individual's family, group, or nation is perceived as valuable in its own right, regardless of immediate and obvious consequences. The attitude is not only one of conformity to personal expectations and social order but of loyalty to it, of actively maintaining, supporting, and justifying the order and of identifying with the persons or group involved in it. At this level, there are two stages:

Stage 3: The interpersonal concordance or "good boy-nice girl" orientation. Good behavior is that which pleases or helps others and is approved by them. There is much conformity to stereotypical images of what is majority or "natural" behavior. Behavior is frequently

judged by intention: "He means well" becomes important for the first time. One earns approval by being
"nice."

Stage 4: The law-and-order orientation. There is
orientation toward authority, fixed rules, and the maintenance of the social order. Right behavior consists of
doing one's duty, showing respect for authority, and
maintaining the given social order for its own sake.

IV. Postconventional, Autonomous, or Principled Level

At this level, there is a clear effort to define moral
values and principles which have validity and application
apart from the authority of the groups or persons holding
these principles and apart from the individual's own identification with these groups. This level has two stages:

Stage 5: The social-contract legalistic orientation.
Generally with utilitarian overtones. Right action tends
to be defined in terms of general individual rights and in
terms of standards which have been critically examined
and agreed upon by the whole society. There is a clear
awareness of the relativism of personal values and opinions and a corresponding emphasis upon procedural rules
for reaching consensus. Aside from what is constitution-
ally and democratically agreed upon, the right is a matter
of personal values and opinion. The result is an emphasis
upon the legal point of view, but with an emphasis upon
the possibility of changing law in terms of rational considerations of social utility (rather than rigidly maintaining it in terms of Stage 4 law and order). Outside the legal
realm, free agreement and contract is the binding element
of obligation. This is the "official" morality of the American government and Constitution.

Stage 6: The universal ethical principle orientation.
Right is defined by the decision of conscience in accord
with self-chosen ethical principles appealing to logical
comprehensiveness, universality, and consistency. These
principles are abstract and ethical (the Golden Rule, the
categorical imperative) and are not concrete moral rules
like the Ten Commandments. At heart, these are universal principles of justice, of the reciprocity and equality
of the human rights, and of respect for the dignity of
human beings as individual persons.

The work of Loevinger, Perry, and Kohlberg (and numerous others not reviewed here) illustrates the potential richness of research on adult stages of development. Whatever the realm of study—ego, cognitive, or moral—developmental stages tend to move in ordered sequence toward increasingly complex capacities. It is this characteristic that makes stage research a challenge to educators, who typically subscribe to the goal of helping each individual develop to his or her highest potential. The theory and implications of developmental-stage research are discussed in Chapter Nine.

CHAPTER 8

How and What Adults Learn— and Want to Learn

Research on the learning preferences and practices of adult learners presents a contrast to the research reviewed in Chapter Seven on cognitive processes and adult development. There we were looking mostly at holistic interpretations of how learners relate to the world about them and how they change and grow over time. In this chapter we will be looking at specific, more easily quantifiable data; we will be taking a snapshot rather than a motion picture of learning activities as adults describe them at a particular point in their lives. The learning may be self-directed, or it may consist of participation in organized instruction.

Self-Directed Learning

Self-directed learning was defined in Chapter Three as deliberate learning in which the person's primary intention is to

186

"gain certain definite knowledge or skills." Researchers identified with self-directed learning (Tough, Penland, and Coolican)
usually include formal learning and class work in their analyses
of learning projects, but when the object of study is *all* of the
deliberate learning efforts of the individual, organized group
learning constitutes a small portion of the total effort. The
question of interest to us here is: When adults plan learning activities to meet their needs, what do they do and how do they
do it? We are also interested in how well they do it and how
satisfied they are with the results, but little information exists
to answer the latter questions.

It would be helpful if the literature on self-directed learning contained more case studies, so that we had a better feel for
what kind of learning we are actually talking about. In an early
study, Tough (1968, p. 20) does provide some examples of
learning projects, and a few from his list are presented below in
order to give the reader a sense of the range and nature of the
learning projects.

· An investment dealer was aware that his company was becoming interested in the possibility of developing an advertis-
ing campaign. Consequently, he offered to learn the knowledge necessary for preparing recommendations concerning
media, content, and budget.
· A man learned about the West Coast in order to decide
whether to take a vacation trip there, where to go and what
to see, and how much to spend.
· A teacher set out to improve his reading speed and comprehension so that he could read more material than before.
· In order to perform more competently and independently in
her work in the public relations office of a large company, a
woman set out to learn what sorts of items the various media
considered newsworthy for their audiences.
· A married secretary in her 30s became more competent at
sewing in order to make and alter her own clothes.
· A man learned how to train his dog to be a good retriever for
hunting and to be obedient in his apartment and in a car.

The possible range of subject matter is infinite in self-

directed projects, but there have been attempts to classify learning projects by subject matter. Across the studies summarized
by Coolican (1974, 1975), the most popular learning projects
usually dealt with vocational subjects, home and family, and
hobbies and recreation, in that order. Penland (1977, p. 59),
using the largest and most representative sample of American
adults to date, asked each respondent to describe one learning
project. The projects were then classified into three subject matter groups as follows:

Formal Topics (6.9 Percent)

Formal learning	English
History	Language
Mathematics	Science

Practical Topics (75.9 Percent)

Business	Child care
Clerical	Hobbies/crafts
Driving	Gardening
Health/beauty	Homemaking
Home repairs	Job search
Job related	Mechanics
Medical	Sports/games
Technical	Travel
Volunteer/civic	Education

Intraself Topics (17.2 Percent)

Sensory awareness	Sociology
Religion	Relationships
Psychology	Politics
Philosophy	Nature
Music	Art

The pragmatism of adult learners is evident, with three
quarters of them choosing practical how-to-do-it projects. This
supports Tough's (1971, p. 72) conclusion that "most adult
learning begins because of a problem or responsibility, or at
least a question or puzzle, not because of a grand desire for a
liberal education." This problem-centered orientation to learning has been identified by Knowles (1978, p. 58) as one of the
basic assumptions about adult learning:

Children have been conditioned to have a subject-centered orientation to most learning, whereas adults tend to have a problem-centered orientation to learning. This difference is primarily the result of the difference in time perspective. The child's time perspective toward learning is one of postponed application.

The adult, on the other hand, comes into an educational activity largely because he is experiencing some inadequacy in coping with current life problems. He wants to apply tomorrow what he learns today, so his time perspective is one of immediacy of application. Therefore, he enters into education with a problem-centered orientation to learning.

Research generally supports the notion that most adults who voluntarily undertake a learning project do so more in the hope of solving a problem than with the intention of learning a subject. Such a conclusion does not, of course, preclude other motivations for learning, as discussed in Chapter Four.

The question of *how* adults learn is interpreted by Tough (1971) to mean how adults go about planning and carrying out their learning projects. Field research on how adult learning is accomplished suggests that the format of traditional education is not often used. Group situations in which a designated person (teacher) is responsible for planning the content, sequence, pacing, and so forth, is present in only 10 percent of the learning projects. In the majority of projects, the learner retains control of the day-to-day decisions about what subject matter to cover, how to cover it, and when and where to carry out the learning efforts. Table 10 is a composite of data from studies of learning projects. In this table, "professional" is used not necessarily in the sense that the person has had training as a teacher but, rather, that he or she is paid or designated by schools, agencies, employers, and the like, to make major decisions about how the learning project will be carried out. "Nonhuman resources," refers to completely planned courses, such as those found in programmed instruction or a television series. Clearly, the great majority of learning projects are, in Tough's words (1979, p.

Table 10. Percentage of Learning Projects Using Various Types of Planners

Self-planned	73
Group	
Led by professional	10
Peers	4
One-to-one helper	
Professional	7
Friend	3
Nonhuman resource	3

Source: Tough, 1978, p. 10.

11), "handled by an amateur." A professional is involved only 20 percent of the time—10 percent in group situations; 7 percent in one-to-one situations; and 3 percent indirectly, through planning a program that is delivered via nonhuman resources.

Penland's data differ substantially from the composite shown in Table 10. Table 11, taken from Penland (1979), shows less control by the learner, with correspondingly more help from nonhuman resources and one-to-one helpers. Group planners, however, maintain the same ratio in both sets of data—about 14 percent.

Table 11. Source of Planning for Learning Projects

	Percent of Learning Projects
Self-planner retains major responsibility for day-to-day decision making about needs and criteria for selecting and using informative data.	25.3
Nonhuman planner, such as series of television programs, programmed instructional materials, a workbook, or other printed matter, can provide a learning blueprint.	22.7
Human planner or "significant other" person helps the learner in a one-to-one situation to fill the gap between the individual's level of competence and the skills necessary to access appropriate resources.	29.0
Group planner, such as a workshop or a class, is accepted in whole or in part by the learner as the source of direction regarding what to do in each episode.	14.6

Source: Penland, 1979, p. 177.

Although Penland's data are more recent and more broadly representative of the adult population than the composite data shown in Table 10, it is doubtful that the differences can be attributed to either the sample or a recent shifting of responsibility from the learner to tutors and nonhuman resources. While observation suggests that audio and videotapes are now in common use by thousands of professionals, and learning exchanges are increasingly common, the discrepancies noted in self-planning and nonhuman planning between Tables 10 and 11 are probably due to differences in categorization of various learning resources. A different approach to the categorization of books, for example, could make a big difference. It is estimated that up to one third of the paperback book industry is devoted to teaching people how to do everything from fixing the plumbing to fixing a marriage. Whether such books are considered nonhuman planners or part of the standard equipment of the self-planner is not made clear by Penland. Tough classifies books as planners only if they are considered primarily (51 percent) responsible for guiding the learning effort.

Books were rated "extremely important" resources by 71 percent of Penland's active learners, exceeded as a preferred resource only by knowledgeable friends and relatives (1977, p. 46). Similarly, 44 percent of Penland's respondents indicated that reading was the best way for them to learn, exceeded slightly by the more social learning mode of "seeing or observing," which was rated best by 45 percent.

Since group learning situations, which represent the predominant learning mode in traditional education, are preferred or used by only a small number of self-directed learners, Penland asked adults why they preferred to learn on their own instead of taking a course. Table 12 shows the results.

There are basically three clusters of reasons represented in Table 12. The first four reasons express a positive desire to have more control over the learning situation. Items 5 and 6 express a rather neutral attitude toward classes, in the sense that they might be satisfactory if they taught what was wanted when it was wanted. The last four items express a negative feeling about the appropriateness of regular classes for the learning

Table 12. Reasons Why People Prefer to Learn on Their Own
Instead of Taking a Course

Category	Most Important (percent)
1. Desire to set my own learning pace	46.8
2. Desire to use my own style of learning	37.4
3. I wanted to keep the learning strategy flexible and easy to change	31.0
4. Desire to put my own structure on the learning project	27.8
5. I wanted to learn this right away and couldn't wait until a class might start	36.2
6. I didn't know of any class that taught what I wanted to know	29.8
7. I don't like a formal classroom situation with a teacher	14.0
8. Lack of time to engage in a group learning program	17.9
9. Transportation to a class is too hard or expensive	5.3
10. I don't have enough money for a course or a class	5.2

Source: Penland, 1979, p. 174.

project, in the sense that, even if an appropriate class existed, the respondent would find it unsatisfactory for one reason or another. Interestingly, the two reasons that are almost always listed on survey questionnaires as major barriers to adult education classes, lack of time and lack of money (see Chapter Four), are not very important in the context of making a choice between self-directed learning and classroom instruction. This suggests that removing the two barriers cited most frequently by survey respondents would not move many people from self-directed learning into the classroom. Permitting learners to start when they want to and to proceed at their own pace would presumably be a far more effective recruiting device than offering transportation or financial aid.

There are probably group differences in the reasons people give for conducting their own learning projects. I would predict, for example, that adults of low educational attainment would be somewhat more likely to express negative attitudes toward classes (check items 7-10 in Table 12), whereas those who went farther in the formal educational system would reflect more positive attitudes, expressing the desirability of having more control over their learning projects (items 1-4). In short, those who liked school, were successful, and went farthest in the educational system would have better self-directed learning skills, and they would also have fewer negative feelings about classes than those who were less successful in school. Some support for this hypothesis exists in Penland's data showing (1977, p. 74) that adults who were taking classes and also conducting self-directed learning projects were more likely than those engaged only in self-directed projects to cite positive reasons (items 1-4) and less likely to cite negative reasons (items 7-10) for conducting self-directed projects.

Penland's failure to include more items related to subject matter appears to be a shortcoming of the choices offered in Table 12. McCatty (1973) found that the desire for individualized subject matter was an important factor in almost half of all self-planned projects. It appears that a major advantage of self-directed learning should lie in the freedom to determine *what* is learned. The man or woman wishing to fix the back patio, for instance, does not want to spend time learning about laying brick or constructing plank flooring if the patio is to be poured cement. At a commonsense level, the efficiency factor seems to be one of the major problems in satisfying problem-oriented learners. By definition, they want to learn enough to solve their rather unique problem (bricks, wood, or cement, but not all three), and they *do* want a solution (how to mix and shape cement, not a lesson on the history or chemistry of cement).

Most learning projects are not as narrowly problem oriented as fixing the back patio, of course; but professional people, who are among the most active self-directed learners in the society, may also have highly focused problems. They usually know what they need to learn, and a course general enough to appeal to sufficiently large numbers would probably contain much that is redundant or irrelevant to the problem-oriented learner. A corollary to the assumption that adults are largely problem-oriented learners is that the more sharply the potential learner has managed to define the problem, the less satisfactory traditional classes will be. At the same time, self-directed learning is likely to be inefficient if the learner cannot define what he wants to know or needs help in locating the relevant resources. In such instances, the learner will be dependent on outside help.

Tough (1971) found that efficiency is often the most important criterion in selecting the planner for learning activities. The first question the learner is likely to ask himself or herself is: What is the fastest, easiest, cheapest way for me to learn whatever I want to learn? The choice of the planner depends heavily on the answer to that question. For research purposes, Tough defines the planner as "the person or thing responsible for more than half of the detailed day-to-day planning and deciding in a learning project. The planner makes the majority of decisions about what to learn (the detailed knowledge and skill) in each learning episode, and/or about how to learn (the detailed strategy, activities, and resources). In addition, the planner may also decide when to begin each learning episode and the pace at which to proceed" (Tough, 1971, p. 77).

Tough contends that there are sixty conceptually distinct steps involved in planning learning projects, and his research has laid them out in some detail (see Tough, 1971, chap. 6). Other studies confirm the existence of a general sequence in planning steps. Morris (1977) orders the planning steps as follows: (1) clarification of the problem, (2) awareness of the need to learn, (3) establishment of general long-term objectives, and (4) identification and securing of resources. When Penland (1977, p. 36) asked his respondents to rank-order their steps in planning, he found considerable personal variation. For example, while 33 percent of the respondents claimed that their first step was to talk with people about their interests, almost as many (29 percent) started their learning project by looking for appropriate information and trying to organize it. This may suggest a difference in learning styles; that is, some people may prefer personal interaction in thinking through a problem, while others prefer a more solitary approach (see Cross, 1976). The nature of the problem, and the extent of the learner's knowledge about where to locate relevant information, also may influence planning sequences. Despite Penland's finding that almost every possible sequence was represented in the planning steps of respondents, the majority of learners followed a sequential planning pattern similar to the one reported by Morris, starting with the clarification of the problem and an awareness of the need for learning. In those two steps lies most of the motivation for undertaking a learning project.

While most self-directed learners decide to maintain complete control over the direction of their learning project, this does not mean that they work alone. Indeed, much self-planned learning involves *more* human interaction than classroom learning does. Tough (1979, p. 4) found that the average adult learner received information, advice, encouragement, and other help from ten people; no one got help from fewer than four persons. Finding competent help, however, turns out to be one of the major problems in self-directed learning projects. Empirical data on "what goes wrong" in learning projects shows that the most frequent source of confusion, frustration, and even anger occurs during the contact with the person, book, or other resource that is expected to be of help (Tough, 1971, p. 105). Such problems are more common than knowing when help is needed or where to find it.

Clearly, the improvement of the help and resources available to self-directed learners is within the domain of professional educators, and the challenge has been set forth. Far from eschewing assistance from educators, most adults are eager for help. "One finding is clear," says Tough (1978, p. 15); "adults want additional competent help with planning and guiding their learning projects." It would be helpful now to have some detailed case studies on why learners are dissatisfied with the help they receive, what kinds of problems they experience, and what they think can be done about providing better help for self-directed learners. To my knowledge, these questions have not been studied in an ordered, comprehensive manner.

In the meantime, it is useful to look at what kinds of resources self-directed learners are using. In Coolican's (1974, 1975) summaries of nine research studies of self-directed learning, the two resources named most often were human resources —intimates (friends, neighbors, or relatives) and paid experts.

The third most common resource was books and pamphlets. Penland (1977, p. 46) found similar results. Resources rated "extremely important" by 40 percent or more of the respondents are shown in Table 13.

Table 13. Resources Rated Extremely Important by Adult Learners

Resource	Percent
Expert who is also a friend or relative	75.2
Books	71.2
Close friend or relative	58.7
Travel	52.5
Individual instruction or tutoring	49.2
Paid expert	48.8
Newspaper	48.1
Television	44.2
Class or lecture series	43.1
Self-formed group of equals	41.8

Source: Condensed from Penland, 1979, p. 46.

There were some interesting differences between learners and nonlearners in the Penland study. Nonlearners (the 21 percent of the sample not engaged in any kind of learning) were likely to rate television and radio considerably higher on the list of extremely important informational resources and books much lower than were those presently engaged in learning activities. This finding confirms what most people already suspect; that is, that better-educated people have learned to use and respect books as important sources of information, whereas those with less education, who probably have more reading handicaps, rely more on the electronic media as sources of information. Books not only serve different segments of the population but also are related to different types of learning projects. To no one's surprise, Penland found that those engaged in formal learning were considerably more likely than those working on so-called practical or intraself projects to depend on books as their best source of information.

Coolican (1974, 1975), in her syntheses of research on self-directed learning, reports that the three methods most commonly used in learning projects are practice, reading, and discussion, in that order. Listening, observation, and instructors are also used but not as frequently. The message should not be lost that the most frequently used methods in self-directed learning are all active, involving the learner directly; the least commonly used techniques are passive—watching or listening to someone else do something. Unfortunately, Penland, who had the opportunity to collect data about what methods people *do* use in their learning projects, chose instead to ask the often-repeated more abstract question: How would you *prefer* to learn? Answers to that question resulted in two top-ranked methods; roughly 45 percent of the respondents indicated that observing and reading were the best methods for them. Talking with someone and asking questions, hearing or listening, and practice or trial and error were the three middle-ranked references, each attracting roughly one third of the respondents. Making notes and solving puzzles or playing games were attractive to fewer than 3 percent of the respondents. Interestingly, the most active modes of learning—asking questions, practicing, making notes, and solving puzzles—were rated lower when Penland asked people about preferences than when other researchers asked about actual behavior in ongoing learning projects. Whether this reflects differences in the research samples or differences between what people say and what they do awaits further investigation. I strongly suspect that what people *say* about learning presents the more stereotypical picture of school learning, whereas what they *do* may be quite different. That is why it is unfortunate that Penland did not find out what people do rather than what they say—which has been studied extensively and will be discussed in the section on research from state and national surveys.

Overall, people appear reasonably well satisfied with their self-planned learning efforts. Sixty-five percent said that they were "very enthusiastic" about having the knowledge or skill learned through their projects, while 6 percent admitted that they were not very enthusiastic about their learning. As to how much they learned, 57 percent said "a great deal," while 10 percent said "little" (Penland, 1977, p. 34).

Tough (1971, p. 90) presented an interesting table sum-

marizing satisfaction with the learning project as a function of
the type of planner used. Table 14 shows some surprising re-

Table 14. Self-Evaluation of Learning Projects by Type of Planner

	Self	Group or Its Leader	Person in One-to-One	Non-human Resource	Mixed
Amount of knowledge/ skill gained	7.0	5.4	7.0	7.5	6.9
Enthusiasm about possessing new learning	7.2	6.0	7.4	5.9	7.3
Number of hours per project	119	47	63	33	141

Source: Abbreviated from Tough, 1971, p. 90.

sults. Tough obtained the ratings in Table 14 by asking people
to rate each of their learning projects on a scale of 1 to 10, with
10 indicating maximum satisfaction. Average satisfaction indices for individuals were then averaged to arrive at the ratings
shown in Table 14. The results are sufficiently interesting to
suggest that the study should be repeated, because without further information about sample size and statistical significance, it
is difficult to say how much credence should be given to the
figures. If the data are confirmed, the implications are considerable.

In the first place, the use of nonhuman planners (such as
study guides, programmed instruction, audio and video cassettes, and television) appears highly efficient in the sense that
they generate the highest ratings on amount learned and they
do it in the fewest hours. On the other hand, the low average
rating for *what* is learned from nonhuman resources may explain their short duration. If, however, nonhuman resources
provide maximum learning in minimal time, further study needs
to be given to what can be done about the skills and knowledge
taught. To address these questions, we need more information
about the congruence between the goals of the learning project
and the particular resources used.

Second, people spend a great deal of time on self-directed projects and those using mixed planners. Is that because those methods are inefficient—that is, people waste time in amateurish efforts to find information—or because people find the projects basically satisfying, as the high ratings on "enthusiasm" suggest? One-to-one learning appears the most satisfactory of all, which should surprise no one if the tutor is good. It offers expertise and personalization and is rated quite satisfactory with respect to both amount and kind of learning. The problem, of course, is that tutoring is expensive and/or an imposition on the time of friends and colleagues unless it is done as an exchange learning project. Its ratings in the Tough data would certainly support an argument for the operation of more learning exchanges, in which, for example, individuals offer guitar lessons in exchange for instruction on financial planning.

Group learning, in which the planning is done by a leader or teacher, appears to be the least satisfactory of all. People feel that their gain in knowledge or skill is relatively low, and they are not especially enthusiastic about what they have learned. Perhaps that explains why so few learning projects involve group planning; only about 15 percent of the deliberate learning efforts of adults use the conventional school model (Tough, 1978).

In a relatively short period of time, the research on self-directed learning has provided a great deal of information about how people go about learning the things they need or want to know. But it has raised far more questions than it has answered. Certainly, it appears to be a very productive avenue of inquiry, one that is basic to the thesis of this book. If we wish to know how to help people become self-directed learners, we need to know in some detail what problems they are encountering, what kinds of help they need, and how they evaluate their learning projects. So far, most pioneer researchers on self-directed learning have left what happens during the learning project virtually unexplored territory. Whether one wants to know how to facilitate learning or how to present information to adults, more in-depth study of how learning actually takes place in everyday settings is a necessity, one that should receive first priority in the 1980s.

State and National Surveys

In the 1970s, far and away the most popular method of finding out how and what adults learn was through surveys that inquired about subjects studied and methods used by adult learners and about the preferences of those who said they were interested in further learning. In the first half of the decade, hundreds of surveys were conducted by colleges attempting to determine the "adult market" for their services, by state offices charged with planning and coordinating educational resources, and by researchers interested in understanding adult learning needs and interests. In addition, the U.S. Bureau of the Census started its triennial surveys of adult education in 1969, and statistical reports describing adult part-time participation in organized learning activities have been issued by the National Center for Education Statistics for data collected in 1969, 1972, 1975, and 1978. Thus, adults have been queried extensively about their learning activities and interests. The purpose of this section is to present an overview and synthesis of recent research from large-scale surveys using adult learners and potential learners as the respondents.[1]

Since *how* people learn is intricately related to *what,* we shall look at both subject matter interests and at preferences regarding teaching/learning methods. One of the frustrations in interpreting survey findings is that related questionnaire variables are generally separated for purposes of analysis. Thus, we have one table for subject matter interests and another for preferences about teaching methods—despite the fact that in the head of the respondent an interest in auto mechanics virtually dictates a preference for "hands-on" methods, while an interest in history suggests a preference for classroom lectures. The reader should keep in mind that the what and the how of learning are inevitably related and that separation exists more in the

---

[1] The data used in this section are from thirty-five large-scale state and national surveys. Syntheses of the data from these surveys have appeared previously in Cross (1978b), Cross and Zusman (1979), and Cross (1979a). Original citations of the state and national surveys used as data sources can be found in those earlier publications.

artificial world of the statistician than in the real world of teachers and learners.

Subject Matter Interests. There are two ways of looking at the subject matter interests of adults. One is through the courses that are actually taken by adult part-time learners; the other is through surveys inquiring about preferences. The most comprehensive data about subjects studied by adult part-time learners are those collected by the Census Bureau every three years. Table 15 shows participants' descriptions of courses they

Table 15. Subject Matter Trends in Adult Education, 1969-1975

Participant Description	1969	1972	1975
Occupational Training	44.6%	46.5%	48.7%
Technical/vocational	22.6	21.8	22.4
Managerial	7.2	7.3	7.0
Professional	16.2	19.0	21.3
General Education	27.2	25.9	20.6
Adult basic education	4.5	4.0	3.9
Citizenship	.7	.6	.3
High school and college credit	22.3	21.5	16.7
Social Life and Recreation	11.9	12.0	15.9
Hobbies and crafts	8.7	8.6	11.4
Sports and recreation	3.4	4.0	5.1
Personal and Family Living	12.1	14.0	14.8
Home and family life	3.4	4.1	3.9
Personal improvement	8.9	10.3	11.3
Community Issues	9.2	9.8	10.0
Civic and public affairs	2.1	2.2	3.0
Religion	5.2	5.1	4.7
Safety	2.0	2.6	2.4
Other	3.9	2.6	2.6
Not Reported	.5	.8	.6

Note: Participants who reported the same course characteristic in regard to two or more courses were counted once within that course characteristic. Participants were counted once, however, in each course characteristic that they reported. Therefore, columns may add to more than 100 percent. Furthermore, details may not add to subtotals because of rounding.

Source: Boaz, 1978, p. 24.

had taken during the previous year that met the NCES definition of adult education: "Organized learning involves a student-teacher relationship in which the learner is supervised or directed in learning experiences over a specified period of time for a recognized purpose. The teacher may be remote, such as on a recording or tape, or in a correspondence school headquarters. Short-term workshops and seminars are considered adult education" (Boaz, 1978, p. 109).

I present these NCES data because they are the best available for studying trends in adult education. Indeed, they are the only comprehensive data available, and many people cite them and rely on them to monitor what is happening nationally in adult education. As mentioned, however, there is considerable risk involved in relying on the triennial surveys of NCES for trend data. In the first place, the definition of who is a "participant" in adult education can change (usually modestly) from one survey to the next. The 1978 preliminary tables give extensive information about the changes in 1978 particularly and warn that plotting trends is "misleading . . . without awareness of the problems involved." In addition, there appear to be even more serious problems in the NCES data. Table 15 suggests a substantial decrease in the percentage of adult part-time learners taking high school and college courses for credit—which is hard to believe given the experience of most colleges with increasing numbers of older students registering for part-time study. Other data collected from colleges and universities by NCES show a clear increase in part-time college enrollments—from 2.8 million students in 1970 to 4.8 million in 1979. Part-time students constituted 32 percent of the college students in 1970 and 41 percent in 1979. (Figures are from Fall Enrollment in Higher Education Series, via personal communication from Andrew Pepin, NCES, July 1980.) Other national data confirm the trend toward increasing numbers of adults registering for college credit (Golladay, 1977, p. 198). In telephone calls to NCES, I found concern and cooperation but no resolution of the conflict in data collected from different sources. Given the personal experiences of colleges over the past decade, it is far easier to accept a trend of increasing rather than decreasing numbers of adults studying for college credit, but the important issue is that our major national data source on adult education leaves an uneasy doubt about what we think we are witnessing. There is an urgent need for a national data bank with the specific charge of monitoring trends in adult education. At the moment, with discussions going on locally and regionally about the necessity of planning for adequate alternatives for adult learners, nothing should be more important than knowing who is providing what services for adults and how adults are changing their learning patterns and preferences.

Table 15 contains no other data that appear questionable, given what we think we know about trends and patterns of adult learning. Thus, I feel reasonably confident in discussing Table 15 as presented, as long as specific figures regarding trends are avoided. I see no reason to question the data regarding the relative popularity of various types of learning or the participation of subgroups in them. Those data correspond with other information collected in state and national research studies. In the discussion to follow, I will concentrate on supplementing the data in Table 15 with my synthesis of information from NCES and other sources about population subgroups and their participation in various kinds of organized instruction.

A number of observations can be made about the subject matter pursued by adult part-time learners. Learning that is relevant to jobs is in the lead and increasing. Occupational training courses are taken by almost half of all adult learners, and it is a fairly safe guess that most of the people studying "general education" are also interested in upgrading their job options. The increase in professional education is easily explained by the growing need for continuing education in the professions (Houle, 1980) and by the recent tendency of states and professional boards to require continuing education for professionals wishing to retain and renew their licenses. (See Chapter Two for a discussion of mandated continuing education.) Approximately one in four white male adult learners are taking professional courses, compared to one in ten black males and about one in six females, black or white.

Participation in courses related to social life and recreation and personal and family living has been on the increase. White women are the major constituents for hobby and handicraft courses, with a 19 percent participation rate, compared to less than 5 percent for white males and less than 3 percent for blacks. The increase between 1969 and 1975 in the numbers of people interested in personal improvement has been substantial. In 1975 white women were the most active seekers after personal improvement (14.4 percent), followed by black men (10.2 percent), white men (8.5 percent), and black women (6.2 percent). Community issues attract relatively few people, but whites are somewhat more likely than blacks to attend classes on civic and public affairs.

The things that people say they would like to learn parallel quite closely the subjects they actually take. Table 16 is typical of the findings regarding what adults say they would like to learn.

Table 16. Learning Interests of Potential Learners

	Percent with First-Choice Interest	Percent with Any Interest
Vocational subjects	43	78
Hobbies and recreation	13	63
General education	13	48
Home and family	12	56
Personal development	7	54
Public affairs	5	36
Religion	3	15
Agriculture	3	11
Other topic	1	3
No response	1	0

Source: Carp, Peterson, and Roelfs, 1974, pp. 18-19.

The high percentages shown in the second column indicate that most people are interested in a wide variety of topics. When they are forced to set priorities (first column), however, vocational subjects are the clear winners. Predictably, interest in vocational/professional subjects is highest for young people. Almost all surveys show a gradual decline in interests in job-related education as people move into their 40s and 50s. At age 55 to 60, there is a sharp drop as older people turn to more interest in avocational subjects and general education. Among the most frequently chosen vocational/professional subjects are business skills or administration, trades or technical subjects, and nursing. Interest in job-related subjects is generally highest among the least well-educated respondents. A California survey, for example, found that 47 percent of the high school graduates selected job-related subjects as their first choice, compared to 31 percent of the college graduates (Hefferlin, Peterson, and Roelfs, 1975). However—and this is an important caution—the less well educated, despite their high interest in vocational education, are actually less likely to be studying job-related subjects than are those with higher educational attainment, who are simply more active participants in all forms of adult education. According to an Iowa statewide survey (Hamilton, 1976, p. 84), "A large portion of those few low-income, low-previous-education respondents who expressed an interest in further learning at all chose technical skills. Yet almost none followed through with a statement of plans to pursue training in these areas." This finding suggests that "demand" for subject matter needs to be interpreted in conjunction with the characteristics of the respondents. The well-intentioned launching of vocational courses to serve the undereducated could well result in substantially lower enrollment than the "interest" data suggest, and there is also a good possibility that actual enrollees will turn out to be better educated and more upwardly mobile than anticipated.

Given the number of reentry women pursuing career-relevant education, it is perhaps surprising that the data in most surveys still show men significantly more interested, and more active, than women in job-relevant education. But the interpretation of survey data can be tricky. When all women are grouped together and contrasted with all men, even a modest number of full-time housewives interested in flower arranging and child care can push the women's data into the traditional stereotype of "feminine interests" when contrasted with a male sample containing no such interest groups. The same phenomenon occurs when the subject matter interests of the elderly are presented. Neugarten (1975) contends that there are marked differences between the young-old (55 to 75 years of age) and the old-old (over 75). Yet, because of small sample sizes, survey researchers are prone to lump "the elderly" together, starting at age 60 or 65. The passive interests of the few old-old in such a sample usually make "the elderly" appear more different from other age groups than most of them really are.

Hobbies, home and family living, and personal development subjects have wide appeal, although not a very strong appeal. Relatively few pick these fields as first-choice subjects, but majorities express some interest. Interest in hobbies and handicrafts is especially high for those 60 years of age or older. In California, for example, one third of potential learners over 60 years of age picked arts and crafts as their first-choice subjects (Hefferlin, Peterson, and Roelfs, 1975). Interest in recreational courses is also usually greater among women, Caucasians, and those with high educational attainment—groups that can generally afford to think about education in uneconomic terms.

Data in Table 16, as well as in other surveys, suggest that there is not a heavy demand among potential learners for general education and traditional academic subjects. The researchers conducting the nationwide study of adult learning needs and interests for the Commission on Non-traditional Study observed:

> Academic professionals will find it somewhat disheartening that adult Americans are so little interested in further study in traditional liberal arts subjects or, for that matter, in such public affairs topics as community and environmental problems. Most people seem mainly oriented toward improved adaptability for simple everyday living (investment, business skills, home repairs, sewing and cooking, gardening, physical fitness), together with a modicum of personal enjoyment and satisfaction (crafts, sports and games, travel) [Carp, Peterson, and Roelfs, 1974, p. 20].

Well-educated potential learners, those interested in college credit or college-level courses, and current adult education participants express more interest in general education than do most other adults. However, when basic skills subjects are included under general education, those with relatively high interest in general education divide into two groups: those with very little formal schooling, who are usually pursuing adult basic education, and those with high levels of formal education, who are pursuing college degrees.

Despite the ability of survey researchers to cluster subject matter interests into reasonably consistent and distinct groups, the wide-ranging diversity of interests is impressive. In the California survey (Hefferlin, Peterson, and Roelfs, 1975), 167 different subjects were mentioned as first-choice selections. Choices ranged from ever popular topics such as art, business, and psychology to more individualistic interests such as Jewish history, kinesiology, and lip reading.

Two broad generalizable conclusions can be drawn about subject matter interests from the extensive collection of survey data in the 1970s:

- Data on the subject matter interests of adult learners are quite consistent from study to study. While there are sometimes regional differences in who participates, once the characteristics of the learners are known, broad areas of interest can be predicted with a fair degree of accuracy, and they are consistent with Maslow's formulation of a needs hierarchy. Extrinsic rewards such as better jobs and more pay appear to dictate subject matter interests until basic needs for security and recognition are met. The people most likely to assign top priority to education for enjoyment or other intrinsic motivations are those who are not interested in career advancement —retired people, spouses who are not in the labor market and not seeking to be, and well-educated people who have attained all the career success that education is likely to provide.
- Adults are highly pragmatic learners. Vocational and practical education that leads to knowledge about how to do something is chosen by more adults than any other form of learning, and no study presents data that would offer an exception to that generalization. Traditional discipline-oriented subjects are not popular with the majority of potential learners. Such subjects are most likely to appeal to those interested in college degrees. Adults interested in liberal learning but without

degree aspirations are more likely to pursue noncredit courses which are especially designed to meet their needs rather than the discipline-based courses offered in college degree programs.

Teaching/Learning Methods Preferred. When the question of how adults learn is raised in the context of survey research, it is interpreted to mean by which methods and under what conditions. Most surveys have polled two groups—learners and would-be learners—to determine how they are learning or would like to learn. Adults who have participated in some form of organized instruction in the year prior to the survey (learners) generally constitute around one third of the respondents, whereas those who express an interest in participating sometime in the future (would-be learners) make up from 60 to 80 percent of the respondents, depending on the sample and definitions used. Frequently, learners are also classified as would-be learners, since most currently active learners also express an interest in future participation.

Method preferences of adult learners show as much variety as subject matter interests, and they too show considerable consistency across studies. As many as 70 to 80 percent of respondents say that they would prefer to learn by some method other than classroom lectures. Nevertheless, lectures usually rank first or second in overall popularity out of the five to ten methods that are generally presented in questionnaires.

Table 17 is typical of survey data. Most surveys show that classes and lectures are preferred by 20 to 35 percent of the respondents, and these rather formal approaches to learning have their greatest appeal to those with college educations, high income, and high-status occupations (Cross and Zusman, 1979). This suggests that those who have done well—that is, advanced farthest in the traditional school system—are those most in favor of continuing to use the methods that have served them well in the past. It is also probable that the subject matter studied by those with more advanced education is more amenable to instruction by the classroom lecture—or at least more frequently taught by that method than by any other.

On-the-job training is usually ranked second in the meth-

Table 17. Percentages of Would-Be Learners Preferring Various Methods
and Percentages of Learners Using the Methods

Method	Preferences of Would-Be Learners	Utilization by Learners
Lectures or classes	28	35
On-the-job training, internship	21	14
Short-term conferences, institutes, or workshops	13	8
Individual lessons from a private teacher	8	6
Discussion groups	8	4
Study on my own, no formal instruction	7	17
Correspondence course	3	5
Group action project	3	2
Travel-study program	2	—[a]
TV or video cassettes	1	—
Radio, records, or audio cassettes	1	—
Other method	—	2
No response	4	8

[a]Less than 1 percent.
Source: Carp, Peterson, and Roelfs, 1974, p. 30.

ods preferences of potential adult learners, and it is attractive to those whom policy planners are especially interested in reaching—the educationally disadvantaged. In a study conducted for the legislature of the state of California, Hefferlin, Peterson, and Roelfs (1975) found that adults with high school diplomas or less, labor or service workers, low-income respondents, and certain ethnic minorities ranked on-the-job training above any other learning mode. As would be expected, potential learners preferring on-the-job training are most often interested in occupational or technical subject matter.

Across the wide variety of surveys, short-term conferences, institutes, or workshops are the first choice of between 10 and 30 percent of the potential learners, usually ranking third or higher in the list of preferences. As might be predicted, these methods are preferred and used largely by professionals and managers. Independent study is selected as first choice by only a small proportion of potential learners (3 to 14 percent across a variety of surveys), and they tend to be among the better-educated adults. In the California study (Hefferlin, Peterson, and Roelfs, 1975), for example, 17 percent of the potential learners with an eleventh-grade education or less, but 49 percent of those with a college degree, said that independent study was an appropriate way for them to learn—although not necessarily their first choice. When the method is defined as "independent study *in consultation with an instructor*" (emphasis added), the percentage of potential learners who respond that they could learn by this method increases substantially. In the California study, where these conditions were met, 32 percent of the would-be learners indicated that independent study with consultation was an appropriate method for them. In considering that about 90 percent of adults conduct their own learning projects, the number of people who express confidence in their ability to learn independently seems low. Independent study, as it is presented in the context of surveys inquiring about interest in classes and other forms of instruction, however, is probably interpreted quite differently from the independence involved in self-directed learning. Most people setting out to learn a course of study (as opposed to problem-oriented learning) seem to feel that they need some human help and stimulation along the way.

The cool reception to media-based education by adult learners is frequently cited as a reason to go slowly in the development of expensive media courses. While it is true that the electronic age has not been embraced by most adult learners (in most surveys fewer than 5 percent select any form of media as their first choice), two factors should be considered. First, significant numbers (from 20 to 40 percent) of adult learners indicate that television, radio, or audio/video cassettes are appropriate ways for them to learn—even though they may not be their first choices. Second, and perhaps more important, evidence is beginning to build that acceptance of television and other nontraditional methods is in direct proportion to the individual's experience with them. To cite one example of how familiarity with instructional method breeds acceptance, and occasionally even enthusiasm, a survey of some 1,300 students enrolled in Coastline Community College instructional television courses in 1976 showed that nearly 80 percent planned to take another instructional television course (California Postsecondary Education Commission, 1979).

Most of the literature on the uses of media in education is still analyzing why the media, especially television, have not been accepted by teachers and students. Meanwhile, the use of television has become widespread in education, and both its familiarity and its acceptability appear to be increasing. A recent study of the use of television in higher education found that 72 percent of the community colleges, 92 percent of the state colleges, and 63 percent of the private colleges and universities responding to the survey were using television for on- and off-campus instruction (reported in *Chronicle of Higher Education,* Nov. 13, 1979, p. 16). Covering the broader uses of television in industry and the professions as well as in schools and colleges, the California Postsecondary Education Commission (1979) points out: "Tens of thousands of Californians, by now, enroll in broadcast 'telecourses' each semester; more than a hundred institutions offer credit as co-sponsors." In the profession of law alone, some sixty thousand attorneys in California are using videotapes to keep abreast of new developments in their profession. Thus, it may be that apologists for the instructional potential of television and video cassettes should cease their preoccupation with explaining why the media are not well received and begin to look at the potential impact of increasing familiarity on the use of media in education. As the children of the electronic age experience the use of television in schools for educational purposes, they may come to prefer it as adult learners.

Table 17 shows some interesting differences in percentages between the "preferences" and "utilization" columns. Those differences can be interpreted in two ways. The major difference is probably attributable to differences between the samples of the 77 percent of the respondents who said they would like to learn something new (would-be learners) and the 31 percent who are currently active learners. In any survey, learners are almost always better educated and hold higher-status jobs than would-be learners; they are also more likely to be pursuing academic subjects in degree-granting institutions. Thus, it is not surprising that learners are more involved in classes and independent study and less involved in on-the-job training than would-be learners. It is also possible, however, to interpret the differences between the two columns in Table 17 as the difference between the methods that are available currently and the methods that people would prefer. Under that interpretation, there is a need for more active forms of learning, such as on-the-job training, workshops, and discussion groups. Notice that the percentages preferring such methods are larger than the numbers currently accommodated. Moreover, if one were to add together the preferences for all active versus passive methods in Table 17, it is clear that methods in which the learner is actively participating (as opposed to watching or listening) are preferred by a two-to-one margin. Since both policy planners and institutional recruiters are interested in attracting a new constituency from the would-be learner group, it can be argued that for whichever reason—to recruit new students or to serve less advantaged populations of adults—there is a need for more participative forms of learning.

It is difficult to document changes or trends in teaching/ learning methods. Johnstone and Rivera (1965) found roughly the same rank order as that shown in Table 17 when they conducted their national survey in the early 1960s, and data from the triennial surveys of adult participation for 1969, 1972, 1975, and 1978 show no significant changes over the past decade. If any "trend" can be discerned at all, it is probably that there is an increase in multimethod activities. NCES asks respondents to the triennial surveys to report all teaching methods used in each course, and totals have shown sizable increases from 1969 to 1978, indicating that respondents are apparently finding it increasingly difficult to classify a course of study by a single method. That trend, if it is one, is a step in the right direction. Given the increasing diversity of the learning force, it seems desirable to offer multiple methods for learning within a given course of study as well as across fields of study.

Preferred Locations. Of all the variables studied in connection with adult learning preferences, the matter of location illustrates better than any other the adage that people tend to like what they know rather than to know what they would like. In the abstract, people say that convenience of learning location is important to them. And in recent years educational providers

have gone to considerable effort to establish convenient locations in shopping centers, work sites, downtown stores and businesses, and even mobile vans. The national survey sponsored by
the Commission on Non-traditional Study (Ruyle and Geiselman, 1974) showed that off-campus locations are the most
common concession made by colleges and universities to nontraditional learners; by 1974 two thirds of the traditional colleges offering nontraditional programs of one sort or another
said that convenience of location was one of their features.
"Taking education to the student" clearly has become one of
the distinguishing characteristics of nontraditional education,
superseding the more traditional practice of "bringing the student to education." All the evidence so far indicates that adults
are responding in encouraging numbers to the convenience of
off-campus locations.

　　　　Yet traditional educational institutions—grade schools,
high schools, trade schools, colleges, and universities—are the
most popular locations for learning, preferred by roughly half
of the would-be learners, and school buildings are currently
used by more than half of the actual learners (Boaz, 1978; Carp,
Peterson, and Roelfs, 1974). Given the popularity of campus
locations with survey respondents, one might ask whether colleges are making a mistake in placing a heavy emphasis on off-
campus locations in the interest of greater convenience to adult
learners. At the same time, off-campus locations have proved
undeniably popular, and some explanation of the differences
between what people say and what they do seems indicated. It
is possible that respondents are confusing location with sponsor,
believing that education offered by "educators" is better or
more credible than that offered (often by the same educators)
in less traditional locations, or that respondents to surveys tend
to opt for the familiar. Perhaps a combination of the two factors is involved; people interpret a course offered in a traditional school building as more credible than one offered in a
church basement.

　　　　While the general tendency of survey respondents to en-
dorse the familiar and possibly to confuse sponsor and location
argues for caution in interpreting the data on "location" prefer-

ences, some findings are universal across studies. First, location is critical to certain groups of learners. The physically handicapped, the geographically isolated, the aged, and others with restricted mobility cannot participate unless learning opportunities are made accessible. The stereotypes about school buildings as the appropriate places to learn are so strong, however, that it is difficult to introduce people to the potential of new locations for learning unless their options are otherwise limited. In a Kansas study, for example, Hoyt (1975) asked respondents to state whether certain locations would be an advantage or a disadvantage to them. Large majorities (over 70 percent) saw advantages to courses offered "at the nearest college," but people were generally skeptical about "convenience" locations, such as courses offered by mail, radio, or amplified telephone. For these options, more people found disadvantages than advantages. Television courses occupied a middle ground, with 47 percent finding advantages, 35 percent disadvantages, and 18 percent uncertain.

Second, preference for learning location is strongly associated with educational attainment and educational aspirations. Preference for a college location increases consistently with level of formal schooling attained. In Colorado (Barlow and Timiraos, 1975) a college site was preferred by only 21 percent of those with seven to twelve years of schooling, 30 percent of the high school graduates, 38 percent of the college graduates, and 41 percent of those with postgraduate education. A college site is also favored by those who wish to undertake "college-level" learning. Similarly, potential learners who want to obtain college credit or to study literature or science or other subjects typically included in a college curriculum are likely to prefer campus locations.

Third, college sites are more likely to be used by learners than preferred by potential learners—a finding no doubt related to the higher educational attainment of learners. Table 18 shows the learning locations of adult education activities in 1975. It is important to keep in mind that certain groups, especially the elderly and those with low educational attainment or low income, are likely to prefer public high schools and adult

Table 18. Locations of Courses Attended by Adults Participating
in Part-Time "Organized Learning" Activities in 1975

Place of Meeting	Percent of Courses
College or university building	30.4
School building	25.1
Hotel or other commercial building	11.4
Place of work	8.3
Other	7.7
Private home	6.7
Church	4.9
Community Center[a]	4.6
Not reported	.9

[a]Includes libraries and museums.
Source: Boaz, 1978, p. 27.

learning centers, in part because these groups tend to favor "noncollege" subject matter, such as vocational or recreational topics, but also perhaps because their lack of college experience makes them uncomfortable on a college campus.

Somewhat surprising is the finding of most preference surveys that work sites, which seem to offer exceptional convenience, are not perceived more often as attractive places to learn. Work locations typically attract between 5 and 15 percent of those interested in learning—at least, such is the finding of the statewide needs assessments. In a special study of the interests of blue-collar workers, however, Botsman (1975b) found that 57 percent of the respondents indicated that the most favored place of learning was on the job. It is possible that this great disparity regarding site preferences between state needs assessments and Botsman's study is attributable more to the context in which the questions were asked (work site versus home) and to conceptions about subject matter (job training versus learning for personal use) than to major differences in populations of respondents (blue collar versus others). Botsman (1975a) found that the profile of learning interests of blue-collar workers is indistinguishable from the profiles of people in the general population with equal educational backgrounds.

When attention is directed to overall rankings, the range and diversity of location preferences may be obscured. Few of the studies reviewed showed a majority of respondents favoring any particular site. While school buildings are typically the most popular locations, frequently more than half of the respondents prefer other locations, and the diversity is even greater if people are asked about sites they are willing to use. Most studies find that potential learners with at least a high school diploma are amenable to a greater variety of educational sites than their less well-educated peers. In addition, the proportion who say that site makes no difference rises with educational level. Perhaps if educated learners blaze the "credibility" trail for more convenient locations, which in the abstract most adults insist they want, *where* one learns will become less important than *what* one learns.

Preferred Scheduling. The oldest, and still one of the most common, modifications of education to accommodate the special needs of adult part-time learners is scheduling learning activities at times when adults are free to participate. The rather simple idea of the evening college has been expanded now to incorporate a vast array of scheduling possibilities. Whether the sponsor of the learning activity is a conventional educational institution, a community agency, an employer, or an informal learning group, there is a definable group of scheduling options, which can be categorized as follows: daytime hours, evening hours, block scheduling (ranging from weekends to a residential week or summer), or self-paced or self-determined scheduling (for example, correspondence courses).

Scheduling probably deserves much more attention than it has received to date. Problems with scheduling are cited as barriers to continuing education by between 15 and 25 percent of all adults expressing an interest in continued learning. Unlike most other conditions of learning, where weakly motivated learners cite the most barriers, strongly motivated learners seem to have the greatest problems with scheduling (Cross and Zusman, 1979)—perhaps because they are more likely to have investigated their options or perhaps because they tend to be professional people with crowded and irregular work schedules. In Massachusetts (Nolfi and Nelson, 1973) 70 percent of those enrolled in evening colleges chose their programs primarily because of convenient scheduling. Program flexibility with respect to scheduling, location, and self-pacing was named as a prime attraction by 62 to 98 percent of the students in the non-traditional college programs examined by Medsker and colleagues (1975). Not only do adults give high priority to scheduling convenience in choosing a program; they also stay away from learning opportunities because of unattractive scheduling options. The self-directed learners studied by Penland (1977), for example, ranked the desire to determine their own learning schedule and pace as the most important reasons for learning on their own rather than taking a course.

Unfortunately, the scheduling options usually offered by survey researchers are limited (morning, evening, or weekend hours) and generally provider biased; that is, they are designed to find out how "classes" can be scheduled to attract or serve the largest number of learners. Rarely do they inquire about self-paced learning preferences or about block scheduling or about other options that would require major structural changes in traditional education. Nevertheless, within the limited survey options offered, there is consistency in the findings. Evening hours are preferred by from 40 to 60 percent of the respondents. Ranking second in scheduling preference are mornings, which are usually popular with those not in the labor market, especially young people and retired people. Rather unpopular with most survey respondents is weekend scheduling. Although there appear to be many extremely successful weekend colleges, the idea of devoting a weekend to scheduled learning activities typically appeals to fewer than 10 percent of the survey respondents (Cross and Zusman, 1979). Part of the resistance to weekend scheduling may be due to a desire to preserve weekends for leisure and family activities, but the spread-out learning that typifies evening colleges (one to three hours per class period) is also frequently perceived as more desirable than the compressed learning (ten to twenty hours at once) of weekend programs (Hoyt, 1975). Most people still think of learning as "courses" dispensed in fifty-minute doses.

Few studies asked respondents whether they would be willing to schedule learning activities in concentrated sessions during summer vacation months or several times a year. Block scheduling is used successfully as one component of nontraditional programs such as Britain's Open University, the University of Oklahoma's Bachelor of Liberal Studies program, and the extremely successful Elderhostel. However, in those studies which did give respondents the option of such schedules, very few desired them; in the Commission on Non-traditional Study survey, for example, only 2 percent indicated that their first choice would be to learn for short, full-time periods during the summer (Carp, Peterson, and Roelfs, 1974). Summer schedules, like weekend schedules, may not offer convenience for adults with continuous home and job responsibilities. Furthermore, most adults apparently do not want learning activities to interfere with valued leisure time, whether on weekends or during vacation periods.

A final alternative is the student-determined schedule. Many adults, especially those with lower levels of educational attainment, question their own ability to maintain self-discipline under a self-determined schedule. Yet we know that highly motivated learners—such as those working on their own self-directed projects—do not regard self-determined scheduling as a problem and, in fact, consider it a substantial advantage. Self-determined schedules seem to work best under conditions of high motivation and clearly defined objectives.

In summary, the evening schedules offered by evening divisions and adult schools appear to meet adult needs for scheduling modifications reasonably well—if one is thinking of rather standard education in the classroom format. However, almost any scheduling convenience that has been offered to adult learners has been eagerly accepted, and programs that are scheduled for the convenience of adult learners have enjoyed considerable competitive advantage in recent years. For traditional institutions of education, however, scheduling is one of the most difficult changes to make because it is a structural change that requires almost everyone from registrar to teacher to do his job differently. (See Cross, 1979b, for a discussion of the pedagogical problems with the fixed time boundaries of traditional education.)

Survey Data: Conclusions. The data from the recent spate of surveys make adult learners appear very conservative in their educational desires. The writings of adult educators notwithstanding, survey responses suggest that large numbers of adults would be satisfied with authoritative lectures delivered by teachers in school and college classrooms at times when working people can attend. Yet experience with adults does not confirm such conservatism. Most of the alternative forms of education that have been offered by imaginative educators in recent years are eagerly accepted by adult learners. Why, then, we might ask, are survey respondents so likely to say they want the traditional and yet sign up for the nontraditional? One reason that must be recognized by anyone designing or interpreting surveys is that surveys are necessarily based on current perceptions and understandings. They are better at telling what is than what might be. It was, after all, only after the electric refrigerator was invented by someone who saw a need not recognized by consumers that a refrigerator became a nearly universal need. Education, like any other enterprise, will probably make progress not solely through responding to "consumer demand" but through being creative and imaginative in developing better ways to teach and to learn.

The point to be made in this overview of survey data is that these findings, when combined with other data, experience, and thoughtful interpretation, are useful in expanding our understanding of how adults learn or would like to learn. We should be cautious, however, about using the data directly to develop learning components into programs for adults—a procedure becoming alarmingly popular among educators conducting "needs assessments" and among legislators requiring evidence of "demand." Educators responding to "demand" as revealed in surveys may find themselves selling the ice box that the learner remembered rather than the refrigerator that the learner wants.

CHAPTER 9

Facilitating Learning

There are pessimists and optimists about where we stand in the 1980s regarding theories of learning in adult education. Of the major writers, Knowles is probably the most optimistic about the current status of theory development. He contends (1978, p. 51) that most of the elements required for a comprehensive theory of adult learning have been discovered and that "andragogy" is the "unifying theory" that can provide the "glue to bind the diverse institutions, clienteles, and activities [of adult education] into some sense of unity." The pessimistic view is probably best expressed by Miller (1967, p. 1): "It is presumptuous to talk . . . about theory building; like most fields of educational research, we are very far from ready for that advanced activity." Although Knowles' optimism comes a decade after Miller's pessimism, I doubt that the difference in perception can be attributed solely to notable progress in theory building during the 1970s.

Chapter Five discussed some of the reasons for the lack of attention to theory in adult education: the enormous diver-

220

sity of adult learning situations, the practitioner domination of
the field, the market orientation of nonsubsidized education,
and, frankly, the lack of desire or perceived need for theory.
Houle (1972, p. 6) observes: "It cannot be said that most of the
work in the field is guided by any . . . system or even by the
desire to follow a systematic theory. The typical career worker
in adult education is still concerned only with an institutional
pattern of service or a methodology, seldom or never catching a
glimpse of the total terrain of which he is cultivating one cor-
ner, and content to be, for example, a farm or home adviser,
museum curator, public librarian, or industrial trainer."

Houle has probably put his finger on the major problem
in developing theory useful in guiding research on teaching and
learning and in formulating systematic guidelines for practice.
Theory broad enough to cover the spectrum of learning situations in adult education is necessarily so broad that it offers
little guidance to either researchers or practitioners. What sort
of theory would be useful—and theory should be useful—to the
disparate learning situations of industrial trainers, YMCA recreation directors, and extension faculty? With all the emphasis
today on self-directed learning, even the notion of a theory for
"teaching" adults is offensive to many.

Ideally, it would seem desirable to conceptualize a framework broad enough to cover almost any situation in adult education, and then depend on a subsequent army of theorists and
researchers to develop the specifics appropriate for the various
classes of situations—one set of principles for group work,
another for media, another for classroom instruction, and so on.
Houle (1972) developed a system that would cover most situations in adult education, but there seems to be no army of aca-
demicians in adult education with the time, interest, and background in research and theory waiting to fill in the cells. While
Houle carefully calls his master design a "system" rather than a
theory, the system presents a framework for analyzing the
learning process in various situations.

Another possible approach to theory development would
be to start with a class of learning situations—say, on-the-job
training or classroom instruction—and attempt to develop some

useful principles about the interactions of teachers and students in such situations, making clear that the concern is with only a small piece of adult education. The problem with this approach is that, even if professionals working in similar situations could develop principles useful to their situation, it would be difficult to fit the separate schemes into an overall framework later—assuming that people think there is, or should be, a common core of knowledge useful to educators working with adults. In any event, and for whatever reasons, little effort has been made to develop conceptualizations that would guide research and practice for specific learning situations.

A third approach is to try to figure out what is unique and distinctive about adults as learners and then to build a theory of adult learning by contrasting adult learners with children as learners. The problem with this approach is that some claim there is no evidence that the process of learning is different for adults than for children. Nevertheless, if adult education is a distinctive field of study at all, it is *adult* learners who make it so, and one of the best-known theories in adult education begins with the assumption that learning for adults (andragogy) is basically different from learning for children (pedagogy). Because andragogy has a long history and a substantial following in adult education, it will be useful to present a brief description of it here and to attempt to assess its usefulness as unifying theory for adult learning.

Andragogy as Theory

The use of the word *andragogy* has been traced back as far as 1833, but Malcolm Knowles is generally credited with the popularization of the term and the concept in the United States. Knowles (1970, p. 38) defines andragogy as "the art and science of helping adults learn" and contrasts it with "pedagogy," which is concerned with helping children learn. According to Knowles (1970, p. 39),

Andragogy is premised on at least four crucial assumptions about the characteristics of adult learners that are different from the assumptions about child learners, on which traditional pedagogy is premised. These assumptions are that, as a person matures, (1) his self-concept moves from one of being a dependent personality toward one of being a self-directing human being, (2) he accumulates a growing reservoir of experience that becomes an increasing resource for learning, (3) his readiness to learn becomes oriented increasingly to the developmental tasks of his social roles, and (4) his time perspective changes from one of postponed application of knowledge to immediacy of application, and accordingly his orientation toward learning shifts from one of subject centeredness to one of problem centeredness.

Table 19 presents a summary of the basic differences between pedagogy and andragogy as Knowles and others have developed it.

Although the word *andragogy* makes a neat contrast with the more familiar and traditional *pedagogy,* the contrast appears difficult to maintain. In his major book setting forth the theses of andragogy, Knowles (1970, pp. 38-39) writes: "I believe that andragogy means more than just helping adults learn; I believe that it means helping human beings learn, and that it therefore has implications for the education of children and youth." Knowles, however, refers frequently in his writings to the "*unique* characteristics of adults as learners" and to andragogy as a "comprehensive theory of *adult* learning" (1978, p. 28; emphases added). Thus, it is not really clear whether Knowles is advocating two distinct approaches to teaching—one for children and a different one for adults—or whether he is suggesting that andragogy should replace pedagogy as a sounder approach to the education of both children and adults. In the latter event, we no longer have a theory of *adult* learning but, rather, a theory of instruction purporting to offer guidance to teachers in general.

Knowles' use of subtitles such as "Farewell to Pedagogy" (1970, p. 37) and "The Millstone of Pedagogy" (1978, p. 53) suggests that andragogy should replace pedagogy for both children and adults. However, in a recent clarification of the

Table 19. Comparison of Assumptions and Designs of Pedagogy and Andragogy

	Assumptions	
	Pedagogy	*Andragogy*
Self-concept	Dependency	Increasing self-directiveness
Experience	Of little worth	Learners are a rich resource for learning
Readiness	Biological development, social pressure	Developmental tasks of social roles
Time perspective	Postponed application	Immediacy of application
Orientation to learning	Subject centered	Problem centered

	Design Elements	
	Pedagogy	*Andragogy*
Climate	Authority oriented, formal, competitive	Mutuality, respectful, collaborative, informal
Planning	By teacher	Mechanism for mutual planning
Diagnosis of needs	By teacher	Mutual self-diagnosis
Formulation of objectives	By teacher	Mutual negotiation
Design	Logic of the subject matter; content units	Sequenced in terms of readiness; problem units
Activities	Transmittal techniques	Experiential techniques (inquiry)
Evaluation	By teacher	Mutual rediagnosis of needs; mutual measurement of program

Source: Knowles, 1978, p. 110.

assumptions of andragogy, Knowles (1979) acknowledges that
it would have been preferable to recognize the continuity of
human development by using the subtitle "From Pedagogy to
Andragogy" rather than "Andragogy Versus Pedagogy," which
implies a dichotomy between childhood and adulthood. The
problem is that a continuum from pedagogy to andragogy really
does not exist. Although some andragogical assumptions (such
as experience) lie on a continuum, others (such as problem-
centered versus subject-centered learning) appear more dichotomous in nature.

    Although in promoting andragogy Knowles is attempting
to meet a quite legitimate need—the need to provide a viable
alternative to traditional "school-like" education—it seems
exceptionally difficult to devise a workable definition of
andragogy. In what may be considered, for the present at least,
a summary statement on andragogy and pedagogy, Knowles
(1979, p. 53) says: "So I am not saying that pedagogy is for
children and andragogy for adults, since some pedagogical
assumptions are realistic for adults in some situations and some
andragogical assumptions are realistic for children in some situations. And I am certainly not saying that pedagogy is bad and
andragogy is good; each is appropriate given the relevant
assumptions." Thus, the current position seems to be that
andragogy consists of a different set of assumptions from pedagogy but that it is neither uniquely suited to adults nor superior
to more traditional education. While Knowles, as the foremost
spokesman for andragogy in the United States, has performed a
valuable service to the profession in at least setting forth a plan
for critique and test in an otherwise barren field, the usefulness
of andragogy as a set of guiding assumptions for adult education
is at present up in the air.

    A spirited exchange carried on in the pages of *Adult Edu-
cation* shows just how up in the air it is. The confusion starts
with the nature of andragogy. There is the question of whether
andragogy is a learning theory (Knowles, 1978), a philosophical
position (McKenzie, 1977), a political reality (Carlson, 1979),
or a set of hypotheses subject to scientific verification (Elias,
1979). McKenzie argues that, until andragogy is subjected to

philosophical analysis, the proponents and opponents of andragogy will continue to "address the issue as if they were sitting around a cracker barrel" (p. 228). He contends that those who see no difference in the education of children and adults base their arguments in classical metaphysics, whereas the supporters of andragogy are approaching the question from the perspective of phenomenology. While McKenzie admits that intelligent and reflective educators can be found on both sides of the issue, he is convinced that there is support for andragogy in more sophisticated philosophical analyses.

Carlson (1979, p. 55) thinks that analysis should proceed along political lines, on the grounds that the legal and educational rights of children are different from those of adults: "Politically it makes sense to set an age—be it 12, 16, 18, 21, or 25—when one is considered an adult with the rights and responsibilities of an adult. Whatever age the society establishes politically for adulthood is a reasonable age for most members of that society to shift from engagement in pedagogy (education of children) to involvement in andragogy (adult education). To allow educators to 'teach' adults on social psychological guidelines alone, including learning theory and socialization theory, is a political act, in my view an unwise political act." The dichotomy that Carlson wishes to maintain is probably more accurately between compulsory and voluntary learning than between children and adults, but the point is that the dichotomy is politically determined.

Elias (1979) takes the position familiar to most social scientists, contending that if andragogy is educational theory it should be validated on the basis of empirical evidence, and he concludes that the assumptions of andragogy have little or no support from research. His interpretation of the evidence is that andragogy "has been a helpful slogan in the adult education movement. But it is not to be taken seriously as education theory" (p. 255).

Still another interpretation question is raised by Kidd (1973, p. 23), who suggests that the appropriate contrast in adult education is not between children and adults but between teaching and learning. He contrasts pedagogy (the science of teaching) with *mathetics,* which he defines as "the science of pupil's behavior while learning, just as pedagogy is the discipline in which attention is focused on the schoolmaster's behavior while teaching." That position is appealing to most adult educators, who understandably wish to capitalize on the ability of adult learners to assume more responsibility for their learning than is possible with schoolchildren. The literature, as well as the practice, of adult education tends to be learner centered rather than instructor centered. Indeed, many adult educators are uncomfortable with the very concept of "instruction" because it suggests that the management of the learning situation is controlled—some would say manipulated—by someone other than the learner. They want to invest the controls in the hands of the learner. Thus, Kidd's call for a science that would help us understand how learners learn instead of how teachers teach seems appropriate enough. The problem is that, if an educator wants to know how to help a learner learn, he needs to know how teachers should behave in order to facilitate learning. That seems to suggest that we *do* need a theory of teaching—or at least a theory for facilitating learning.

   Gage (1972, p. 19) discusses the relationship between theories of learning and theories of teaching in this lucid passage: "Teaching becomes the process of providing for the learner what a given learning theory regards as essential. For the conditioning theorists, the teacher must provide cues for a given response and reinforcement of that response. For the modeling theorist, the teacher must provide a model to be observed and imitated. For the cognitive theorist, the teacher must provide a cognitive structure or the stimuli that will produce one." Against that description, andragogy is probably closer to a theory of teaching than to a theory of learning, since it consists largely of suggestions to teachers of adults about what they can do to help adults learn.

   Whether andragogy can serve as the foundation for a unifying theory of adult education remains to be seen. At the very least, it identifies some characteristics of adult learners that deserve attention. It has been far more successful than most theory in gaining the attention of practitioners, and it has been

moderately successful in sparking debate; it has not been especially successful, however, in stimulating research to test the
assumptions. Most important, perhaps, the visibility of andragogy has heightened awareness of the need for answers to
three major questions: (1) Is it useful to distinguish the learning
needs of adults from those of children? If so, are we talking
about dichotomous differences or continuous differences? Or
both? (2) What are we really seeking: Theories of learning?
Theories of teaching? Both? (3) Do we have, or can we develop,
an initial framework on which successive generations of scholars
can build? Does andragogy lead to researchable questions that
will advance knowledge in adult education?

Humanistic Theories

The environment of adult education is, by history and
structure, more accepting and less authoritarian than conventional education. Traditionally, adult education has regarded
learners as volunteers. (For a discussion of the growing trend
toward compulsory education for adults, see Chapter Two.)
They learn whatever they want to learn without faculty committees' determining whether or not it meets externally imposed standards, and there are no grades or examinations to
serve as rewards or punishments. That environment springs
largely from humanistic theories of learning.

The humanist assumes that there is a natural tendency for
people to learn and that learning will flourish if nourishing, encouraging environments are provided. Implementing humanistic
theory in the learning society would mean providing multiple
options of people, resources, and materials; making them freely
available to everyone; helping learners to think through what
they want to learn and how they want to learn it; and making
few value judgments about the nature or quality of the learning
experiences.

There is considerable support for this theory in the research of Allen Tough on self-directed learners. Tough has demonstrated that there is indeed a natural tendency for adults to

learn—90 percent or more of them do so. Although Tough and others interested in self-directed learning have made little effort to relate their research findings to any theory, their approach to the accumulation of knowledge is to find out how people learn and what they choose to learn when they direct their own learning. That is basically a humanistic orientation, since the implication is that educators should try to enhance or facilitate the natural learning process without imposing their will on the direction that learning should take. The UNESCO report, *Learning to Be* (Faure and others, 1972), is another example of the strong humanistic influence in adult education. The authors recommend that educational activities should be centered on the learner in order to allow him "greater and greater freedom, as he matures, to decide for himself what he wants to learn and how and where he wants to learn it" (p. 220). Learning contracts, as they are utilized by Empire State College and other nontraditional colleges established specifically for adult learners, also reflect humanist traditions; the learner is presumably in a better position than anyone else to plan an appropriate learning program.

Developmental Theories

Another theoretical position that seems compatible with the environment of adult education is that of the developmentalists. As we have seen (Chapter Seven), some developmentalists see the various stages and phases of human development as an inevitable unfolding of predetermined patterns. While the environment may influence the *rate* of growth, it has little effect on form and sequence. Other developmentalists place more emphasis on the role of the environment in shaping growth. They are interactionists, who believe that education can play a critical role in "pulling" the individual into ever higher levels of development. Where environmental stimulation is lacking, the individual may stagnate at lower levels of development. Some developmentalists take the position that difficulties will occur if a given phase of development does not emerge "on time." Others, most commonly those concerned about stages of development, take the position that rates of development show extreme variation. Indeed, most people never reach the highest stages of development. While the order of succession is common for all people, some people may pass through two stages of development in a lifetime, whereas others may pass through nine or ten stages.

Developmental interactionists are not as willing to suspend judgment as humanists are. While they too would give considerable attention to creating an environment rich in educational resources and encouragement, they would take a more active role in deciding what kinds of learning experiences are most likely to advance the individual to the next stage of growth. They would emphasize challenge and stimulation in the environment, whereas humanists would stress acceptance and encouragement. Despite some differences in the importance attached to environmental factors, developmentalists subscribe to four basic presuppositions: (1) Each stage of development is an integrated whole. (2) A particular stage is integrated into the next stage and finally replaced by it. (3) Each individual acts out his own syntheses; he does not merely adopt a synthesis provided by family or society. (4) The individual must pass through all previous stages before he can move on to the next stage. Thus, the order of succession of stages is constant and universal (Craig, 1974).

As we have seen (Chapter Seven), there is plenty of support in the research literature for theoretical positions with respect to both phases and stages of adult development. Common plateaus have been demonstrated, transition points identified, and sequences documented. Moreover, research supports the notion that environmental challenges provide times when adults are especially receptive to new learning. Aslanian and Brickell (1980) found that the stimulation and challenge of the inevitable transitions in life—marriage, job changes, retirement, and so on—account for most adult learning. The findings from this study would lead us to conclude that adults learn not so much because it is "natural" for human beings to learn, a humanist position, but because transitions are an inevitable part of life, and change creates the challenges and stimulation that promote learning, and therefore development.

Challenge and stimulation are inevitable conditions of life, but they can also be deliberately invoked. Perry (1970, p. 35) illustrates from his research how a good teacher can help college students advance to the next stage of intellectual development through challenge:

> We gather from what our students have told us that the educational impact of diversity can be at its best when it is deliberate. When a teacher asks his students to read conflicting authorities and then asks them to assess the nature and meaning of the conflict, he is in a strong position to assist them to go beyond simple diversity into the disciplines of relativity of thought through which specific instances of diversity can be productively exploited. He can teach the relation, the relativism, of one system of thought to another. In short, he can teach disciplined independence of mind. . . . Henry Adams said that if he were ever to do college lecturing again it would be in the company of an assistant professor whose sole duty would be to present to the students an opposite point of view.

The role of the teacher (or facilitator) in the Perry scheme is to help the individual advance to the next level of cognitive development through designing educational experiences that will challenge the learner to "reach" for growth-enhancing cognitive experiences.

Another variation on the developmental theme is represented in Mezirow's (1978) concept of perspective transformation—a term he uses to suggest that, at some point, new learning is not just additive to what we already know but, rather, transforms existing knowledge to bring about a new perspective. One of the most significant aspects of adult learning, in Mezirow's view, is that "we are caught in our own history and are reliving it. . . . New experience is assimilated to—and transformed by—one's past experience" (p. 101). Such learning is different in kind from most school learning, and it is developmental in orientation. Mezirow cites the consciousness-raising experiences of the women's movement as an example of perspective transformation. In such learning, women—and men—come to perceive the role of women in society in a different light. Freire (1970) uses the term *conscientization* to describe the new level of awareness that occurred as villagers in rural Brazil and Chile became aware that they had options and could make choices about things that they had formerly seen as beyond their control.

Although Mezirow is primarily concerned about the role of perspective transformation in personal growth, the concept can also be applied in more academic learning situations. Most academics have had experiences where something "clicked" and the learning changed suddenly from additive learning to transformed learning, in which the subject was seen from a new perspective. Most creative thought seems to be of this nature. It is not that the individual with the new idea knows more content than anyone else but, rather, that he or she has put it together in new ways that transformed an idea.

Behaviorism

While behaviorist positions of learning sometimes seem at odds with the well-publicized, student-centered attitudes of many adult educators, behaviorism is frequently the foundation for one of the largest segments of adult education, namely job and skills training. Many of the self-instructional packages prevalent in occupational and professional programs are direct applications of theories formulated by behaviorists. Such learning materials usually have the following characteristics, as Srinivasan (1977, p. 12) notes:

1. Objectives must be clearly stated in specific and measurable behavioral terms.
2. The learning tasks must be analytically designed in relation to desired end behaviors.
3. Content must be broken into small steps which are easy to master. These steps must be designed to encourage self-instruction and require an overt response by the learner (for example, filling in the blanks or selecting a response from multiple options.)
4. The materials should provide a means for immediate feedback so that the learner will know if his response

was correct and so that he can be aware of the pace of his progress.

5. The subject matter and activities must adhere to a set sequence and process conducive to mastery.
6. The successful completion of each step and the chain of steps must provide its own reward or incentive.
7. The responsibility for ensuring that learning takes place must rest with the materials themselves as learning instruments and not with any instructor, leader, or helper.

Programmed instruction, computer-assisted instruction, personalized systems of instruction (PSI) and other applications of behaviorism have been growing rapidly in traditional education (see Cross, 1976), and their convenience for off-campus learners plus their general effectiveness with well-motivated, self-disciplined adults makes them likely candidates for growth in adult education as well.

Although variations on the theme of programmed instruction are dramatic applications of behaviorism, the general principles of behaviorism are present in most skills training where the learning task is broken into segments or tasks and there is a "correct response," which is rewarded. Such reward, according to behaviorists, assures learning and repetition of the desired behavior.

Relevance of Existing Learning Theories

This overview of some of the more prevalent learning theories does not pretend to be a comprehensive review of all the theoretical formulations that might contribute to the development of a theory to facilitate adult learning. Indeed, with the exception of andragogy, there is no assumption that the characteristics of the learner need to be considered.

Most existing learning theories are more easily applied to *what* is learned than to *who* is doing the learning. Whereas it would be foolish to argue that adults should be approached with humanistic, behavioristic, or developmental learning theories, it does make sense to argue that, generally speaking, humanistic theory appears relevant to learning self-understanding; behaviorism seems useful in teaching practical skills; and developmental theory has much to offer to goals of teaching ego, intellectual, or moral development. Thus, the theoretical orientation of teachers may be related more to the characteristics of their subject matter than to the characteristics of their students. I believe, however, that the profession of adult education will be advanced if adult educators are encouraged to think about the special characteristics of adult learners and the context in which learning takes place. As the research review in Chapters Seven and Eight suggests, there is now a great deal of research information about the learning processes, practices, and preferences of adults and about developmental stages and phases. The problem is that investigators in these different areas all follow completely separate lines of investigation. With the possible exception of stage and phase research, there is almost never any attempt to relate one stream of research findings to any other. Maybe there should not be, but if the ultimate goal is to facilitate the learning of adults, then adult educators will have to merge all these streams of research and theory into their own practice—or the field as a whole will have to attempt some synthesis.

I offer the following model as *a* tentative framework to accommodate current knowledge about what we know about adults as learners, in the hope that it may suggest ideas for further research and for implementation. I shall simply call the following framework CAL—Characteristics of Adults as Learners. The explicit purpose of CAL is to elucidate differences between adults and children as learners and ultimately to suggest how teaching adults should differ from teaching children—basically the position of andragogy. CAL is a bare-bones, rather than a comprehensive, model, since at this early stage of development the skeletal structure will be more evident if it is not fleshed out with details.[1]

[1] It should be obvious that no "new" formulation is without great debt to the past, and my debt to past researchers, theoreticians, and practitioners is intentionally great. The hope is to build on past and present knowledge to the maximum extent possible.

Characteristics of Adults as Learners (CAL):
A Conceptual Framework

The CAL model, shown in Figure 5, consists of two classes of variables. Those describing the learner are called *per-*

Figure 5. Characteristics of Adults as Learners (CAL)

Personal Characteristics

— — — — — — —▶Physiological/Aging — — — — — — — —▶
— — — — — —▶ Sociocultural/Life Phases — — — — — — —▶
— — — —▶Psychological/Developmental Stages — — — — —▶

Situational Characteristics

Part-Time Learning Versus Full-Time Learning
Voluntary Learning Versus Compulsory Learning

sonal characteristics, whereas those describing the conditions under which learning takes place are called *situational character-istics.* Two characteristics sharply differentiate the learning *situation* of the adult from that of the child or adolescent; adults are typically part-time learners, and they are usually volunteers. Although the situational variables of CAL are not quite as discrete as they appear on the surface, they are usually expressed as dichotomies: part-time versus full-time learning and voluntary versus compulsory learning. The personal variables of CAL, in contrast, are almost always considered continuous. They represent the gradual growth of children into adults and are expressed as growth or developmental continua along three dimensions: physical, psychological, and sociocultural. These dimensions correspond roughly to the research dimensions reviewed in Chapter Seven.

Personal Characteristics. We now know something about the physiological correlates of aging, about the stages of ego and other forms of personal development, and about the phases of the life cycle in our culture. I am not going to argue, in this initial framework, the relative weights of internal and external influences in personal and phasic development. Most phasic researchers support some measure of internal unfolding, influenced by sociocultural factors. Most stage theory posits internal unfolding, influenced by personal and educational experience. And, of course, almost everyone accepts the notion of a universal sequence in physiological aging, influenced by health practices and health care. Given our present state of knowledge, then, we can assume some form of underlying, predetermined code of human development that is relatively impervious to external influence. Educators can do little to change the inner code; but, understanding it, they can adapt to it, capitalize on it when desirable, and compensate for it when necessary. To take the simplest example, educators cannot do much about physiological aging. Knowing its cycle, however, they can capitalize on the growing strength of crystallized intelligence with age or on the rising interest in nutrition on the part of the elderly. They can compensate for the decline in reaction time by stressing power rather than speed in learning, and they can adapt to declines in vision by making sure that illumination is adequate for learners past middle age (see Chapter Seven for research evidence).

Each of the personal characteristics continua has a different shape as far as education is concerned. Physiological aging and life phases are both related to chronological age. But the physiological dimension would show a smooth rising curve up to roughly the 20s, a slowly declining curve to somewhere around the age of 60, and a more sharply declining curve thereafter—depending, of course, on which functions are being graphed. As the research in Chapter Seven shows, the graph for vision has a little different shape from that for hearing. In general, a graph of life phases, while also generally related to age, would consist of a series of plateaus separated by transitions. Although one phase leads to another and is incorporated into it, one life phase is not higher or better than another, only more appropriate for a given age. Thus, the life-phase continuum is essentially horizontal. Developmental stages, in the opinion of current researchers, are not necessarily related to age but, like life phases, show a pattern of plateaus and transitions. In this case, however, succeeding stages are higher—that is, show greater growth or maturity—than preceding stages, and so the developmental stage continuum has a vertical dimension to the plateaus and transitions. The shape of the three continua in the CAL model might look something like those depicted in Figure 6.

Figure 6. Characteristics of Adults as Learners (CAL):
Personal Characteristics Schemata

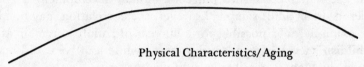

Physical Characteristics/Aging

Sociocultural Characteristics/Life Phases

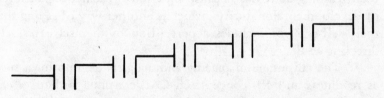

Psychological Characteristics/Developmental Stages

In the CAL model, the position of an individual on the physiological and life-phase dimensions is to some extent a function of chronological age. A 25 year old, for example, is typically physically vigorous, somewhat stronger in fluid than in

crystallized intelligence, ready to perceive himself or herself as
an adult, and in the process of building for the future (see Chapter Seven). Knowing chronological age tells us something about
the position of the learner on the physiological continuum and
in the phases of the life cycle.

While developmental-stage researchers deny an age relationship, most would probably admit that a child is generally
incapable of the highest forms of ego or cognitive development;
hence, there is some relationship between developmental stage
and age when the entire range of human development is considered. In an adult sample, however, the correlation may be nil;
for example, it is possible for a 50-year-old adult to remain at a
"childish" level of ego development, while a 30 year old may
attain the highest possible level of ego maturity.

Some of the assumptions of andragogy can be incorporated into these CAL continua. Readiness, for example, appears to be largely a function of the sociocultural continuum of
life phases (see Table 8, Chapter Seven). The implication is that
educators should capitalize on the "teachable moments" presented by the developmental tasks of the life cycle. A 60 year
old, for example, is "ready" to learn about retirement, about
the aging process, and about mellowing personal relationships.
Self-concept, another andragogical assumption, would be
aligned with the developmental-stage continuum in CAL. Adults
at the higher levels of ego, moral, or cognitive development are
able to assume increasing responsibility for the direction of
their learning activities because they have reached higher levels
of developmental maturity—which is another way of saying that
their self-concept includes a perception of themselves as self-
directing adults.

The advantage of placing andragogical assumptions, such
as readiness and self-concept, on CAL continua is that we can
now account for the low level of self-direction on the part of
some adults. The andragogical assumption that calls for treating
adults as though they are self-directing while children are not—
or at least treating adults as though they are *more* self-directing
than children—flies in the face of the experience of many teachers who have worked with dependent adults and independent

children. The CAL model calls for considering self-concept a function of developmental growth rather than a matter of childhood versus adulthood. Similarly, the assumption of readiness, interpreted as motivation for learning tasks associated with the life cycle, is placed on a sociocultural continuum which is related to age or at least to societal expectations regarding age-appropriate behaviors.

Educators need to think somewhat differently about each of the personal characteristics in the CAL model. The physiological continuum calls for an educational stance that is largely adaptive and adjustive. Physical aging, for instance, requires careful attention to transportation and delivery systems, greater illumination, less auditory confusion in the classroom, slower speech in presenting new ideas, and so forth (see Chapter Seven). While educational adaptation to the physiological continuum is usually stated in *compensatory* terms, educators can also accept what is and *capitalize* on it. For example, traditional education consistently fails to capitalize on wisdom and life experience; most school learning tasks are designed to emphasize fluid rather than crystallized intelligence. Research suggests, however, that adult educators should give relatively more attention to designing educational tasks that call for crystallized intelligence (see Chapter Seven). Crystallized intelligence is not only a valuable asset to society; it is also a type of intelligence that is especially characteristic of more mature learners with some experience to their years. Thus, "adaptation" to the physiological processes of aging can, in many cases, be treated as active "capitalization." By using the words *adaptive* and *adjustive* to describe the primary educative roles on the physiological dimension, I do not intend to imply educator passivity. Most adaptation requires a knowledgeable, creative response to a given situation. And aging presents "a given situation" that needs to be programmed into educational activities for adults.

The educator's role on the sociocultural continuum of CAL is also adaptive and adjustive, this time with the emphasis on adjustment. One of the challenges of the life-cycle dimension is adjustment to new life phases for adults. There is considerable evidence that the transition points in the life cycle generate especially high motivation for learning (Aslanian and Brickell, 1980; Havighurst, 1972). Because the greatest opportunities for learning occur at transition points, the educator's stance on this dimension is adjustive in the sense that educators who understand the life phase being left behind and the one to come can design learning experiences to aid in the transition to a new phase of the life cycle. Once again, I should caution that the word *adjustive* does not imply passivity on the part of the educator. To help an adult make an active transition to new and unfamiliar territory is a challenging and creative educational task, calling for deep understanding of the research and considerable sensitivity to individual situations.

There are differences in opinion about what the educative stance should be with respect to the developmental-stage continuum. My personal evaluation of the theory and research convinces me that the role of the educator on this continuum of CAL should be described as *challenger*. If one accepts a hierarchy of developmental stages, and if one believes that the role of educators is to help each individual develop to the highest possible level, then the role of educators is to challenge the learner to move to increasingly advanced stages of personal development. This may mean creating the motivation for learning through making the learner uncomfortable in her present assumptions. She is thus forced to examine her present assumptions and to redefine and reshape them at increasingly higher levels of development.

Notice that the same educator operating across all three continua might create a warm and accepting environment on the physiological dimension; a cooperative, adventuresome environment on the life-phase continuum; and a challenging environment for stimulating developmental growth on the developmental-stage continuum. The problem for implementation arises when the same educator (used in the broad sense of anyone facilitating learning) must consider all three dimensions at once for a diverse group of adult learners. However, that probably is not as difficult in practice as it is conceptually. Most adult educators operate intuitively on all three levels of adult development without articulating which educational tasks call for which approaches. But progress in providing improved education for adults will be made only when it is possible to articulate and analyze the elements that go into effective practice. The CAL model provides one possible framework in which to organize and interrelate present knowledge and to identify research gaps where more knowledge is needed.

Situational Characteristics. The situational variables of the CAL model are usually treated as dichotomous because they differentiate adult education from education for children more sharply than other variables, and they provide much of the flavor and distinction of adult education. Strictly speaking, however, neither part-time versus full-time study nor voluntary versus compulsory learning are true dichotomies. Part-time learners can merge into full-time learners statistically when they cross the magic boundary of twelve credit hours or some other equally arbitrary figure. Nevertheless, there is a common understanding that the major "full-time" responsibility of children and adolescents is "going to school," whereas for adults commitment to job and family is the primary full-time responsibility, and participation in adult education is a secondary (part-time) commitment. One could, I suppose, call the variable "primary" versus "secondary" commitment to learning, but that seems to suggest that learning is less important for adults than for children, which would distort the values of many adult learners. Hence, we shall retain the common, if not quite precise, dichotomy of full-time versus part-time learning as a major situational characteristic of adult learners.

A similar analysis could be applied to the situational category of voluntary versus compulsory learning. There is a common understanding that school is compulsory for children and voluntary for adults. There is, however, a continuum of "voluntariness" in adult learning. Some learning is completely voluntary, as in most of Allen Tough's self-directed learning projects (see Chapters Three and Eight); some is mandated, as in relicensure requirements for nurses and accountants (see Chapter Two); and some falls in between. Some argument could be generated, for example, on how "voluntary" most job-related learning really is. In most cases, the employer does not require employees to update skills or to keep abreast of their field of expertise. Nevertheless, there is coercion present in the knowledge that career mobility is frequently linked to adult learning. Thus, one could conclude that learning is required *if* the adult wants to get ahead on the job. Indeed, part of the argument for lifelong learning is that learning is increasingly a *requirement* for living comfortably and productively in the learning society.

Thus, while some argument can be made for the existence of continua underlying the CAL situational variables, the continua are quite different from those of the personal variables. They do not represent the continuous growth of children into adults; rather, they represent differences in the extent to which the variable operates in the adult learning situation. Some adults are virtually full-time learners, and some are under as much compulsion to learn as children are. In such cases, the common situational characteristics of adult learners cease to distinguish the uniqueness of adults as learners, and the CAL model would call for inactive situational variables—while still giving full consideration to the adult's position on the three personal continua. In short, a full-time adult learner would still be treated differently from a schoolchild because of his or her position on the personal characteristics continua. For the overwhelming majority of adults, however, both personal and situational characteristics would be considered in educational programming.

Most of the research reviewed in Chapter Eight is related to the situational characteristics of voluntary and part-time learning. Survey research, for example, tends to emphasize procedures, schedules, locations, and other administrative arrangements that make it possible for part-time learners, with major adult responsibilities elsewhere, to participate in organized learning activities. The research on self-directed learning is especially relevant to the voluntary nature of adult learning. Indeed, the major reason for the intense interest in research on self-directed learning is precisely because it is largely voluntary.

One of the kingpins of andragogy, the problem-centered orientation of adult learners, would enter the CAL framework largely through the situational variable of voluntary learning. In fact, one of the hypotheses that might be suggested is that learner orientation is problem centered *to the extent* that it is voluntary. As the learning situation moves toward coercion or compulsion, the power to determine what is studied moves from learner to teacher, and learner orientation moves from solving the learner's problem to satisfying the teacher's requirements. A corollary is that the more sharply the learner has defined the problem, the less satisfactory traditional group-oriented education is likely to be. If, for example, a mother has an autistic child, she wants to know how to work with *that* child and is unlikely to be satisfied with a traditional course on child development, or maybe even a course on handicapped children. A teacher studying for certification, on the other hand, may be quite content to study whatever leads to certification.

Implications of the CAL Model. While the CAL model is certainly not simple, it does seem to have the initial advantage of incorporating the major existing theories of *adult* learning (andragogy and developmental-stage and phase theory) into a common framework, and it does provide a mechanism for thinking about a growing, developing human being in the context of the special situations common to part-time volunteer learners. Much of the research on the three personal characteristics continua is ongoing and can be directly inserted into CAL by those studying aging, life cycles, and developmental stages. Similarly, recent research on situational characteristics (most of it since 1970) can be incorporated into CAL, although those lines of inquiry might be more fruitful if they focused not on differences between the learning activities of adults and children but on the effect of part-time commitment and voluntary status of learning.

There are multiple pressures, as we enter the learning society, to blur the historical distinctions between voluntary and compulsory learning, and we need to know how the interests and accomplishments of voluntary adult learners differ from those of adults who are coerced or required to learn. Similarly, the moves toward "recurrent education" for adults tend to press for periods of full-time commitment as opposed to the historical part-time learning situations characteristic of adult learners. Is there something to be gained from full-time immersion in learning that cannot be accomplished through part-time study? In traditional education, there is considerable research now to show that full-time resident college students gain more from their college experience than part-time commuting students do (Astin, 1977; Chickering, 1974). Is this also true for adult learners—or do the positions of mature adults on the personal characteristics continua suggest different conclusions in the case of adults? Realistically, of course, most adults *are* going to be part-time learners, but if that status tends to result in a lower quality of learning, what steps can be taken to provide greater depth and enrichment for part-time students? Do block periods of a summer, a week, or a weekend result in enriched learning experiences? We really do not know the answers to many questions lying within the five dimensions of CAL.

As for research *across* variables in the CAL model, the situation is even worse. If one thinks of the three personal characteristics continua plus the two situational variables as forming the warp of the fabric for understanding adult learners, then some woof is needed to define interrelationships across and between CAL variables. Research combining two or more CAL variables in adult learning appears only sporadically in the literature. There is some work in gerontology, however, which uses "the elderly" as the woof across the warp of physical, psychological, and social aging. Because such theory serves as a fine example of what can be done to work across CAL variables, a brief review of one set of theories about the motivations of the elderly will be given here.

Disengagement theory was first proposed by Cumming and Henry (1961), who argued that the withdrawal of elderly people from the activities of society is not an imposed condition resulting from retirement, poor health, and low income but, rather, is an inevitable, gradual, and mutually satisfying process for both society and older individuals. Disengagement is inevitable because death is inevitable, and the gradual withdrawal of the elderly prevents their death from being disruptive to the equilibrium of society. Society is thus prepared for the death of the older generation and so, goes the argument, is the individual who can face death with relative equanimity having said his "goodbyes" to his responsibilities and engagements with the society (Rose, 1968). In disengagement theory, there is also the implication that preoccupation with self and decreased emotional investment in others on the part of the elderly is indicative of a new and quite normal and productive level of personal development (Havighurst, Neugarten, and Tobin, 1968). To the extent that disengagement theory holds up, it suggests that we may be unwise to attempt to engage the elderly in education and other forms of active participation in society—unless the education were to take the developmental approach, teaching people that disengagement is a healthy response to aging and a part of the developmental scheme for "growing old gracefully."

Disengagement theory, of course, flies directly in the face of the prevailing American "activity theory," which holds that those who age successfully are those who keep active and in touch with the life of the community. Education, under the activity theory, would seek to keep the elderly current and active in the life of the community, through programs carried out in social settings, lectures on current events, discussions of new life styles, participation in recreational learning, and the like.

Somewhere between disengagement theory and activity theory is the "theory of margin" proposed by McClusky (1971). In this theory, "older people are constantly engaged in a struggle to maintain the margin of energy and power they have enjoyed in earlier years" (p. 1). "Margin" refers to keeping one's capacity to deal with life (power) a little in excess of the problems (load). The "theory of margin" calls for neither withdrawal nor maintenance of former activity but for substitution of the satisfactions of old age for the earlier satisfactions of youth. Education under the "theory of margin" would replace education for upward mobility, for example, with education for community service or creative handwork, which might provide the "margin" necessary to enhance self-esteem and growth. In the words of McClusky, "the preeminent and universal educational need of the aging is the need for that kind of education that will assist them in creating margins of power for the attainment and maintenance of well-being, and continuing growth toward self-fulfillment" (p. 2).

While disengagement theory might explain the low rate of

participation and interest in education on the part of the elderly, there is probably more research support for the theory of
margin, and perhaps something that might be called a "theory
of continuity." Research to date offers general support for the
notion that people tend to continue the behavior pattern they
developed earlier in life. Socially active people tend to remain
so throughout life, and those who are withdrawn in old age tend
to be those who were withdrawn at younger ages (Reichard,
Livson, and Peterson, 1968; Videbeck and Knox, 1965; Williams and Wirths, 1965). In a study conducted in 1975 for the
National Council on the Aging, Louis Harris concluded: "At no
point in one's life does a person stop being himself and suddenly turn into an 'old person,' with all the myths that that
term involves. Instead, the social, economic, and psychological
factors that affect individuals when they were younger often
stay with them throughout their lives. Older people share with
each other chronological age, but factors more powerful than
age alone determine the conditions of their later years" (quoted
by Weinstock, 1978, p. 34).

Research and theory in gerontology are somewhat more
advanced than research and theory in adult education, but this
example of testing competing theories through research shows
how knowledge can be built up if there is some framework in
which to accumulate it. The questions that should be raised by
working across CAL variables are numerous. Is there, for example, a relationship between the rise of crystallized intelligence
and the mellowing phase in the life cycle? Do people in the
more mature stages of ego development accomplish the transitions of the phases of the life cycle more easily? How can cognitive development best be promoted for part-time learners—a
goal that is rarely considered in adult education, which tends
more toward piecemeal skills training than intellectual growth.

Placing the variables of adult learning in some kind of
framework—not necessarily CAL, but it may help until something better comes along—shows us how far we have to go in
understanding and providing for adults as learners, but it also
shows us how far we have come and where we stand at present.
I assess the present as showing considerable knowledge on the

warp variables, especially on the physiological and phasic dimensions of personal development. Work on the phases of the life cycle seems to be proceeding productively in that researchers and practitioners are both active, if not always in concert, in seeking improved understanding and practical implementation. Theory and research are reasonably strong in developmental-stage research, but implementation is difficult, given the pragmatic, piecemeal orientation of adult education. How realistic is it to entertain visions of ego development or cognitive development when time and contact with adults are limited? Perhaps, however, intellectual challenge, sufficient to stimulate significant cognitive growth, can be built into televised instruction and other forms of "nonhuman" instruction.

Research on situational variables is new and is heavily consumer oriented at the present time—which means among other things that it is usually implemented out of context of any depth of understanding of the nature of the adult learner. If a survey shows that there appears to be a consumer demand for elementary accounting, a course is forthwith arranged and adults recruited for it, with due consideration given to registration procedures, scheduling, and location. True, the voluntary nature of most adult learning dictates a consumer orientation, but not necessarily the simplistic one now in vogue, which seems to consist of putting discrete item responses together in a whole that is no more than the sum of the parts. As we observed elsewhere, the success of Elderhostel is not predictable from the item responses of older people to survey questionnaires. It *is* understandable, however, in the context of practitioner sensitivities and in-depth research about the physical/psychological/sociocultural characteristics of older learners. The point is not that highly quantitative survey research is not useful; it is extremely helpful when viewed from the perspective of a deeper understanding of adults as learners. That means taking into consideration the personal and situational characteristics of adult learners, and interpreting research on any single dimension in the context of knowledge about other dimensions.

Whatever the shortcomings of research and practice on the warp variables of CAL, the woof variables remain virtually unexplored at present. Except for researchers who start with a particular kind of learner (gerontologists studying the elderly, for example), there has been little attention to the interrelationships across variables. Some fascinating research could be derived by using *any point* on the warp variables of CAL as woof. What is the relationship, for example, of mature ego development to physiological development, phasic adjustment, or amount and kind of volunteer learning? Or consider another point on the warp of CAL—the situation of the volunteer learner. Research on the ultimate volunteer—the self-directed learner—is in its infancy, but its promise is enormous and its potential for adding to understanding of adults as learners almost unlimited. I suspect that there is a strong relationship between stage of ego development and voluntary participation in learning. It is also probable that transition points in either phase or stage of development generate extra amounts of volunteer learning. But there may also be certain phasic plateaus which are especially conducive of voluntary learning. The answers to these questions are only hinted at in the early stages of research on voluntary learning.

Conclusion

Chapters Six and Nine are the appropriate summaries for this book. In those two chapters, I have attempted to integrate existing research and theory into two frameworks for understanding adults as learners. The purpose of the Chain of Responses (COR) model developed in Chapter Six is to explain *who* participates in adult learning activities and *why*. The Characteristics of Learners (CAL) model developed in this chapter provides a framework for thinking about *what* and *how* adults learn.

The development of the models constituted a conscious and difficult choice. The alternative—one to which I thought I was committed at the start of this project—was to review the research and emerge with a final chapter on "implications" and "applications." But it is clear to me now that to make a list of all the recommendations implied in the research reviewed would result in piecemeal, elemental understandings.[2] I believe that we are on the brink of massive change in the role of education in society. With such a possibility, it is important to develop thoughtful educators who are able to assess constantly changing conditions. The need, as I perceive it, is for conceptual models capable of accommodating new knowledge and shifting questions. To draw the implications of current research for today's questions is a useful but limited function. In periods of escalating change, the result is yesterday's answers to tomorrow's questions. I hope and believe that many of the questions educators have about adult learning will be illuminated by the research reported in this book, but I hope even more strongly that readers will be helped to formulate new questions and to think in new ways about the future of the learning society. Summary Chapters Six and Nine should prove useful as organizing frameworks.

In the preface, I quoted the definition of lifelong learning adopted by the General Conference of UNESCO (1976), which calls for three things: a restructuring of the existing system of education, the full development of all educational potential outside the formal system, and the development of self-directing learners, capable of serving as the active agents of their own education. I have seen no better call for action.

I believe that the single most important goal for educators at all levels and in all agencies of the learning society is the development of lifelong learners who possess the basic skills for learning plus the motivation to pursue a variety of learning interests throughout their lives. There is some danger that the present educational system is geared to creating dependent rather than independent learners. Students in the formal educational system are rarely asked to think about what they should learn or how they should learn it. Most classroom teachers

[2]Another reason for not presenting my own list of recommendations for action is my cynical observation that lists of recommendations are legion in the lifelong learning movement, and few if any seem to result in implementation (see, for example, Cross, 1978b, Appendix B for a summary of recommendations from state and national commissions and reports on lifelong learning).

define the subject matter, assign readings, and test for subject matter mastery, despite the fact that such an antiquated model is increasingly incompatible with the demands of the learning society. Few adults, on the job or in their role as citizens and family members, are ever told what they need to know or where the answers will be found. Much more commonly, the learner is required to define the problem, locate appropriate learning materials, and demonstrate not just subject matter comprehension but the ability to apply the knowledge on the job, in the home, or for personal development. These needs call for thoughtful, autonomous learners rather than dependent learners. Moreover, they call for people who know how to select and use the multiple resources in the learning society. They call for discriminating consumers of educational services.

Many educators deplore the "consumerism" that seems to characterize the competition for students today (Carnegie Foundation for the Advancement of Teaching, 1977). The complaint implies that the "low tastes" of the educational consumer will compromise educational quality. But if young people coming out of the formal school system have low educational tastes, educators have largely themselves to blame. Ideally, the task of educators is to develop the taste for good learning—to develop gourmet learners who are able to tailor and utilize the resources in the learning society to their own needs.

There is every reason to think that the presence of a critical mass of gourmet learners in the society would stimulate the education industry in much the same way that gourmet cooks or physical fitness buffs have sparked remarkable vitality in the industries that serve them. Without question, knowledgeable cooks with developed tastes have stimulated the imagination and improved the quality of the cooking and dining industry. The more people know about foods, cooking, and nutrition, the more imaginative and responsive the industry must become. The gourmet cooking movement has demanded and received a tremendous response from restaurateurs, manufacturers of cooking equipment, cooking schools, and publishers of specialized cookbooks and magazines. A similar analogy can be made in certain sports. The more knowledgeable runners and joggers are regarding their needs, the more likely they are to demand forty varieties of running shoes over the all-purpose sneaker of a decade ago. Were we as educators really about the business of developing gourmet learners and responding to their needs, we would not be worried about educational consumerism or competition between "adult education" and "traditional education" or about the survival of institutions of education. We would be pushed to be responsive to a public demanding new developments, better services, and improved products—and I believe that society would be willing to pay for them. Ten years ago, the sneaker industry would have said that was no market for greater variety in active sport shoes. The difference between yesterday and today is that the society now consists of large numbers of runners and joggers and tennis players able to assess their individualistic needs and willing to pay large dividends to the industry responding. Some will complain that education has the problem of generating *collective* willingness to pay, but the principle remains the same. People are willing to pay, individually and collectively, for that which meets their needs.

While some teachers insist that nothing will ever replace the standard classroom lecture as sound and efficient pedagogical technique, that is a little like saying that nothing will ever replace sneakers as the standard American sport shoe, or meat and potatoes as the universal American diet. Tastes do develop and change, and as people are exposed to alternatives, whether in physical fitness, cooking, or in education, large numbers are likely to find something that suits their particular needs better than the standard fare. The role of educators in the learning society is to develop gourmet learners and to be responsive to their interests by providing a wide range of high-quality educational options.

Appendices

The term *lifelong learning* is used internationally, yet, throughout the world, its definition has proved slippery. Appendix A contains a representative sample of the definitions concocted for lifelong learning. Lifelong learning is variously described as a slogan, a process, a set of activities, a conceptual framework, a rallying cry, and a philosophy of education. Frustration with the task of converting the ideal of lifelong learning into practical suggestions for action is also illustrated in the collection of statements in Appendix A. The term "lifelong learning" is described as slippery, strikingly inconsistent, and subject to varying interpretations.

Appendix B is the best scholarly work I have seen that describes the concept of lifelong learning. Dave (1973), working for UNESCO, conducted a careful review of the extensive international literature on lifelong learning, interviewed leaders worldwide, and finally arrived at the twenty characteristics listed in Appendix B. His integration of those characteristics into a single definition appears in Appendix A.

APPENDIX A

Lifelong Learning: Comments and Definitions

"There is gradually emerging . . . a conception of education as a lifelong process beginning at birth and ending only with death, a process related at all points to the life experiences of the individual, a process full of meaning and reality to the learner, a process in which the student is active participant rather than passive recipient" (Leigh, 1930, p. 123).

"Lifelong learning includes, but is not limited to, adult basic education, continuing education, independent study, agricultural education, business education and labor education, occupational education and job training programs, parent education, postsecondary education, preretirement and education for older and retired people, remedial education, special educa-

255

tional programs for groups or for individuals with special needs, and also educational activities designed to upgrade occupational and professional skills, to assist business, public agencies, and other organizations in the use of innovation and research results, and to serve family needs and personal development" (Higher Education Act of 1965, Title I, Part B, Section 132).

"There is no such thing as a separate 'permanent' part of education which is not lifelong. In other words, lifelong education is not an educational system but the principle on which the overall organization of a system is founded, and which should accordingly underlie the development of each of its component parts" (Faure and others, 1972, p. 182).

"Adult *learning* is a major, continuing mode of adult behavior permeating the major categories of human experience and the major sectors of society. It takes place in a 'natural societal setting.' Adult *education* refers to organized and sequential learning experiences designed to meet the needs of adults. It takes place in the context of 'learning organizations.' To be sure, all adult education then involves adult learning, but all adult learning is not adult education" (Delker, 1974, p. 24).

"Adult education refers to any activity or program deliberately designed by a providing agent to satisfy any learning need that may be experienced at any stage in his life by a person who is over the normal school-leaving age and no longer a full-time student. Its ambit spans nonvocational, vocational, general, formal, nonformal, and community education, and it is not restricted to any academic level" (Organization for Economic Cooperation and Development, 1975, p. 12).

"Lifelong education seeks to view education in its totality. It covers formal, nonformal and informal patterns of education, and attempts to integrate and articulate all structures and stages of education along the vertical (temporal) and horizontal (spatial) dimensions. It is also characterized by flexibility in time, place, content and techniques of learning and hence calls for self-directed learning, sharing of one's enlightenment with others, and adopting varied learning styles and strategies" (Dave, 1976, pp. 35-36).

"The term 'lifelong education and learning,' for its part, denotes an overall scheme aimed both at restructuring the existing education system and at developing the entire educational potential outside the education system; in such a scheme men and women are the agents of their own education, through continual interaction between their thoughts and actions" (UNESCO, 1976, p. 2).

" 'Lifelong learning' is a banner for a movement around which various educational and social interests have rallied" (Green, Ericson, and Seidman, 1977, p. 3).

"Lifelong learning means self-directed growth. It means understanding yourself and the world. It means acquiring new skills and powers—the only true wealth which you can never lose. It means investment in yourself. Lifelong learning means the joy of discovering how something really works, the delight of becoming aware of some new beauty in the world, the fun of creating something, alone or with other people" (Gross, 1977, p. 16).

"So far as definition is concerned, 'lifelong learning' is taken here as meaning this: the distribution of educational opportunity over the entire life experience so as to maximize both the individual and the system interests that are involved—with particular recognition of the potentially *reciprocal* values of education and other human experiences. So the distribution and allocation of work and service and leisure, as well as educational opportunities, are to be taken into consideration" (Wirtz, 1977, p. 2).

"By now readers can appreciate the slipperiness of 'lifelong learning' as a guideline for federal policymakers. It is not just that the phrase provokes disagreements about details—any generalization does that—but that its implications for different users are strikingly inconsistent. It is used as a slogan by those who advocate expanding institutional programs *and* by those who want to 'deschool' society; by those who emphasize recurrent education to help workers adjust to their jobs *and* by those who emphasize education as a means of self-fulfillment; by those who attack overreliance on degrees and credentials *and* by those who want to expand the system of degrees and credentials via continuing education units; by those who perceive schools as oriented too little toward the job market *and* by those who perceive them as crassly dehumanizing; by those who wish to target educational opportunities toward well-defined age groups *and* by those who wish to maximize interaction among different age groups within the same classroom setting. To be sure, these positions are not in every case contradictory, but they pull in opposite directions" (Baldwin, 1977, pp. 23-24).

"The term 'lifelong learning' refers to the purposeful activities people undertake with the intention of increasing their knowledge, developing and updating their skills, and modifying their attitudes throughout their lifetimes. This may happen in formal settings, such as schools, or in less formal settings—for example, in the home or at work; the teacher may be a professional educator or some other knowledgeable person—a master craftsman, a business person, a peer; the 'instructional materials' may be traditional texts and books or may include the newer technologies, such as television and computers; learning experiences may occur in a classroom or they may be field experiences, such as museum visits or internships" (Advisory Panel on Research Needs in Lifelong Learning During Adulthood, 1978, p. 17).

"Lifelong Education. Learning activities, including all skills and branches of knowledge, using all possible means, and giving the opportunity to all people for full development of their personalities. It considers the formal and nonformal learning processes in which children, young people, and adults are involved during their lives. (See also adult education, career education, continuing education, continuing professional education, lifelong learning, and recurrent education.)

"Lifelong Learning. (1) The process by which a person acquires knowledge and skills through his/her life span, in order to maintain or improve occupational, academic, or personal development. (2) It includes, but is not limited to, adult basic education, continuing education, independent study, agricultural education, business education and labor education, occupational education and job training programs, parent education, postsecondary education, preretirement and education for older and retired people, remedial education, special educational programs for groups or for individuals with special needs, and also educational activities designed to upgrade occupational and professional skills, to assist business, public agencies, and other organizations in the use of innovation and research results, and to serve family needs and personal development (Higher Education Act of 1965). (See also adult education, career education, continuing education, continuing professional education, lifelong education, and recurrent education)" (Sell, 1978, p. 183).

"*Lifelong learning* refers to the process by which individuals continue to develop their knowledge, skills, and attitudes over their lifetimes" (*Lifelong Learning and Public Policy*, 1978, p. 1).

"Lifelong learning is a conceptual framework for conceiving, planning, implementing, and coordinating activities designed to facilitate learning by all Americans throughout their lifetimes. We believe this framework should consist for the present of the following seven priority goals:

1. To invent and test entirely new kinds of learning programs, involving new combinations of services and new organizational arrangements, in order to better meet identified needs of populations of learners.
2. To assist all adults—particularly those with young children— to become literate and otherwise competent to function in American society.

3. To assist all individuals—particularly school-age children and youths—to become resourceful, autonomous, continuous learners in their various future roles.
4. To develop learning programs that will attract and serve people having poor educational backgrounds.
5. To involve nonschool organizations providing educational services—museums, for example—in planning learning programs.
6. To include other human services organizations—social welfare, housing, and transportation, for example—in planning and implementing learning programs.
7. To maintain high standards of educational practice in all programs; to guard against fraudulent practice."

(Peterson and Associates, 1979, p. 5).

" 'Lifelong learning' [is used] in Washington to describe educational opportunities designed to meet the varied needs of Americans past compulsory school age, with special emphasis on those not served by existing educational programs" (Hartle and Kutner, 1979, p. 277).

" 'Lifelong education' means anything you want it to mean" (Richardson, 1979, p. 48).

Appendix B

Characteristics of Lifelong Education

1. The three basic terms upon which the *meaning* of the concept is based are *life, lifelong,* and *education.* The meaning attached to these terms and the interpretation given to them largely determine the scope and meaning of lifelong education. *(Meaning* and *Operational Modality)*
2. Education does not terminate at the end of formal schooling but is a *lifelong process.* Lifelong education covers the entire life span of an individual.
3. Lifelong education is not confined to adult education but it encompasses and unifies all stages of education—preprimary, primary, secondary, and so forth. Thus, it seeks to view *education* in its *totality.*
4. Lifelong education includes *formal, nonformal, and informal patterns of education.*

Source: Dave, 1973, pp. 14-25.

5. The *home* plays the first, most subtle and crucial role in initiating the process of lifelong learning. This process continues throughout the entire life span of an individual through *family learning*.

6. The *community* also plays an important role in the system of lifelong education right from the time the child begins to interact with it. It continues its educative function both in professional and general areas throughout life.

7. *Institutions of education,* such as schools, universities, and training centers, are important, but only as one of the agencies for lifelong education. They no longer enjoy the monopoly of educating the people and can no longer exist in isolation from other educative agencies in their society.

8. Lifelong education seeks continuity and articulation along its vertical or longitudinal dimension. *(Vertical Articulation)*

9. Lifelong education also seeks integration at its horizontal and depth dimensions at every stage in life. *(Horizontal Integration)*

10. Contrary to the elitist form of education, lifelong education is *universal* in character. It represents *democratization of education.*

11. Lifelong education is characterized by its *flexibility* and *diversity* in *content, learning tools* and *techniques,* and *time* of learning.

12. Lifelong education is a *dynamic approach* to education which allows adaptation of materials and media of learning as and when new developments take place.

13. Lifelong education allows *alternative patterns* and forms of acquiring education.

14. Lifelong education has two broad components: *general* and *professional.* These components are not completely different from each other but are *interrelated* and *interactive* in nature.

15. The *adaptive* and *innovative functions* of the individual and society are fulfilled through lifelong education.

16. Lifelong education carries out a *corrective function*: to take care of the shortcomings of the existing system of education.

17. The ultimate goal of lifelong education is to maintain and improve the *quality of life.*
18. There are three major *prerequisites* for lifelong education; namely, *opportunity, motivation,* and *educability.*
19. Lifelong education is an *organizing principle* for all education.
20. At the *operational level,* lifelong education provides a *total* system of *all* education.

References

Abrahamsson, K. "The Effects of Work Experience on the Educational Process—Some Theoretical Considerations." In K. Abrahamsson, L. Kim, and K. Rubenson, *The Value of Work Experience in Higher Education.* Paris: UNESCO, 1980.

Adult and Continuing Education Today, July 2, 1979, *9* (11), 60-61.

Advisory Panel on Research Needs in Lifelong Learning During Adulthood. *Lifelong Learning During Adulthood.* New York: Future Directions for a Learning Society, College Board, 1978.

Anderson, R. E., and Darkenwald, G. G. *Participation and Persistence in American Adult Education.* New York: College Board, 1979.

Arbeiter, S. "Mid-Life Career Change: A Concept in Search of Reality." Paper presented at the 1979 National Conference on Higher Education, Washington, D.C., April 18, 1979.

265

Arbeiter, S., and others. *40 Million Americans in Career Transition: The Need for Information.* New York: Future Directions for a Learning Society, College Board, 1978.

Arenberg, D., and Robertson-Tchabo, E. A. "Learning and Aging." In J. E. Birren and K. W. Schaie (Eds.), *Handbook of the Psychology of Aging.* New York: Van Nostrand Reinhold, 1977.

Armstrong, D. "Adult Learners of Low Educational Attainment: The Self-Concepts, Backgrounds, and Educative Behavior of Average and High Learning Adults of Low Educational Attainment." Unpublished doctoral dissertation, University of Toronto, 1971.

Aslanian, C. B., and Brickell, H. M. *Americans in Transition: Life Changes as Reasons for Adult Learning.* New York: Future Directions for a Learning Society, College Board, 1980.

Astin, A. W. *Four Critical Years: Effects of College on Beliefs, Attitudes, and Knowledge.* San Francisco: Jossey-Bass, 1977.

Atkinson, J. W., and Feather, N. T. *A Theory of Achievement Motivation.* New York: Wiley, 1966.

Atkinson, R. C. "Futures: Where Will Computer-Assisted Instruction (CAI) Be in 1990?" *Educational Technology,* April 1978, pp. 60-63.

Baldwin, F. *"Lifelong Learning" and Public Policy.* Washington, D.C.: Lifelong Learning Project, U.S. Department of Health, Education, and Welfare, 1977.

Baltes, P. B., and Schaie, K. W. (Eds.). *Life-Span Developmental Psychology: Personality and Socialization.* New York: Academic Press, 1973.

Barlow, B. M., and Timiraos, C. R. *Colorado Adult Needs Assessment.* Final Technical Report. Denver: Colorado Department of Education and State Board for Community College and Occupational Education, 1975.

Bashaw, W. L. "The Effect of Community Junior Colleges on the Proportion of Local Population Who Seek Higher Education." *Journal of Educational Research,* 1965, *58* (7), 327-329.

Best, F., and Stern, B. *Lifetime Distribution of Education,*

Work, and Leisure. Washington, D.C.: Institute for Educational Leadership, Postsecondary Convening Authority, 1976.

Birren, J. E. (Ed.). *Handbook of Aging and the Individual: Psychological and Biological Aspects.* Chicago: University of Chicago Press, 1959.

Birren, J. E., and Schaie, K. W. (Eds.). *Handbook of the Psychology of Aging.* New York: Van Nostrand Reinhold, 1977.

Bishop, J., and Van Dyk, J. "Can Adults Be Hooked on College?" *Journal of Higher Education,* 1977, *48* (1), 39-62.

Bloom, B. S. "Mastery Learning." In J. H. Block (Ed.), *Mastery Learning: Theory and Practice.* New York: Holt, Rinehart and Winston, 1971.

Bloom, B. S. *Human Characteristics and School Learning.* New York: McGraw-Hill, 1976.

Boaz, R. L. *Participation in Adult Education, Final Report 1975.* Washington, D.C.: National Center for Education Statistics, 1978.

Boshier, R. "Motivational Orientations of Adult Education Participants: A Factor Analytic Exploration of Houle's Typology." *Adult Education,* 1971, *21,* 3-26.

Boshier, R. "Educational Participation and Dropout: A Theoretical Model." *Adult Education,* 1973, *23* (4), 255-282.

Boshier, R. "Factor Analysts at Large: A Critical Review of the Motivational Orientation Literature." *Adult Education,* 1976, *26* (1), 24-47.

Boshier, R. "Review of R. H. Dave (Ed.), *Foundations of Lifelong Education.*" *Adult Education,* 1978, *28* (2), 132-135.

Botsman, P. B. *An Analysis of the Continuing Education Interests and Needs of Blue-Collar Factory Workers.* Ithaca, N.Y.: Institute for Research and Development in Occupational Education, Cornell University, 1975a.

Botsman, P. B. *The Learning Needs and Interests of Adult Blue-Collar Factory Workers.* Ithaca: New York State College of Human Ecology, Cornell University, 1975b.

Botwinick, J. "Intellectual Abilities." In J. E. Birren and K. W. Schaie (Eds.), *Handbook of the Psychology of Aging.* New York: Van Nostrand Reinhold, 1977.

Boulding, K. *The Meaning of the 20th Century*. New York: Harper & Row, 1964.

Bowen, H. R. "Higher Education: A Growth Industry?" *Educational Record*, Summer 1974, *55* (3), 147-158.

Bowen, H. R. *Investment in Learning: The Individual and Social Value of American Higher Education*. San Francisco: Jossey-Bass, 1977.

Brecht, D. L. "The Difference Between Day and Night." *Liberal Education*, 1978, *64*, 373-376.

Breneman, D. W. "Economic Trends: What Do They Imply for Higher Education?" *AAHE Bulletin*, Sept. 1979, *32* (1), 1-5.

Bretz, R. G., Rutledge, S. B., and Richards, J. G. "Continuing Professional Education Uses ITV." *Audiovisual Instruction*, Jan. 1978, pp. 40-41.

Brim, O. G., Jr. "Major Contributions: Theories of the Male Mid-life Crisis." *The Counseling Psychologist*, 1976, *6* (1), 2-9.

Broschart, J. R. *Lifelong Learning in the Nation's Third Century: A Synthesis of Selected Manuscripts About the Education of Adults in the United States*. HEW Publication No. (OE) 76-09102. Washington, D.C.: U.S. Government Printing Office, 1977.

Bryan, D., and Forman, D. C. *Characteristics of SUN Learners*. Statistical Summary No. 4. Lincoln, Neb.: University of Mid-America, March 1977.

Burgess, P. "Reasons for Adult Participation in Group Educational Activities." *Adult Education*, 1971, *22*, 3-29.

Calearo, C., and Lazzaroni, A. "Speech Intelligibility in Relationship to the Speed of the Message." *Laryngoscope*, 1957, *67*, 410-419.

California Postsecondary Education Commission (CPEC). *Using Instructional Media Beyond Campus*. Sacramento: California Postsecondary Education Commission, 1979.

Carlisle, R. D. B. *Patterns of Performance: Public Broadcasting and Education, 1974-1976*. Washington, D.C.: Corporation for Public Broadcasting, 1978.

Carlson, R. A. "The Time of Andragogy." *Adult Education*, Fall 1979, *30* (1), 53-57.

Carnegie Commission on Higher Education. *Less Time, More*

Options: Education Beyond the High School. New York: McGraw-Hill, 1971.

Carnegie Foundation for the Advancement of Teaching. *Missions of the College Curriculum: A Contemporary Review with Suggestions.* San Francisco: Jossey-Bass, 1977.

Carp, A., Peterson, R., and Roelfs, P. "Adult Learning Interests and Experiences." In K. P. Cross, J. R. Valley, and Associates, *Planning Non-Traditional Programs: An Analysis of the Issues for Postsecondary Education.* San Francisco: Jossey-Bass, 1974.

Cattell, R. B. "Theory of Fluid and Crystallized Intelligence: A Critical Experiment." *Journal of Educational Psychology,* 1963, *54* (1), 1-22.

Center for Educational Research and Innovation (CERI). *Recurrent Education: Recent Developments and Future Options.* Paris: Organization for Economic Cooperation and Development, 1977.

Chamberlain, M. N. (Ed.). *New Directions for Continuing Education: Providing Continuing Education by Media and Technology,* no. 5. San Francisco: Jossey-Bass, 1980.

Chapanis, A. "Prelude to 2001: Exploration in Communications." *American Psychologist,* 1971, *26,* 949-961.

Chickering, A. W. "The Impact of Various College Environments on Personality Development." *Journal of the American College Health Association,* 1974, *23,* 82-93.

Chickering, A. W., and Associates. *The Modern American College: Responding to the New Realities of Diverse Students and a Changing Society.* San Francisco: Jossey-Bass, 1981.

Chickering, A. W., and Havighurst, R. J. "The Life Cycle." In A. W. Chickering and Associates, *The Modern American College: Responding to the New Realities of Diverse Students and a Changing Society.* San Francisco: Jossey-Bass, 1981.

"Colleges Expect Increased Commitment to CLEP Policies in Next 3-5 Years." *College Board News,* May 1979, p. 1.

Collins, G. "The Good News About 1984." *Psychology Today,* Jan. 1979, *12* (8), 34-48.

Commission on Non-Traditional Study. *Diversity by Design.* San Francisco: Jossey-Bass, 1973.

Committee on the Financing of Higher Education for Adult

Students. *Financing Part-Time Students: The New Majority in Postsecondary Education.* Washington, D.C.: American Council on Education, 1974.

Coolican, P. M. *Self-Planned Learning: Implications for the Future of Adult Education.* Syracuse, N.Y.: Educational Policy Research Center, Syracuse University Research Corporation, 1974.

Coolican, P. M. *Self-Planned Learning: Implications for the Future of Adult Education.* An addendum to the 1974 paper. Washington, D.C.: Division of Adult Education, U.S. Office of Education, 1975.

Craig, R. "Lawrence Kohlberg and Moral Development: Some Reflections." *Educational Theory,* Spring 1974, *24,* 121-129.

Craik, F. I. M. "Age Differences in Human Memory." In J. E. Birren and K. W. Schaie (Eds.), *Handbook of the Psychology of Aging.* New York: Van Nostrand Reinhold, 1977.

Cross, K. P. *Beyond the Open Door: New Students to Higher Education.* San Francisco: Jossey-Bass, 1971.

Cross, K. P. *Accent on Learning: Improving Instruction and Reshaping the Curriculum.* San Francisco: Jossey-Bass, 1976.

Cross, K. P. "The Adult Learner." In *The Adult Learner: Current Issues in Higher Education.* Washington, D.C.: American Association for Higher Education, 1978a.

Cross, K. P. *The Missing Link: Connecting Adult Learners to Learning Resources.* New York: Future Directions for a Learning Society, College Board, 1978b.

Cross, K. P. "Adult Learners: Characteristics, Needs, and Interests." In R. E. Peterson and Associates, *Lifelong Learning in America: An Overview of Current Practices, Available Resources, and Future Prospects.* San Francisco: Jossey-Bass, 1979a.

Cross, K. P. "Old Practices and New Purposes." *Community and Junior College Journal,* 1979b, *50* (1), 4-8.

Cross, K. P. "The State of the Art in Needs Assessment." Paper presented at the Conference on Lifelong Learning: Assessing the Needs of Adult Learners, Akron, Ohio, April 27, 1979c.

Cross, K. P., and Zusman, A. "The Needs of Nontraditional Learners and the Response of Nontraditional Programs." In

C. B. Stalford (Ed.), *An Evaluative Look at Nontraditional Postsecondary Education.* Washington, D.C.: National Institute of Education, 1979.

Cumming, E. M., and Henry, W. *Growing Old.* New York: Basic Books, 1961.

Dave, R. H. *Lifelong Education and School Curriculum.* Hamburg: UNESCO Institute for Education, 1973.

Dave, R. H. (Ed.). *Foundations of Lifelong Education.* Elmsford, N.Y.: Pergamon Press, 1976.

deCharms, R., and Muir, M. S. "Motivation: Social Approaches." *Annual Review of Psychology,* 1978, *29,* 91-113.

Dede, C. J. "Educational Technology: The Next Ten Years." *World Future Society Bulletin,* Nov.-Dec. 1979, pp. 1-7.

Delker, P. V. "Governmental Roles in Lifelong Learning." *Journal of Research and Development in Education,* Summer 1974, 7 (4), 24-33.

Dickinson, G., and Rusnell, D. "A Content Analysis of *Adult Education.*" *Adult Education,* 1971, *21* (3), 177-185.

Dirr, P. J., and Pedone, R. J. *Uses of Television for Instruction, 1976-77.* Washington, D.C.: Corporation for Public Broadcasting, 1979.

Dresch, S. "Demography, Technology, and Higher Education: Toward a Formal Model of Educational Adaptation." *Journal of Political Economy,* 1975, *83,* 535-569.

Drucker, P. F. "The Surprising Seventies." *Harper's Magazine,* July 1971, pp. 35-39.

Dubin, S. S. "Obsolescence or Lifelong Education: A Choice for the Professional." *American Psychologist,* May 1972, *27* (5), 486-498.

Elias, J. L. "Androgagy Revisited." *Adult Education,* Summer 1979, *29* (4), 252-256.

Empire State College. *Self-Study Report.* Saratoga Springs, N.Y.: Empire State College, n.d.

Erikson, E. H. *Childhood and Society.* New York: Norton, 1950.

Erikson, E. H. *Identity and the Life Cycle.* Psychological Issues Monograph 1. New York: International Universities Press, 1959.

Faure, E., and others. *Learning to Be: The World of Education Today and Tomorrow.* Paris: UNESCO, 1972.

Footnotes to the Future, Feb. 1980, *9* (2).

Forman, D. C., and Brown, L. A. "The Roles of Television in Adult Educational Programs." *National Society for Performance and Instruction Journal,* March 1978, pp. 7-25.

Frankel, M. M. *Projections of Education Statistics to 1986-87.* Washington, D.C.: National Center for Education Statistics, 1978.

Freeman, R. B. *The Declining Economic Value of Higher Education and the American Social System.* Palo Alto, Calif.: Aspen Institute for Humanistic Studies, 1975.

Freire, P. *Pedagogy of the Oppressed.* New York: Herder and Herder, 1970.

Froomkin, J. *Needed: A New Federal Policy for Higher Education.* Policy Paper 6. Washington, D.C.: Institute for Educational Leadership, George Washington University, 1978.

Fry, C. L. "The Ages of Adulthood: A Question of Numbers." *Journal of Gerontology,* 1976, *31* (2), 170-177.

Gage, N. L. *Teacher Effectiveness and Teacher Education.* Palo Alto, Calif.: Pacific Books, 1972.

George, J. L., and Dubin, S. S. *Continuing Education Needs of Natural Resource Managers and Scientists.* University Park: Department of Planning Studies, Continuing Education, Pennsylvania State University, 1972.

Ghiselli, E. E. "The Relationship Between Intelligence and Age Among Superior Adults." *Journal of Genetic Psychology,* 1957, *90,* 131-142.

Gilder, J. *Policies for Lifelong Education.* Washington, D.C.: American Association of Community and Junior Colleges, 1979.

Gilligan, C. "Moral Development." In A. W. Chickering and Associates, *The Modern American College: Responding to the New Realities of Diverse Students and a Changing Society.* San Francisco: Jossey-Bass, 1981.

Glaser, R. *Adaptive Education: Individual Diversity and Learning.* New York: Holt, Rinehart and Winston, 1977.

Golladay, M. A. *The Condition of Education: A Statistical*

Report on the Condition of Education in the United States. Washington, D.C.: National Center for Education Statistics, 1976.

Golladay, M. A. *The Condition of Education 1977.* Vol. Three, Part One. Washington, D.C.: National Center for Education Statistics, 1977.

Gould, R. "The Phases of Adult Life: A Study in Developmental Psychology." *American Journal of Psychiatry,* Nov. 1972, *129* (5), 521-531.

Gould, R. "Adult Life Stages: Growth Toward Self-Tolerance." *Psychology Today,* Feb. 1975, pp. 74-78.

Grant, W. V., and Lind, C. G. *Digest of Education Statistics 1977-78.* Washington, D.C.: National Center for Education Statistics, 1978.

Green, T. F., Ericson, D., and Seidman, R. H. *Lifelong Learning and the Educational System: Expansion or Reform?* Washington, D.C.: Lifelong Learning Project, U.S. Department of Health, Education, and Welfare, 1977.

Gross, R. *The Lifelong Learner.* New York: Simon & Schuster, 1977.

Haan, N., and Day, D. "A Longitudinal Study of Change and Sameness in Personality Development: Adolescence to Later Adulthood." *International Journal of Aging and Human Development,* 1974, *5* (1), 11-39.

Hamilton, I. B. *The Third Century: Postsecondary Planning for the Nontraditional Learner.* Report prepared for the Higher Education Facilities Commission of the State of Iowa. New York: College Board; Princeton, N.J.: Educational Testing Service, 1976.

Hargreaves, D. *Adult Literacy and Broadcasting: The BBC's Experience.* New York: Nichols, 1980.

Hartle, T. W., and Kutner, M. A. "Federal Policies: Programs, Legislation, and Prospects." In R. E. Peterson and Associates, *Lifelong Learning in America: An Overview of Current Practices, Available Resources, and Future Prospects.* San Francisco: Jossey-Bass, 1979.

Havighurst, R. J. *Developmental Tasks and Education.* (3rd ed.) New York: McKay, 1972.

Havighurst, R. J., Neugarten, B. L., and Tobin, S. S. "Disengagement and Patterns of Aging." In B. L. Neugarten (Ed.), *Middle Age and Aging*. Chicago: University of Chicago Press, 1968.

Heath, R. *The Reasonable Adventurer*. Pittsburgh: University of Pittsburgh Press, 1964.

Hefferlin, J. L., Peterson, R. E., and Roelfs, P. J. *California's Need for Postsecondary Alternatives*. First Technical Report, Pt. I: Postsecondary Alternatives Study. Sacramento: California Legislature, 1975.

Henderson, C., and Plummer, J. C. *Adapting to Changes in the Characteristics of College-Age Youth*. Washington, D.C.: American Council on Education, 1978.

Hiemstra, R. *The Older Adult and Learning*. Lincoln: Department of Adult and Continuing Education, University of Nebraska, 1975.

Hilton, W. J. *State Visitation Program, Final Report*. New York: Future Directions for a Learning Society, College Board, 1979.

Holmstrom, E. I. " 'Older' Freshmen: Do They Differ from 'Typical' Undergraduates?" *ACE Research Reports*, Oct. 1973, *8* (7, entire issue).

Holt, J. *How Children Fail*. New York: Dell, 1970.

Horn, J. L. "Organization of Data on Life-Span Development of Human Abilities." In L. R. Goulet and P. B. Baltes (Eds.), *Life-Span Developmental Psychology: Research and Theory*. New York: Academic Press, 1970.

Houle, C. O. *The Inquiring Mind*. Madison: University of Wisconsin Press, 1961.

Houle, C. O. *The Design of Education*. San Francisco: Jossey-Bass, 1972.

Houle, C. O. *Continuing Learning in the Professions*. San Francisco: Jossey-Bass, 1980.

Hoyt, D. P. *Appraisal of Interest in Continuing Education Opportunities Among Kansas Adults*. Manhattan: State Education Commission of Kansas and Kansas Board of Regents, 1975.

Huberman, M. "Live and Learn: A Review of Recent Studies in

Lifelong Education." *Higher Education,* March 1979, *8* (2), 205-215.

Hunter, C., and Harman, D. *Adult Illiteracy in the United States: A Report to the Ford Foundation.* New York: McGraw-Hill, 1979.

Jencks, C., and others. *Who Gets Ahead? The Determinants of Economic Success in America.* New York: Basic Books, 1979.

Johnstone, J. W., and Rivera, R. J. *Volunteers for Learning.* Chicago: Aldine, 1965.

Jones, H. E., and Conrad, H. S. "The Growth and Decline of Intelligence." *Genetic Psychology Monographs,* 1933, *13,* 223-298.

Kangas, J., and Bradway, K. "Intelligence at Middle Age: A Thirty-Eight-Year Follow-Up." *Developmental Psychology,* 1971, *5,* 333-337.

Kanter, R. M. "The Changing Shape of Work: Psychosocial Trends in America." In *The Adult Learner: Current Issues in Higher Education.* Washington, D.C.: American Association for Higher Education, 1978.

Kelly, J. T., and Anandam, K. "Nationwide Prime-Time Television in Higher Education." *International Journal of Instructional Media,* 1977-78, *5* (3), 219-228.

Kemp, F. B. *Noncredit Activities in Institutions of Higher Education for the Year Ending June 30, 1976.* Washington, D.C.: National Center for Education Statistics, 1978.

Kidd, J. R. *How Adults Learn.* New York: Association Press, 1973.

Kidd, J. R. "Adult Learning in the 1970's." In R. M. Smith (Ed.), *Adult Learning: Issues and Innovations.* Information Series No. 8. DeKalb: Information Program in Career Education, Northern Illinois University, 1977.

Knowles, M. S. *The Modern Practice of Adult Education: Andragogy Versus Pedagogy.* New York: Association Press, 1970.

Knowles, M. S. *The Adult Learner: A Neglected Species.* (2nd ed.) Houston: Gulf, 1978.

Knowles, M. S. "Andragogy Revisited Part II." *Adult Education,* Fall 1979, *30* (1), 52-53.

Knox, A. B. *Adult Development and Learning: A Handbook on Individual Growth and Competence in the Adult Years for Education and the Helping Professions.* San Francisco: Jossey-Bass, 1977.

Kohlberg, L. "Stage and Sequence: The Cognitive-Developmental Approach to Socialization." In D. A. Goslin (Ed.), *Handbook of Socialization Theory and Research.* Chicago: Rand McNally, 1969.

Kohlberg, L., and Mayer, R. "Development as the Aim of Education." *Harvard Educational Review,* Nov. 1972, *42,* 449-496.

Kohlberg, L., and Turiel, E. "Moral Development and Moral Education." In G. S. Lesser (Ed.), *Psychology and Educational Practice.* Glenview, Ill.: Scott, Foresman, 1971.

Koos, L. V. "Local Versus Regional Junior Colleges." *School Review,* 1944, *5,* 525-531.

Korman, A., Greenhaus, J. H., and Badin, I. J. "Personal Attitudes and Motivation." *Annual Review of Psychology,* 1977, *28,* 175-196.

Kuhlen, R. G. "Developmental Changes in Motivation During the Adult Years." In B. L. Neugarten (Ed.), *Middle Age and Aging.* Chicago: University of Chicago Press, 1968.

Kurland, N. D. (Ed.). *Entitlement Studies.* Washington, D.C.: National Institute of Education, 1977.

Lasker, H. M., and Moore, J. F. *Current Studies of Adult Development: Implications for Education.* Report prepared for the National Institute of Community Development. Cambridge, Mass.: Harvard Graduate School of Education, 1979.

Lehman, T. "Educational Outcomes from Contract Learning at Empire State College." Paper presented at the 30th National Conference on Higher Education, American Association for Higher Education, Washington, D.C., 1975.

Lehman, T., and Lester, V. *Adult Learning in the Context of Adult Development.* Empire State College Research Series. Saratoga Springs, N.Y.: Empire State College, 1978.

Leigh, R. D. "Reducing Academic Formalism." *Journal of Adult Education,* April 1930, *2* (2), 122-127.

Levine, H. A. *Strategies for the Application of Foreign Legisla-*

tion on Paid Educational Leave to the United States Scene. Washington, D.C.: National Institute of Education, 1974.

Levinson, D. J. *The Seasons of a Man's Life.* New York: Knopf, 1978.

Levinson, D. J., and others. "The Psychosocial Development of Men in Early Adulthood and the Mid-Life Transition." In D. F. Ricks, A. Thomas, and M. Roff (Eds.), *Life History Research in Psychopathology.* Vol. 3. Minneapolis: University of Minnesota Press, 1974.

Lewin, K. "Frontiers in Group Dynamics: Concept, Method and Reality in Social Science." *Human Relations,* June 1947, *1,* 5-41.

Lifelong Learning and Public Policy. Report prepared by the Lifelong Learning Project. Washington, D.C.: U.S. Government Printing Office, 1978.

Lisman, D., and Ohliger, J. "Must We All Go Back to School?" *The Progressive,* Oct. 1978, *42* (10), 35-37.

Lister, I. "The Threat of Recurrent Education, and the Nightmare of Permanent Education." Speech to the 3rd International Conference on Higher Education, University of Lancaster, England, 1975.

Loevinger, J. *Ego Development: Conceptions and Theories.* San Francisco: Jossey-Bass, 1976.

Loevinger, J., Wessler, R., and Redmore, C. *Measuring Ego Development.* (2 vols.) San Francisco: Jossey-Bass, 1970.

Lowenthal, M. F., and others. *Four Stages of Life: A Comparative Study of Women and Men Facing Transitions.* San Francisco: Jossey-Bass, 1975.

Luxenberg, S. "Education at AT&T." *Change,* Dec.-Jan. 1978-79, *10* (11), 26-35.

McCatty, C. "Patterns of Learning Projects Among Professional Men." Unpublished doctoral dissertation, University of Toronto, 1973.

McClusky, H. Y. *Education: Background.* Report prepared for the 1971 White House Conference on Aging, Washington, D.C., 1971.

McCoy, V. R. "Adult Life Cycle Change: How Does Growth

Affect Our Education Needs?" *Lifelong Learning: The Adult Years,* Oct. 1977, pp. 14-18, 31.

McCoy, V. R., Ryan, C., and Lictenberg, J. W. *The Adult Life Cycle: Training Manual and Reader.* Lawrence: University of Kansas, 1978.

McIntosh, N. E., and Woodley, A. "Excellence, Equality and the Open University." Paper presented to the working party on "Teaching and Learning and the New Media," 3rd International Conference on Higher Education, University of Lancaster, England, 1975.

McKenzie, L. "The Issue of Andragogy." *Adult Education,* Summer 1977, *27* (4), 225-229.

McMahon, H. F., Anderson, J. S. A., and Anderson, T. H. *The Computer in the Management of Open Learning Systems.* Champaign: University of Illinois, 1978.

McNeil, D. R. *Future Directions of the University of Mid-America.* Lincoln, Neb.: University of Mid-America, 1978.

Maeroff, G. I. "Fight on Illiteracy Found to Lag Badly." *New York Times,* Sept. 9, 1979.

Magarrell, J. "The Social Repercussions of an 'Information Society.'" *Chronicle of Higher Education,* June 30, 1980, *20* (18), 1.

Maslow, A. H. *Motivation and Personality.* New York: Harper & Row, 1954.

Mazza, G. "Tailor-Made Education." *Council of Europe Forum,* Jan. 1979, p. xxiii.

Medsker, L., and others. *Extending Opportunities for a College Degree: Practices, Problems, and Potentials.* Berkeley: Center for Research and Development in Higher Education, University of California, 1975.

Mezirow, J. "Toward a Theory of Practice." *Adult Education,* 1971, *21* (3), 135-147.

Mezirow, J. "Perspective Transformation." *Adult Education,* 1978, *28* (2), 100-110.

Miles, C. C., and Miles, W. R. "The Correlation of Intelligence Score and Chronological Age from Early to Late Maturity." *American Journal of Psychology,* 1932, *44,* 44-78.

Miller, H. L. *Participation of Adults in Education: A Force-*

Field Analysis. Boston: Center for the Study of Liberal Education for Adults, Boston University, 1967.

Minnesota Metropolitan State College. *Self-Study Report.* Minneapolis: Minnesota Metropolitan State College, 1975.

Moenster, P. A. "Learning and Memory in Relation to Age." *Journal of Gerontology,* 1972, *27,* 361-363.

Monette, M. L. "Need Assessment: A Critique of Philosophical Assumptions." *Adult Education,* 1979, *29* (2), 83-95.

Morris, J. F. "The Planning Behavior and Conceptual Complexity of Selected Clergymen in Self-Directed Learning Projects Related to Their Continuing Professional Education." Unpublished doctoral dissertation, University of Toronto, 1977.

Morstain, B. R., and Smart, J. C. "Reasons for Participation in Adult Education Courses: A Multivariate Analysis of Group Differences." *Adult Education,* 1974, *24* (2), 83-98.

National Center for Education Statistics. *Statistics of Trends in Education: 1966-67 to 1986-87.* Washington, D.C.: Office of Education, U.S. Department of Health, Education, and Welfare, 1978.

National Center for Education Statistics. *News Release: Adult and Continuing Education in Colleges and Universities.* Washington, D.C.: Office of Education, U.S. Department of Health, Education, and Welfare, Aug. 6, 1979.

National Center for Education Statistics. *Preliminary Data, Participation in Adult Education, 1978.* Washington, D.C.: Office of Education, U.S. Department of Health, Education and Welfare, 1980.

National Center for Educational Brokering. "An Important Client Group: Displaced Homemakers." *Bulletin,* May/June 1979, *4* (4).

National Commission on the Observance of International Women's Year. *The Spirit of Houston: The First National Women's Conference.* Washington, D.C.: National Commission on the Observance of International Women's Year, 1978.

Neugarten, B. L. "Adult Personality: Toward a Psychology of the Life Cycle." In B. L. Neugarten (Ed.), *Middle Age and Aging.* Chicago: University of Chicago Press, 1968.

Neugarten, B. L. (Ed.). "Aging in the Year 2000: A Look at the Future." *Gerontologist,* Feb. 1975, *15* (1), 4-9.

Neugarten, B. L. "Personality and Aging." In J. E. Birren and K. W. Schaie (Eds.), *Handbook of the Psychology of Aging.* New York: Van Nostrand Reinhold, 1977.

Neugarten, B. L., Moore, J. W., and Lowe, J. C. "Age Norms, Age Constraints and Adult Socialization." In B. L. Neugarten (Ed.), *Middle Age and Aging.* Chicago: University of Chicago Press, 1968.

Nickerson, R., and Teachman, G. *Potential for Television-Based Learning Systems.* Final Report. Toronto: Office of Project Research, Ontario Educational Communications Authority, 1979.

Nisbet, J. D. "Intelligence and Age: Retesting with Twenty-Four Years' Interval." *British Journal of Educational Psychology,* 1957, *27,* 190-198.

Nolfi, G. J., Jr., and Nelson, V. I. *Strengthening the Alternative Postsecondary Education System: Continuing and Part-Time Study in Massachusetts.* Vol. 1: *Summary Report and Recommendations.* Cambridge, Mass.: University Consultants, 1973.

Nollen, S. D. "The Current State of Recurrent Education." In D. W. Vermilye (Ed.), *Relating Work and Education: Current Issues in Higher Education 1977.* San Francisco: Jossey-Bass, 1977.

O'Keefe, M. *The Adult, Education, and Public Policy.* Cambridge, Mass.: Aspen Institute for Humanistic Studies, 1977.

Okes, I. E. *Participation in Adult Education 1969.* Washington, D.C.: National Center for Education Statistics, 1971.

Okes, I. E. *Participation in Adult Education: Final Report, 1972.* Washington, D.C.: National Center for Education Statistics, 1976.

Organization for Economic Cooperation and Development. *Recurrent Education: A Strategy for Lifelong Learning.* Paris: Organization for Economic Cooperation and Development, 1973.

Organization for Economic Cooperation and Development. *Framework for Comprehensive Policies for Adult Education.*

Paris: Education Committee, Organization for Economic Cooperation and Development, 1975.

Owen, J. D. "Workweeks and Leisure: Analysis of Trends, 1948-1975." *Monthly Labor Review,* Aug. 1976.

Owens, W. A. "Age and Mental Abilities." *Genetic Psychology Monographs,* 1953, *48,* 3-54.

Owens, W. A. "Age and Mental Abilities: A Second Adult Follow-Up." *Journal of Educational Psychology,* 1966, *57,* 311-325.

Paltridge, J. G., and Regan, M. C. *Mid-Career Change: Adult Students in Mid-Career Transitions, and Community Support Systems Developed to Meet Their Needs.* Final Report. Berkeley: School of Education, University of California, 1978.

Penland, P. *Individual Self-Planned Learning in America.* Washington, D.C.: Office of Education, U.S. Department of Health, Education,and Welfare, 1977.

Penland, P. "Self-Initiated Learning." *Adult Education,* 1979, *29* (3), 170-179.

Perry, W. G., Jr. *Forms of Intellectual and Ethical Development in the College Years.* New York: Holt, Rinehart and Winston, 1970.

Perry, W. G., Jr. "Cognitive and Ethical Growth: The Making of Meaning." In A. W. Chickering and Associates, *The Modern American College: Responding to the New Realities of Diverse Students and a Changing Society.* San Francisco: Jossey-Bass, 1981.

Peterson, R. E., and Associates. *Lifelong Learning in America: An Overview of Current Practices, Available Resources, and Future Prospects.* San Francisco: Jossey-Bass, 1979.

Peterson, R. E., and Hefferlin, J. L. *Postsecondary Alternatives to Meet the Educational Needs of California's Adults.* Final Report, Postsecondary Alternatives Study. Sacramento: California Legislature, 1975.

Peterson, R. E., and others. *Community Needs for Postsecondary Alternatives.* First Technical Report, Pt. II, Postsecondary Alternatives Study. Sacramento: California Legislature, 1975.

Phares, E. J., and Lamiell, J. T. "Personality." *Annual Review of Psychology,* 1977, *28,* 113-140.

Purdy, L. N. "The History of Television and Radio in Continuing Education." In M. N. Chamberlain (Ed.), *New Directions for Continuing Education: Providing Continuing Education by Media and Technology,* no. 5. San Francisco: Jossey-Bass, 1980.

Reichard, S., Livson, F., and Peterson, P. G. "Adjustment to Retirement." In B. L. Neugarten (Ed.), *Middle Age and Aging.* Chicago: University of Chicago Press, 1968.

Rest, J. "Developmental Psychology as a Guide to Value Education: A Review of 'Kohlbergian' Programs." *Review of Educational Research,* Spring 1974, *44,* 241-259.

Richardson, P. L. "Lifelong Education and Politics." In *Policies for Lifelong Education.* Washington, D.C.: American Association of Community and Junior Colleges, 1979.

Riessman, F. *The Culturally Deprived Child.* New York: Harper & Row, 1962.

Rockhill, K. "The Past as Prologue: Toward an Expanded View of Adult Education." *Adult Education,* 1976, *26* (4), 196-207.

Rockhill, K. "The Mystique of Certification, Education and Professionalism: In the Service of Whom?" In *Yearbook of Adult and Continuing Education.* (3rd ed.) Chicago: Marquis Academic Media, 1977-78.

Roelfs, P. J. "Teaching and Counseling Older College Students." *Findings,* 1975, *2* (1).

Rose, A. M. "A Current Theoretical Issue in Social Gerontology." In B. L. Neugarten (Ed.), *Middle Age and Aging.* Chicago: University of Chicago Press, 1968.

Rothstein, L. *New Directions in Mass Communications Policy: Implications for Citizen Education and Participation.* Washington, D.C.: Office of Education, U.S. Department of Health, Education, and Welfare, 1978.

Rubenson, K. "Participation in Recurrent Education: A Research Review." Paper presented at meeting of National Delegates on Developments in Recurrent Education, Paris, March 1977.

Ruyle, J., and Geiselman, L. A. "Non-traditional Opportunities and Programs." In K. P. Cross, J. R. Valley, and Associates, *Planning Non-traditional Programs: An Analysis of the Issues for Postsecondary Education.* San Francisco: Jossey-Bass, 1974.

Schaie, K. W. "Rigidity-Flexibility and Intelligence: A Cross-Sectional Study of the Adult Life-Span from 20 to 70." *Psychological Monographs,* 1958, *72* (9, entire issue).

Schaie, K. W. "External Validity in the Assessment of Intellectual Development in Adulthood." *Journal of Gerontology,* 1978, *33,* 695-701.

Schaie, K. W., and Parr, J. "Intelligence." In A. W. Chickering and Associates, *The Modern American College: Responding to the New Realities of Diverse Students and a Changing Society.* San Francisco: Jossey-Bass, 1981.

Schaie, K. W., and Willis, S. L. "Life-Span Development: Implications for Education." In L. S. Shulman (Ed.), *Review of Research in Education.* Itasca, Ill.: Peacock, 1979.

Sell, G. R. *A Handbook of Terminology for Classifying and Describing the Learning Activities of Adults.* Denver: National Center for Higher Education Management Systems (NCHEMS), 1978.

Sharp, L. M., and Sosdian, C. P. "External Degrees: How Well Do They Serve Their Holders?" *Journal of Higher Education,* Sept./Oct. 1979, *50* (5), 615-649.

Sheehy, G. *Passages: Predictable Crises of Adult Life.* New York: Dutton, 1976.

Solmon, L. C., Gordon, J. J., and Ochsner, N. L. *The Characteristics and Needs of Adults in Postsecondary Education.* Los Angeles: Higher Education Research Institute, 1979.

Sosdian, C. P. *External Degrees: Program and Student Characteristics.* Washington, D.C.: National Institute of Education, 1978.

Sosdian, C. P., and Sharp, L. M. *The External Degree as a Credential: Graduates' Experiences in Employment and Further Study.* Washington, D.C.: National Institute of Education, 1978.

Srinivasan, L. *Perspectives on Nonformal Adult Learning.* North Haven, Conn.: Van Dyck, 1977.

Staley, E. J. "The Struggle for Significance." In *Leisure Today,* special editorial insert in *Journal of Physical Education and Recreation,* March 1976.

Stern, M. R. "Compulsory Continuing Education for Professionals—or the Gold Rush of '76." In J. S. Long and R. Boshier (Eds.), *Certification, Credentialing, Licensing and the Renewal Process.* Seattle: Northwest Adult Education Association, 1976.

Stern, M. R. "Competition in Continuing Education in the '80's." Speech to the annual conference of the Universities Council for Adult Education, University of Keele, England, April 11, 1979.

Thorndike, E. L., and others. *Adult Learning.* New York: Macmillan, 1928.

Toffler, A. *Future Shock.* New York: Random House, 1970.

Tough, A. *Why Adults Learn: A Study of the Major Reasons for Beginning and Continuing a Learning Project.* Monographs in Adult Education, No. 3. Toronto: Ontario Institute for Studies in Education, 1968.

Tough, A. *The Adult's Learning Projects: A Fresh Approach to Theory and Practice in Adult Learning.* Research in Education Series, No. 1. Toronto: Ontario Institute for Studies in Education, 1971.

Tough, A. "Major Learning Efforts: Recent Research and Future Directions." In *The Adult Learner: Current Issues in Higher Education.* Washington, D.C.: American Association for Higher Education, 1978.

Tough, A. "Choosing to Learn." In G. M. Healy and W. L. Ziegler (Eds.), *The Learning Stance: Essays in Celebration of Human Learning.* Final report of Syracuse Research corporation project, National Institute of Education No. 400-78-0029. Washington, D.C.: National Institute of Education, 1979.

Tough, A., Abbey, D., and Orton, L. "Anticipated Benefits from Learning." Unpublished manuscript, 1979.

Trent, J. W., and Medsker, L. L. *The Influence of Different Types of Public Higher Institutions on College Attendance from Varying Socioeconomic and Ability Levels.* Berkeley:

Center for Research and Development in Higher Education, University of California, 1965.

UNESCO. *Recommendation on the Development of Adult Education.* Recommendation adopted at General Conference, Nairobi, Kenya, Oct.-Nov., 1976. Paris: UNESCO, 1976.

UNESCO. *The Economics of New Educational Media.* Paris: UNESCO, 1977.

U.S. Bureau of the Census. *Historical Statistics of the United States: Colonial Times to 1970.* Part I. Washington, D.C.: U.S. Government Printing Office, 1975.

U.S. Bureau of the Census. *Educational Attainment in the United States: March 1977 and 1976.* Current Population Reports, Series P-20, No. 314. Washington, D.C.: U.S. Government Printing Office, 1977a.

U.S. Bureau of the Census. *Projections of the Populations of the United States: 1977 to 2050.* Current Population Reports, Series P-25, No. 704. Washington, D.C.: U.S. Government Printing Office, 1977b.

U.S. Bureau of the Census. *Social Indicators 1976.* Washington, D.C.: U.S. Government Printing Office, 1977c.

U.S. Bureau of the Census. *School Enrollment—Social and Economic Characteristics of Students: October 1977.* Current Population Reports, Series P-20, No. 333. Washington, D.C.: U.S. Government Printing Office, 1979a.

U.S. Bureau of the Census. *School Enrollment—Social and Economic Characteristics of Students: October 1978.* Current Population Reports, Series P-20, No. 335. Washington, D.C.: U.S. Government Printing Office, 1979b.

Videbeck, R. E., and Knox, A. B. "Alternative Participatory Responses to Aging." In A. M. Rose and W. A. Peterson (Eds.), *Older People and Their Social World.* Philadelphia: F. A. Davis, 1965.

Vogel, B. "Professional Retraining in Flux." *New York Times,* Sept. 9, 1979.

von Moltke, K., and Schneevoigt, N. *Educational Leaves for Employees: European Experience for American Consideration.* San Francisco: Jossey-Bass, 1977.

Vroom, V. *Work and Motivation.* New York: Wiley, 1964.

Watkins, B. T. "Certification of Professionals: A Bonanza for Extension Programs." *Chronicle of Higher Education,* April 11, 1977, p. 8.

Watkins, B. T. "Continuing Education for Professionals." *Chronicle of Higher Education,* Sept. 4, 1979, p. 9.

Weathersby, R. "Life Stages and Learning Interests." In *The Adult Learner: Current Issues in Higher Education.* Washington, D.C.: American Association for Higher Education, 1978.

Weathersby, R. P. "Ego Development." In A. W. Chickering and Associates, *The Modern American College: Responding to the New Realities of Diverse Students and a Changing Society.* San Francisco: Jossey-Bass, 1981.

Wechsler, D. *The Measurement of Adult Intelligence.* (Rev. ed.) Baltimore: Williams and Wilkins, 1955.

Wechsler, D. *The Measurement and Appraisal of Adult Intelligence.* (4th ed.) Baltimore: Williams and Wilkins, 1958.

Weinstock, R. *The Graying of the Campus.* New York: Educational Facilities Laboratories, 1978.

Welford, A. T. *Skill and Age: An Experimental Approach.* London: Oxford University Press, 1951.

Wilcox, J., Saltford, R., and Veres, H. *Continuing Education: Bridging the Information Gap.* Ithaca, N.Y.: Cornell University, and Albany: New York State Education Department, Dec. 1975.

Williams, R. H., and Wirths, C. G. *Lives Through the Years.* New York: Atherton, 1965.

Willingham, W. *Free-Access Higher Education.* New York: College Board, 1970.

Wilson, D. L., and Goerke, G. "Education for New Times: The Video Cassette Revolution." *International Journal of Instructional Media,* 1978-79, *6* (1), 1-11.

Wirtz, W. *Lifelong Learning and Living.* Washington, D.C.: Lifelong Learning Project, U.S. Department of Health, Education, and Welfare, 1977.

Woodruff, D. S., and Birren, J. E. "Age Changes and Cohort Differences in Personality." *Developmental Psychology,* 1972, *6* (2), 252-259.

Ziegler, W. L. *The Future of Adult Education and Learning in the United States.* Syracuse, N.Y.: Educational Policy Research Center, Syracuse University Research Corporation, 1977.

Index